PUBLIC LOVES, PRIVATE TROUBLES

CONTEMPORARY ISSUES AND METHODS IN INDIGENOUS STUDIES

PUBLIC LOVES, PRIVATE TROUBLES

Migration, Technology, and Intimacy in Rural Indigenous Guatemala

MEGHAN FARLEY WEBB

THE UNIVERSITY OF ALABAMA PRESS
Tuscaloosa

For Hannah

The University of Alabama Press
Tuscaloosa, Alabama 35487-0380
uapress.ua.edu

Typeface: Arno Pro

Cover images: tiles by ckybe/stock.adobe.com and
phone by suriyapong/stock.adobe.com
Cover design: Sandy Turner Jr.

Cataloging-in-Publication data is available from the Library of Congress.
ISBN: 978-0-8173-2229-8 (cloth)
ISBN: 978-0-8173-6201-0 (paper)
E-ISBN: 978-0-8173-9553-7

Contents

Illustrations

Figures

Table

Preface

This book focuses on the experiences of undocumented transnational migration from the perspective of those who do *not* migrate. The women profiled herein referred to their shared situation using the phrase *yojkanäj wawe'* (We remain here). Magda, my Kaqchikel teacher, helped me think through how to best convey the sentiments of this phrase. It describes their geography, remaining in Guatemala. But the phrase captures much more; *-kanäj* (to remain) also describes their perseverance in the face of new challenges associated with being part of a transnational family. Magda agreed that here *-kanäj* means more than to remain. She suggested *aceptar* (to accept) as part of the translation. We thought "resigned oneself to the situation" might be the best, albeit lengthy, translation, because as Magda pointed out, "for them, there aren't any alternatives."

Telling these women's stories presents a challenge. It is difficult to impart the nuance of opportunity and constraint shaping their worlds. Ethnography, no matter how descriptive, flattens and simplifies. This challenge is amplified as I try to situate my writing within scholarship that encourages exploration of all the spaces of agency that (Indigenous) women have as they navigate patriarchal systems of oppression and often violence. Though speaking from a different context, I am reminded of the late physician-anthropologist Paul Farmer's caution that academics should not overstate people's agency.[1] This, along with numerous discussions with my students (especially the anthropology majors who graduated in 2021), helped me to think through what it is anthropologists aim to do: to translate and amplify voices. As such, the chapters that follow offer stories of women's lives as they told them to me. They are overwhelmingly told from the point of view of women, more specifically migrants' wives. I present their voices as their own and serve as a cultural and linguistic translator, helping to make their lives, the struggles and successes, legible to a reader who may be far removed from rural Indigenous Guatemala.

Several women's stories stand out as I describe the impacts of men's transnational migration on their wives who remain in Guatemala. The complexity of these women's lives reflects the realities faced by many women in transnational households. The willingness of these women to deeply share the details of their situation means that their stories feature prominently in the book. Summary information about these five women is presented in table P.1.[2]

Table P.1. Name, Age, Residence, and Number of Children of Five Women Profiled

Name	Age	Residence	Number of Children
Dolores	35	aldea	4
Flora	29	aldea	3
María	34	city center	2
Nohemy	29	aldea	2
Rosa	43	city center	2

The research I conduced for the book spans the years 2010–2022. During this period, I made nearly annual trips to Guatemala, ranging from weeks to months. The longest period of continuous fieldwork was from June 2013 through May 2014. In 2015, 2017, and 2019 I returned to Guatemala for formal follow-up research. During these research trips I conducted participant-observation coupled with formal interviews and informal chats. I carried out semistructured interviews with more than one hundred individuals representing three key populations in transnational households: migrants' wives, migrants' parents, and return migrants. These interviews provided insights on the experience of more than forty transnational households, roughly divided between those living in aldeas and those residing in the city center. In addition to these interviews that focused on migration, I conducted guided life histories with seven migrants' wives. They were selected because of rapport I was able to establish with them and because their personal situation reflected outcomes commonly seen among transnational households.

I conducted interviews in both Spanish and Kaqchikel Mayan; most interviews featured a mixture of both. I am fluent in Spanish and proficient in Kaqchikel. During my work in communities, I was almost always accompanied by a community member who made introductions and vouched for me. Sometimes this person provided support in the form of translation. After initial introductions and as people became more comfortable with my presence in the community, I conducted follow-up interviews individually. However, these personal introductions were critical for gaining entrée into the intimate spaces of transnational families' daily lives. Talking to Tecpanecos about their undocumented migrant family members was delicate. The sensitive nature of the interviews meant that I did not usually digitally record them; instead, I took copious notes.

Another catalyst for gaining trust in the communities was my initial willingness, and later ability, to speak Kaqchikel. In the city center Tecpán, Spanish and Kaqchikel are both widely spoken, meaning Kaqchikel was not necessary for communication. However, my willingness to speak Kaqchikel with my host family and friends as we went to the market and church made me memorable and, in some cases, less threatening. Questions about my learning Kaqchikel started conversations and friendships. In aldeas, my ability to speak Kaqchikel was critical for communication with older women who were more likely to be monolingual or exhibit a strong preference for Kaqchikel. Interviews and informal chats most often were a mixture of Kaqchikel and Spanish and filled with laughs when I mispronounced and misused Kaqchikel words. These moments of levity in otherwise heavy interviews, and my willingness to laugh at myself, created friendships and demonstrated that, as one woman explained, "Ak'ux man kow ta" (Your heart isn't hard).

My interest in women's handicrafts, especially textiles such as traditional weaving and cross-stitch, further enabled my entrée into Tecpán. I learned to weave on a backstrap loom. Weaving, although practiced in my home's patio, made me fit within traditional conceptions of Kaqchikel femininity and provided an opportunity for me to perform this femininity as I purchased threads and designs in town. Other female scholars working in rural Latin America have noted the importance of handicrafts to their successful incorporation into gendered spaces.[3] While weaving was a genuine interest, I strategically brought cross-stitch kits with me from the United States to help me fill rainy afternoons and perform "appropriate" gendered behaviors.

While I regularly make return trips to Tecpán for both research and pleasure, I also maintain contact with several transnational families through the same social media and communication technologies I research. These technologies mean I am never fully out of the field. WhatsApp messages maintain friendships and provide me the opportunity to check in about my interpretations of observations and interviews. I also stay up-to-date on the happenings of daily lives of community members through Facebook posts.

Casual keeping up with friends and acquaintances in Tecpán changed into formal digital ethnography in 2020–2021, as COVID-19 changed the conditions of life and of research. With international travel restricted, I conducted Zoom and telephone interviews from the United States. I also had the help of three student research assistants (two from the city center and one from an aldea) who carried out an additional thirty interviews on technology use. I supplemented these structured interviews with a digital survey on technology carried out in 2021. These research assistants also conducted an additional twenty interviews on the dynamics of courtship and marriage.

The various stages of research underwent human subjects review from institutional review boards at the University of Kansas, Wuqu Kawoq|Maya Health Alliance, Universidad del Valle, and Albion College. Research approvals were also given by local *auxiliaturas* (local community governmental committees).

Acknowledgments

The protections of anonymity mean that I cannot offer the most important thank yous individually. I am deeply indebted to those who so graciously trusted me to tell the stories of their lives.

Countless individuals in Guatemala provided friendship and guidance. Wuqu' Kawoq|Maya Health Alliance facilitated my introduction into the communities with which I worked. Anne Kraemer Diaz and Peter Rohloff encouraged my investigations at both a theoretical and logistical level. I also thank the Wuqu' Kawoq health promotors and translators who started out as colleagues and quickly became friends. Although I did not have the opportunity to officially participate in Oxlajuj Aj, teachers there welcomed me and helped me acquire the Kaqchikel language skills needed for the project. I especially thank Ixq'anil (Judie Maxwell), Ixkamey (Magda Sotz Mux), Ixim Nikte (Carmela Rodríguez), and Lajuj Batz (Edy Rene Guajan Car). The project also benefited from institutional support at Universidad del Valle, especially from María del Pilar Graciozo. In Tecpán, research assistants Florencio, Sonia, Alicia, and Alex helped with interviews when COVID-19 prevented my travel to Guatemala. Many friends in Guatemala have helped me in my work over the years and made Guatemala feel like home. I especially thank Ruth, Sonia, Rolando and Ingrid, German and Magdalena, Eufemia, Cristi, Magali, and Ernesto. The greatest support for the project came from the Calí and Ajquijay families. They accepted me as one of their own, tolerated my endless questions, and taught me how to be *choj tecpaneca. Janila matyöx chiwe*, Florencio, Lidia, Alex, Cristian, Francis, and Josue.

I am lucky to be part of a larger community of academics who have shaped my development as a scholar and been supportive of this work: Rick Axtell, Heather Betz, Terri Castaneda, Brad Chase, Rebecca Crosthwait, Nancy Demerdash, Andrea Ploucher Francis, Majid Hannoum, Alli Harnish, Allison Jendry James, Phyllis Passariello, Ebenezer Obadare, Katey Price, Krista

Quesenberry, Katie Rhine, Silvia Sánchez Díaz, Matt Schoene, Ximena Sevilla, Bill Staples, Akiko Takeyama, Raghu Trichur, Anna Weiser, and Laura Wylie. A very special thanks go to Taylor Tappan for making the maps.

The Guatemalanists have always been a warm and welcoming group. Several members of this community deserve special recognition. Brent Metz's mastery of the ethnographic literature and dedication to all communities he inhabits (both in the field and at home) is inspirational; I couldn't have asked for a better mentor as I navigated graduate school, being a new faculty member, and now my postacademic work. Joyce Bennett has served as a cheerleader since my first day in the field, offering encouragement and "tough love" over the course of the research and writing of this book. Tiffany Creegan Miller and I met as graduate students. We have been writing partners ever since. Lisa Munro's editing and intimate knowledge of Tecpán made this a better book. Finally, I had the excellent luck to begin my fieldwork at the same time as Anita Chary. As we learned about the nuances of Kaqchikel women's worlds, we cried until we laughed and laughed until we cried. Over the years she has been an excellent field companion, editor, and confidant as well as a sister-cousin and partner-in-crime.

It was a pleasure to work with the University of Alabama Press. Special thanks go to my editor Wendi Schnaufer, who patiently worked with me as I navigated the publication of my first book. Thanks also go to the two anonymous reviewers who helped me find my argument in a sea of ethnographic examples.

Portions of chapter 5 are derived in part from an article published in *Human Organization* 77, no. 1 (2018): 32–41, available online.

In a book that pays so much attention to affective labor it would be an oversight to not recognize those who have nurtured my own family. Stephanie Head visited me during long stretches of research in Guatemala. She also served as my nonacademic reader. In Lawrence, Kansas, the members of my weekly Spanish conversation group offered encouragement. Gracias a Quica, Dani, Emily, Elim, Jen, MariaAna, Rebecca, Stephanie, Tita, and Ximena. I was lucky to find a group of other new moms who supported each other unconditionally. I am especially grateful for Alex, Meredith, and Nina. In Ann Arbor, Michigan, my incredible friends helped me with both childcare and *ánimo*, ensuring I could *mostly* meet my manuscript deadlines. I especially thank Andi, Heather, Melanie, Rosa, Santhi, and Sheetal. Finally, I owe a debt of gratitude to my daughter's teachers at the Discovery Center and Emerson School and her babysitters: Lauren, Kelly, Maggie, and Peach.

The biggest thanks go to my family: Eric, John, Lauren, and Bob and Dianna. My parents, Linda and Jim Farley, taught me to love people's stories and travel, awakening the ethnographer in me at an early age. My daughter, Hannah, celebrated all our adventures in Guatemala and patiently tolerated hours of writing and editing while she watched every episode of *Bluey* (thanks Disney+). Finally, thanks go to my husband, Nick, who has supported me through the writing of the chapters of this book and our lives. I am grateful to have your love through the happy and sad moments of both.

The research for this book received financial support from the Wenner-Gren Foundation, the University of Kansas's Center for Latin American and Caribbean Studies and the Anthropology Department, and Albion College's Hewlett-Mellon Faculty Development Fund.

PUBLIC LOVES, PRIVATE TROUBLES

Introduction

Glimpses of lush green cornfields and puffy white clouds are visible as the camera adjusts to fit everyone into frame. A large box, roughly six feet tall, covered in colorful wrapping paper sits in front of some balloons. A man in a red T-shirt and jeans arranges an older couple and a younger woman on either side of the box. Both women are wearing *traje* (handwoven dress worn by Maya women). It is hard to pick what is the most vibrant: the wrapping paper, the balloons, or the women's *huipiles* (woven blouses) typical of K'iche' region.[1] The accompanying Facebook post describes the video as "a man surprises his wife by arriving in a gift box after seven years in the United States." I assume that the younger woman, probably in her mid- or late thirties, is the migrant's wife; the older couple, in their fifties or sixties, must be the migrant's parents. Unlike the transnational videos of previous generations that were sent directly between family members, this two-minute video was shared publicly on Facebook. It has gotten almost 22,000 views, 116 likes, and 50 shares in the month since it was posted. I can see that several members of transnational families I know in Tecpán have liked the video, even though none of us know the family in the video. One woman even sent it to me in Facebook's messaging app, suggesting that it might be helpful for my research. I keep watching.

Recorded marimba music plays in the background. From out of frame, a man (seemingly standing in the crowd) serves as the emcee for the event, held on a makeshift stage that has been erected in the middle of town. In Spanish, he tells the wife, "Now it is your turn to unwrap this other present. But be careful while you're unwrapping it . . . there isn't any other like it, not *any* other." The woman laughs, tucking her smartphone into her *faja* (woven belt) so her hands are free to unwrap the last present her migrant husband has sent. To her side you can see the corner of what appears to be a gas grill—maybe another present? The video does not say.

The emcee then asks, "Are you ready for the surprise?" To which the crowd energetically responds, "Yes," and applauds. The family gently pulls away the bright paper to reveal a refrigerator box. They seem happy, but the revelation is anticlimactic; although a luxury, a refrigerator is not unique. As the excitement wanes, the man in the red T-shirt lifts the box to reveal the returned migrant. The migrant, dressed in a button-down shirt and black dress pants, immediately embraces his wife. They hold each other as the crowd cheers and his parents clap. No one can believe that he is really home. I am so caught up in the unfolding reunion that I hardly notice the emcee saying, "Your dad is here," as he helps a boy of about ten to the stage. The video ends with the entire family holding each other, wiping tears from their eyes as the emcee says, "How beautiful. . . . This is what love looks like . . . and of course happiness."

This Facebook video of a K'iche' transnational family was so similar and yet so unlike the experiences of the Kaqchikel Maya transnational families I know. In both cases the transnational families were Indigenous, speaking one of Guatemala's twenty-two Mayan languages. In both cases it was the man who migrated in the hopes of improving daily life in Guatemala. These migrants spend around seven years working in the United States to create economic opportunities for their families. However, the work they put in planning, filming, and posting a surprise return after years away reminded me more of reunification videos made and shared on social media by US military families than of Maya communities in Guatemala.

When I first arrived in Tecpán in 2010, Kaqchikel friends instructed me not to share my phone number with others and told me that it was always best to respond to strangers' questions with vague—sometimes evasive—answers. Women modeled a preference for discretion, obscuring signs of status as they covered market purchases in woven cloths and avoided outward displays of wealth. I rarely saw married Kaqchikel couples openly embrace in public displays of affection. Given local preferences for conformity and outward stoicism, I was left wondering why the family in the video would share a moment as intimate as a family reunion seven years in the making for just anyone to watch? Why make such a private moment so public? The fact that the woman who sent me the video and the women who liked the post were the same ones who had socialized me into cultural norms of privacy and conformity when I began living in Guatemala amplified these questions. The wives of transnational migrants I knew valued their privacy as they moved through their daily lives in Guatemala, but many also spent significant time on social media liking and sharing videos like this one. Was their interest in the video voyeuristic or an attempt to document the potentiality of men's migration? Regardless of motivation, the video resonated with Indigenous transnational families in Tecpán.

Roughly one third of Guatemalans benefited from the $18.2 billion in remittances that were sent home in 2022.[2] The ethnographic literature on Indigenous Guatemalan migrations has focused primarily on K'iche', Q'anjob'al, and Mam Maya communities from the Western Highlands and how economic and ethnic violence have driven flows of Maya peoples into diasporic communities in Los Angeles, North Carolina, Texas, New England, and Florida.[3] While the Central Highlands have not figured prominently in the literature on Maya migrations, there has been significant migration from Kaqchikel communities.[4] Men from Tecpán, a *municipio* and city in the Central Highlands, have engaged in undocumented transnational economic migration for the past thirty years.[5] Tecpanecos primarily migrate to Los Angeles and New Jersey. Today, in a pattern that has held steady for three decades, it is overwhelmingly married men who migrate without documentation. They temporarily leave their wives and children in Guatemala in the hopes that their families will be able to achieve *algo más* (something more).[6] These men migrate not as a rite of passage or to prove their manhood, as is the case with communities in Mexico and the western Highlands of Guatemala, but *salir adelante* (to get ahead; to succeed).

Outside of the migrant context, anthropologist Edward Fischer has explored how Kaqchikel Maya farmers pursue the personal and community project of the good life, noting that in Tecpán, markers of the good life include land, a house, a business, and maybe a car.[7] Despite a shared understanding of what the good life looks like on the ground, families go about achieving it in different ways. Some Tecpanecos look to in-home garment factories, others look to growing broccoli, snow peas, or other nontraditional crops, and still others seek out jobs in Guatemala City.[8] Transnational migration is increasingly becoming a way that young Kaqchikel families pursue the good life.

The expenses of daily life in Guatemala drive many families to consider undocumented transnational migration. Guatemalans, especially rural men, are chronically underemployed. Additionally, most families in Tecpán do not have enough land to engage in subsistence agriculture. In 2013 (when I was finishing my longest stint of fieldwork), the cost of the Canasta básica alimentaria (the thirty-four food products required to maintain the *minimum* dietary needs of a family of five for a month) was Q2900.10 ($374.21 USD). In 2022, the cost of the Canasta Básica Alimentaria was Q3,134.40 ($405.36 USD), making it the most expensive in Latin America.[9] Given these costs, it is unsurprising that food insecurity and stunting (chronic malnutrition) are widespread in Maya communities.[10]

While not as bad as neighboring Honduras, violence ranging from extortion to murder permeates daily life in Guatemala. Local gangs and those acting in concert with drug cartels are seen as responsible for this increased uncertainty and violence. Traveling to Guatemala City for work has become both more expensive and more dangerous. This new calculus of risk means that many Kaqchikel men from Tecpán no longer see taking these jobs as "worth it" or a viable economic strategy. Additionally, the cost of land is also increasing, making it harder and harder for young families to get ahead. This reality prompts those who can to migrate.

Migration has historically been an economic strategy in rural Indigenous Guatemala. The colonial-era tributary labor systems of *encomienda* and *repartimiento* created a tradition of temporary domestic migration. The use of Indigenous labor for public works continued after Guatemala's independence, when both conservatives and liberals created policies to mobilize Maya communities' participation in various infrastructure projects to "improve" the nation.[11] In the early 1900s, government policies, including vagrancy laws, facilitated seasonal migration from the Indigenous highlands to coffee plantations, creating an odd symbiosis between the regions and allowing for the maintenance of a peasant lifestyle for most people living in the countryside.[12] Sebastian, an elder from the aldea of Paquip, remembered his father and older brothers working under Ubico's vagrancy laws (1934–1944) and recalled his own migration to work on coffee plantations in the 1960s and 1970s: "Everyone went with their little bags to the coast."[13] But he pointed out that such migrations were different from the migrations undertaken today: "In the old days every member of the family went together." The new patterns of migration referenced by Sebastian are remaking Tecpán and its inhabitants, as objects, people, and ideas move between sending and receiving communities.

Transnationalism, the way migrants "develop and maintain multiple relations—familial, economic, social, organizational, religious, and political that span borders," reshapes origin and destination communities.[14] The boundaries between *aquí* (here) and *allá* (there) become blurred. While migrants themselves are often the subject of transnational analyses, the inherent relationality of transnationalism means that those in "home" communities likewise live transnational lives, even when they never cross a physical border.[15] For example, anthropologist David Stoll and geographers Michelle Moran-Taylor and Matthey Taylor describe how transnational migration has altered the financial and physical landscapes in Western Guatemala as the cost of land continues to increase.[16]

The work of anthropologists Patricia Foxen, Debra Rodman, and Joyce N. Bennett has paid special attention to the ways that transnational migration shapes ethnic and gender identities. All note the role of local jealousies and (transnational) gossip in shaping expressions of personhood. Foxen's multisited ethnography traces the reworking of postwar ethnic identities and memories as migrants and ideas move between Providence, Rhode Island, and Xinxuc, Quiché, Guatemala. She notes the variability of expressions of Mayaness, with many K'iche' preferring to express a Guatemalan or Latino identity in Rhode Island. Female migrants may avoid wearing traje or speaking K'iche' in the United States. Foxen also notes the nostalgia and loss many residents have for a Xinxuc that has changed during their time away.[17] In contrast, Joyce N. Bennett's work in Kaqchikel communities on Lake Atitlán explores how women's domestic and transnational migration influences the expression of Kaqchikel womanhood. She notes that migration results in women investing more heavily in the wearing of traje and speaking of "Kaqchikel puro" (pure Kaqchikel).[18]

Farther from Tecpán, in eastern Guatemala, Rodman's work suggests that men's transnational migration increased the subordination of their wives despite financial remittances, noting that often women were not in control of how remittances were spent.[19] Rodman notes that the communication technologies available to transnational families at the time of her fieldwork (1999–2001) did not foster intimacy. Instead, they were experienced as impersonal because the focus was on communicating immediate household needs.[20]

Today, readily available cell phones that provide access to social media platforms like WhatsApp and Facebook mean that transnational communication can occur almost instantaneously. These new technologies alter forms and models of intimacy. Mediation considers how various mediums of communication, in this case forms of communication technologies, facilitate or restrict flows of information and emotion. This does not imply technological determinism but rather highlights the flexibility of both media and society. Communities remake technologies as they "domesticate" them in ways that are locally relevant.[21]

Anthropologists Daniel Horst and Heather Miller pioneered ethnographic studies of digital media, the mediations they bring about, and how they impact daily life.[22] They describe how Jamaicans incorporated cell phones into existing networking practices, demonstrating the ways that society integrates new technologies.[23] In Mexico, text messages have altered courtship patterns among Tzotzil Maya youth, due to their private nature and the fact that they are written in Spanish. In South America, Baird Campbell and Nell Haynes note the way that online spaces, especially Facebook and YouTube, become places where the archive of the self is constructed.[24] Importantly, as Horst and Miller note, the virtual cultural spaces are no less real than the "real" world.[25] Others have similarly noted that the emotionality of virtual parenting or breaking up via text messages is as authentic as the experiences would be offline.[26] While all relationships are mediated, the role of mediation is especially evident in those relationships characterized by a prolonged absence, like the case of transnational families, where relationships depend entirely on digital communication technologies.[27]

This is an ethnography of transnational migration in the digital age, examining how communications technologies are reshaping ideas on family, intimacy, and selfhood in Kaqchikel Maya communities in Guatemala. Members of transnational communities use available technologies to mediate lives and maintain the tenuous bonds of intimacy and define selfhood.[28] I argue that among Kaqchikel transnational households, the intimacies of family are created over WhatsApp messages and Facebook posts. Facebook provide migrants' wives a novel way to do the affective work of marriage and personhood. These mediations attempt to replicate the intimate, often in the profoundly nonintimate settings like publicly viewable social media posts. Transnational families also use social media posts to consciously self-construct locally relevant and socially acceptable identities. These women look to Facebook to perform their femininity, demonstrating that they are "good" Kaqchikel women. Social media allow women to explore and assert their selfhood and aspire to the good life.

This is also an ethnography about what happens when the pursuit of "something more" and "the good life" makes life not so good, at least temporarily, and how migrants' wives negotiate the struggles associated with migration. The hope of the good life—despite its contribution to disappointment, unhappiness, and oppression—is the crux of what Lauren Berlant terms "cruel optimism." Berlant describes cruel optimism as "a relation of attachment to compromised conditions of possibility." They point out that optimisms become cruel because "the very vitalizing or animating potency of an object/scene of desire contributes to the attrition of the very thriving that is supposed to be made possible in the work of attachment in the first place."[29] On the surface, the case of Kaqchikel transnational migration embodies cruel optimism. Migration promises optimism in the potentiality of *algo más*. But this optimism is cruel because the pursuit of something more means that transnational families endure the loneliness of years of separation. The wives of migrants who remain in Guatemala face the additional cruelty stemming from the loss of their husbands' protection and the additional gossip and monitoring of their behavior that often results in the constriction of their physical worlds. Many migrants 'wives are bound to the fantasy of migration, despite the reality that makes life unlivable. For others, daily life in Tecpán is livable despite the incredible difficulties associated with men's migrations. Some women's lives improve in the absence of controlling and abusive husbands, especially if these women are willing to, at least nominally, comply with traditional expectations of Kaqchikel femininity that value motherhood, wearing traje, and speaking Kaqchikel. Additionally, new forms of social media create not only spaces for maintaining proximity to the desired good life but also new spaces for female empowerment and agency.

Drawing from the work of cultural theorist Lauren Berlant and anthropologist Zoë H. Wool, I suggest that social media posts maintain the potentialities of the good life.[30] Women's Facebook posts attempt to maintain the proximity of the "cluster of desires" promised by men's transnational migration. Social media present migrants' wives with the opportunity to imagine a future that makes life in the present livable. These posts overwhelmingly mobilize traditional images of Kaqchikel femininity. Deployment of such images of femininity is not about reifying patriarchal gender roles, though it may inadvertently do so. Instead, these images are deployed to garner respect and protect women from malicious gossip so common in transnational communities.[31] In the absence of their migrant husbands, women must be especially mindful to protect their reputations as their behavior is under extra scrutiny. However, local expectations of good womanhood, especially those related to motherhood, are overwhelmingly practiced in the intimate spaces of the home, rendering them invisible to community members and migrant husbands.

Social media present migrants' wives with a way of proving their goodness because the porous boundaries of social media mean that the private is always at least a little public. Indeed, social media provide an ideal space for presentations of self and constructions of identity.[32] Additionally, social media become a key space for these definitions of self because migrants' wives often experience a constriction of their physical worlds as they find themselves subject to additional scrutiny and local monitoring, often at the hands of their mothers-in-law, with whom they live.

TECPÁN: HERE AND THERE

Anna-Maria Walter notes that the virtual world is never uncoupled from the material social worlds.[33] The experiences of transnational households are defined by the local context of Tecpán. Tecpán is the largest municipality in Chimaltenango as measured by geography and second largest as measured by population (fig. I.1). Guatemala's 2018 National Census lists the population of the municipality as 91,927. This includes the 34,519 living in the city center, which sits on the Pan-American Highway, just fifty miles from Guatemala City. The remaining 57,408 people live in Tecpán's thirty-four aldeas (small towns) and twenty-seven *caseríos* (rural hamlets) dotting the surrounding hills and mountains (fig. I.2).[34] Tecpán's aldeas range in size and rurality. Some aldeas, like Pueblo Viejo, are hardly distinguishable from the city center. Others, like Palamá, are isolated in mountains covered in *milpa* (corn and bean) agriculture (fig. I.3). The physical isolation of aldeas like Palamá results in their being seen, by their residents and others, as *olvidadas* (forgotten). Adding to this perception is the fact that aldeas are overwhelmingly home to Indigenous peoples.

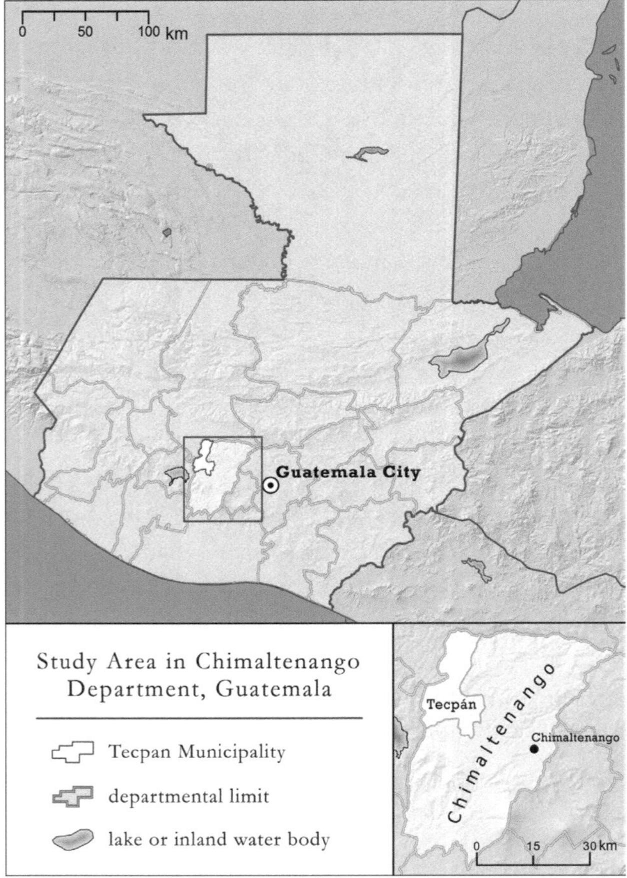

Figure I.1. Map of Chimaltenango. Data from ASTER Global Digital Elevation Model V003 and Instituto Geográfico Nacional, Guatemala. Map courtesy of Taylor Tappan.

Figure I.2. Map of Tecpán. Data from ASTER Global Digital Elevation Model V003 and Instituto Geográfico Nacional, Guatemala. Map courtesy of Taylor Tappan.

Figure I.3. Men picking strawberries just outside the city limits. The field behind awaits the planting of corn. Photo by Meghan Farley Webb.

Figure I.4. Tecpán's city center. The Catholic church and large pine trees mark the central plaza. Photo by Meghan Farley Webb.

Ninety-two percent of the municipality of Tecpán is Kaqchikel.[35] Among the most salient divisions in Tecpán, like the rest of Guatemala, are the ethnic, economic, and social divide between *ladinos* (non-Indigenous people) and *indígenas* (Indigenous peoples). In Guatemala, ethnoracial identity is most often indexed through language and dress.[36] The traditional dress for Kaqchikel men (white pants and shirt worn with an apron-like, black wool *xerka* or *rodillero*) is increasingly rare and typically used by elders. The majority of the city's Kaqchikel female residents wear traje daily, publicly.[37] This means that overwhelmingly, men's ethnic identity is not visually marked, but that of women is. As anthropologist Diane Nelson notes, "gender is raced and race is gendered."[38] Originating in the Spanish colonial *casta* system, Guatemala's racial hierarchy continues to privilege ladinos, despite inroads made by Maya activists. Anthropologist Charles R. Hale characterizes contemporary ethnic relations in Chimaltenango as "racial ambivalence," where ladinos are not overtly racist as in the past but still fight to maintain their position of privilege.[39] Although my work focused on the experience of Kaqchikel transnational families, I observed this racial ambivalence while living in Tecpán and conducting the more than twenty-five months of ethnographic research from 2010 to 2022.[40]

The vibrancy of the textiles worn by Maya women and the stunning vistas of pine-covered mountains shrouded in mist prompted *capitalinos* (residents of Guatemala City) to remark "¡Ay, Tecpán es preciosa!" (Tecpán is precious) when they learned where I was living. The countryside of the municipality is beautiful, yet it is unlikely any of those making this remark had actually been to the city of Tecpán.[41] Despite abutting the Pan-American Highway, the city is not a destination for outsiders, even those tourists passing through town on their way to the archaeological site of Iximché.

The city of Tecpán, which sits in the mountains (~7,500 ft; 2,300 m), does not fit the image of a "precious" bucolic community, nor does it have the "colonial charm" of Antigua, a tourist destination roughly thirty miles away. Nearly all the buildings in Tecpán are cinderblock (fig. I.4). The city was rebuilt after its near total destruction by a 7.5 magnitude earthquake that occurred in the early morning hours of February 4, 1976.[42] All the cinderblock makes it easy to forget that Tecpán was once the capital of the Kaqchikel kingdom and the first capital of colonial Guatemala.[43]

The beauty of the city of Tecpán is hard to see beneath the frenetic movement of people, buses, and red *tuk-tuks* (moto taxis). Cipresales—the second, but busier, entrance to the city—boasts a constant presence of *camionetas* (brightly painted US school buses), *micros* (micro buses; vans), *filetes* (commissioned pickup trucks), and tuk-tuks waiting to transport people and their goods to the surrounding villages and beyond. Living on Cuarta Calle, the road to Cipresales, made me acutely aware of Tecpán's connection to the rest of Guatemala as the tranquility of the early morning was broken at 4:30 a.m. when buses began honking their horns and *ayudantes* (assistants) began yelling, "Guate, Guate, Guate," advertising their trips to Guatemala City.

Tecpán's connections to the rest of Guatemala make the city a thriving commercial center. Stores selling agricultural products, including seeds, fertilizers, and pesticides, dominate the city. While agriculture and its related economy have prospered in Tecpán since the eighteenth century and feature prominently in Tecpán's Thursday market, today the city is locally known for its garment production.[44] Since the 1950s families in Tecpán have produced sweaters in home workshops. While these domestic workshops are out of sight, behind the high cinderblock walls of Tecpán's homes, they are a driving force in the city's economy.[45]

Figure I.5. One of Tecpán's larger aldeas to the north of the city. The recently paved road that was cut into the side of the mountain is visible. Photo by Meghan Farley Webb.

In addition to these garment workshops, Tecpán has a thriving Indigenous bourgeois class of teachers, intellectuals, bankers, accountants, and lawyers.[46] Edward Fischer and Carol Hendrickson note that upward mobility of Tecpanecos generally requires working in Chimaltenango—the department capital—or Guatemala City, as well-paying, skilled jobs are not plentiful in the city center.[47] In the early 2020s, Tecpán experienced incredible growth. The blocks around the central park boast several coffee shops and restaurants where young people and middle-aged residents alike meet to hang out after work and/or school. Several NGOs have offices in Tecpán, and it is no longer odd to see foreigners living in town. In 2023, Pollo Campero, Guatemala's fried chicken chain restaurant, opened a location at the Cipresales entrance.

In contrast to the bustling nature of the city center, the economies of most aldeas revolve around agriculture (fig. I.5). Men in aldeas identify as *agricultores* (farmers) or *campesinos* (peasants), even when they do not own land and primarily work as *jornaleros* (agricultural day laborers).[48] While milpa agriculture is the most common, local farmers also grow coffee and nontraditional

agricultural exports, like broccoli and snow peas, because family plots can no longer support subsistence agriculture.[49] Nontraditional agricultural exports are pursued here as a way out of poverty and social suffering.[50] However, the shift to nontraditional agricultural exports and the decreasing productivity of the land continue to marginalize those who survive on agriculture. These realities translate into poverty for most residents of remote aldeas. For example, 45 percent of those living in one of Tecpán's northern aldeas live in poverty (defined by the World Bank as less than $2 USD/day) and 5 percent live in extreme poverty (defined by the World Bank as less than $1 USD/day).[51]

Pa ri jay, Pa ri b'ey

Although it is not often explicitly expressed using the terms "public" and "private," there is a locally understood distinction between those things are *de la calle, pa ri bey* (of the street; public) and those things that are more intimate and private. Kaqchikel-speaking families contrasted *pa ri b'ey* with *pa ri jay* (of the house).[52] The street is the public domain. It is a place of precarity, as demonstrated by nearly everyone telling me "tachajij cuenta pa ri b'ey" (be careful on the road; travel safe) when I left the house. In contrast, the home is a space of intimacies and security. Such understandings of public and private play out in the definition of spaces as well as gender expression.

Throughout most of the city, a *portón* (gate) and high walls obscure daily life from those passing by. The most common arrangement of homes in the city is a series of buildings built around a paved patio. Patios serve as places to hang laundry, weave, grow plants, and park a car. They are the lively shared space of intergenerational households. Children use the patio as a place to ride bikes, play soccer, or draw with chalk. The house's *pila* (outdoor sink; water source) is in this courtyard, making the patio also the place where clothes and dishes are washed. The rooms constructed around the patio serve as bedrooms, a kitchen, bathrooms, a room for receiving visitors, and, if the family is Catholic, a shrine. Even within private domestic space, not all have equal access. How far a visitor is let into the house reflects the level of trust placed in them.[53] Sitting around the hearth, sharing meals occurs in the most intimate of spaces.[54] It is these intimate spaces of home that transnational families try to replicate in phone calls, WhatsApp messages, and Facebook posts.

Although the most common arrangement is buildings surrounding a patio, homes in the city center take other forms as well. Some homes, particularly those near the *plaza central* (central park; downtown), are multiple-story buildings built right on the edge of the road.[55] One enters this style of homes by passing through a portón into a paved or tiled parking space. Even families that do not own a car have this area in their homes. From here, one passes into a "living room" for receiving guests. Depending on the house, this room may also hold a shrine, a TV, or both. The primary kitchen area is also on the ground floor of the home.[56] Often this type of structure has a small patio or garden area at the rear of the home where the pila is and where clothes can be hung to dry. The bedrooms are upstairs. Regardless of style, it is common for houses to be reconfigured as family size and economic status change.

In aldeas, most families live in intergenerational households, with multiple dwellings built on the same parcel of land. In contrast to homes in the city center, buildings are primarily one story and made from either cinderblock or adobe. Some homes have both types of construction, with older buildings made of adobe and more recent construction made of cinderblock. This construction pattern is common in households receiving remittances from the United States. As in the city center, homes have an internal patio area (almost always pressed earth) where the pila is located. Aldea homes do not have a portón separating public and private space. Instead, homes are built slightly away from the main dirt road or path. Plants and buildings mark the entrance to the home. Entry into a patio is unrestricted except by behavioral norms and the household's dog(s). Instead of ringing a doorbell or knocking on the portón, visiting involves walking into the edge of the patio and calling the name of the person one is looking for or saying "Xqa q'ij nan" (Good afternoon, elder woman). Intergenerational households and gendered divisions of labor mean that houses are rarely empty; typically an older female family member is almost always home.

The dynamics of public and private spaces are also reflected in local approaches to gender socialization: men belong in the public sphere, participating in formal employment and politics. Women's power lies in the domestic sphere, where they concern themselves with caring for children and the household. Such clear divisions represent an idealized version of the world. Socioeconomic status, race, and personality all influence how much this idealized version matches reality.[57] Even when women leave the physical space of the house to perform domestic duties, like caring for animals, helping in the fields, gathering firewood, buying food at the market, or washing clothes at a public pila, these duties are locally understood as being within the realm of the "home."

Feminist anthropologist Helen I. Safa notes that in much of Latin America the public-private divide has primarily applied to the rich, giving the image of the *mujer encerrada* (sequestered woman) an aspirational quality.[58] Lois Paul's ethnography of the women in the Kaqchikel community of San Pedro notes that Pedranas see themselves as aristocratic (as compared with women of other Lake Atitlán communities). They take pride in the fact that they do not engage in manly activities like carrying heavy loads or working in the fields. Given the special status Tecpanecos afford themselves, it is unsurprising that a similar affinity for la mujer encerrada is articulated within the community.[59] I found this out when Tecpanecas encouraged me to not be out in the streets, "paseando" (walking around). Kaqchikel women stressed the importance of staying at home as a requirement of being a "good," "responsible" woman, even when they worked outside the home.[60] Thus, the local dynamics of public and private reflect larger power dynamics and histories of power.

Ethnographic and historical works have demonstrated the ways power structures the intimate.[61] In *Carnal Knowledge and Imperial Power*, Ann Stoler demonstrates how monitoring the intimate was critical to establishing the colonial apparatus in Indonesia. Sanctions on sexual relation and reproduction served to protect the (white) fragility of European women and allow for the "patriotic manhood" of European men.[62] These laws emphasized women's domesticity and positioned women as sites of morality and cultural reproduction that had to be protected due, in large part, to the social dangers created by European men's promiscuity resulting in *métissage* (racial mixing).[63] Similarly, Spanish colonial practices required the protection of European women through an emphasis on cloistering and virginity. This model of a mujer encerrada became the model of ideal femininity in the colonies. At the same time, European men's sexual exploits were a means of "improving" the colonies through *blanquimiento* (whitening). Guatemalan sociologist and historian Marta Elena Casaús Arzú has similarly shown that colonial laws relegating sexuality in Guatemala made Maya women's bodies the site of the whitening of the nation, with ladino men engaging in extramarital affairs and/or rape of Indigenous women.[64] Spanish colonial practices created a fascination, which continues today, with Indigenous bodies as simultaneously titillating and "dirty."[65]

Indigenous peoples of Latin America are underrepresented in ethnographic descriptions of romance, sex, and sexuality, but there are some notable exceptions. In Bolivia, Andrew Canessa describes how Aymara men take on a mestizo sexuality, often through service in the military, to prove their manhood and counter the historical processes that have rendered Indigenous (male) sexuality invisible.[66] Throughout Latin America, investigations of courtship and marriage patterns document a local preference for premarital chastity for women.[67] Maud Oakes's 1950's ethnography of highland communities showed that despite a valuing of chastity, women engaged in premarital sex and infidelities. However, these women were often labeled problematic locally.[68] Lois Paul's ethnography of the Kaqchikel community San Pedro La Laguna notes that while men are expected to enjoy and desire sex, Kaqchikel women are not.

Paul describes how many young brides experience (initial) sexual encounters as a violation of privacy and something that must be endured.[69] More recent scholarship has focused on linguistic investigations of romance and sexuality. Lourdes de León's analysis of messages sent between Tzotzil Maya youth demonstrates how texting in Spanish creates a (virtual) space where couples can explore romance through talk of kissing, touching, and desire. These messages create a discourse of romantic love that was not previously part of courtship in the Tzotzil language.[70] In Guatemala, Diane Nelson analyzes sexual jokes about K'iche' Maya Nobel Peace Prize winner Rigoberta Menchú. These jokes include plays on words that describing Menchú as an *indita desenvulta* (articulate Indian; unwrapped Indian, unwrapped here refers to removing of *corte* [skirt]). These jokes also suggest that male genitals hide below Menchú's corte. Similarly, anthropologist Brent Metz shows the prevalence of sexual joking among Ch'orti' Maya of eastern Guatemala. Despite this joking, he notes that substantive discussion of sexuality and reproduction is rare in Ch'orti' households.[71] Locally, then, Maya women present a set of contradictions. They are strong dedicated workers but need protection from men. They are the site of biological and cultural reproduction but are not agentive whole persons with intimate desires and fantasies who enjoy sex.[72]

MIGRATION FROM TECPÁN: IN PURSUIT OF "SOMETHING MORE"

As is true for other migrant groups, in Tecpán, today's patterns of migrations are shaped by larger social, historical, and economic forces. While patterns of domestic migration were long established in the highlands, Guatemala's thirty-six year civil war represents the beginning of Tecpán's transnational migrant flows.

The effects of Guatemala's civil war arrived in the highlands in earnest soon after the 1976 earthquake. *La violencia* (the violence), as these most brutal years of anti-Indigenous military violence are known, coincided with administration of General Efraín Ríos Montt (president from 1982 to 1983).[73] During his presidency, Ríos Montt orchestrated a scorched earth campaign in the highlands, which killed many and made refugees of others. Individuals the government labeled subversive were eliminated in extrajudicial killings.[74] Maya fled the violence and the food shortages that resulted from the military's burning of their crops. Numerous Tecpanecos, including members of my host family, fled Tecpán for the relative anonymity and safety of Guatemala City. Some Tecpanecos left the country altogether, seeking asylum in the United States and Canada. The violence of the civil war was the first time Tecpanecos migrated beyond the temporary seasonal migrations to pick coffee or cut sugarcane; however, families tended to migrate together as a unit during this time.[75]

Following years of war, Guatemalans have sought to create a stable and equitable nation, with limited success; a culture of impunity and corruption continues. Many military leaders, most notably Ríos Montt and Otto Perez Molina, remained in active in Guatemalan politics, ensuring their immunity from prosecution for crimes committed during the civil war.[76]

Neoliberal economic policies aimed at increasing regional peace and economic prosperity, like the System de la Integración Centroamericana (SICA; 1991) and Central American Free Trade Agreement (CAFTA-DR; 2004), have done little to change previous patterns of marginalization. Several return migrants, now in their forties and fifties, remarked to me that the changes in Tecpán's economy due to neoliberal treaties prompted their migration in the early 2000s. Privatization and low tax rates mean that the state provides few services, especially in rural (Indigenous) communities, resulting in the need for an extensive NGO network to provide services.[77] Land-holding patterns remain skewed: 2 percent of the population controls 60 percent of arable land.[78] This figure that has hardly changed since 1945. The lack of available land and employment in Guatemala's cities has prompted many to look to migration as a means of economic survival. This economic strategy has profound impacts on expressions of intimacy and selfhood for those who do not migrate.

STRUCTURE OF THE BOOK

This book on intimacy, technology, and migration explores the impacts of thirty years of neoliberal economic policy that gives rural Kaqchikel families few options for achieving the good life. Neoliberal capitalism has sold them a vision, a desire, for life that is largely unachievable without migration. This new pattern of migration has important consequences for Kaqchikel familial dynamics and personhood.

To understand how migration and technology are remaking selfhood and intimacy it is necessary to understand the institutions that structure women's worlds in Tecpán. Drawing its title from the Guatemalan adage "The destiny of women is to endure," chapter 1 outlines the central ideologies and institutions that shape Kaqchikel women's worlds and their images of themselves. The chapter highlights local women's own perspectives on what it means "to endure" in rural Indigenous Guatemala. It discusses their understanding of marriage, family, and religion. Under the precarious conditions of men' migration that leaves women at home in Tecpán, these structures and institutions enable some women while constraining others.

Chapter 2 describes the various technologies that mediate daily life in Tecpán. While the use of digital technology is widespread today, transnational households were among the first to live mediated lives, being early adopters of information communication technologies. The chapter describes three technological generations of transnational households and how the available technologies (beginning with letters and public phones and ending with WhatsApp and individually owned smartphones) have impacted the nature of communication in transnational households and with it the nature of family and personhood.

Chapter 3 examines how Kaqchikel Maya transnational families make use of Facebook, locally known as "Face." The platform has transformed from a technology primarily used by men to secure extramarital affairs to a space in which women and men can imagine together a shared life worth living in the future. The public performance of digital photo collages and inspirational posts allows men and women to "do family" despite physical separation.

Chapter 4 explores the contradictions inherent to contemporary transnational migration. Women's family lives are largely lived out on publicly accessible social media, but their physical worlds are often shrinking as they are subject to additional monitoring in Guatemala. This chapter investigates the forms of monitoring and social control launched against migrants' wives on the ground at home. It focuses on local—often malicious gossip—and its rapid spread through communication technologies like WhatsApp. The chapter reveals *suegras* (mothers-in-law) to be key agents of monitoring in transnational households in rural Indigenous Guatemala.

Chapter 5 describes the common "outcomes" of men's transnational migration for Kaqchikel Maya families. Revisiting stories introduced throughout the text reveals that men's migration and the subsequent "doing family" through communication technologies can result in women's emancipation during the prolonged absence of their husbands, family reunifications—both happy and unhappy, the abandonment of families in Guatemala, and extended periods of uncertainty and/or depression. The chapter focuses on the psychosocial impacts of men's migration on their wives.

Chronology

Key Dates in Guatemalan History

1470–1524: Precolonial Period

1470: Iximché founded as capital of Kaqchikel Kingdom

1524–1530: Conquest of Guatemala

1524–1821: Colonial Period

1525: Tecpán named Capital

1527: Capital moved to Ciudad Vieja

1773: Capital moved to Guatemala City

1821: Independence

1821–1870: Establishing New Republic

1871–1944: Planter Period

1930: Ubico's vagrancy laws

1944–1954: Ten Years of Spring

1944: October Revolution

1952: Land expropriation

1952: US CIA launches Operation PBSuccess

1954: Coup d'état

1960–1996: Civil War

1976: Earthquake

1980: Burning of the Spanish Embassy

1981: Extrajudicial killings of Tecpán's priest and Maya activists

1982–1983: Rios Montt's presidency and genocidal scorched-earth campaign

1990 to Present: Neoliberal Reforms

1991: Central American Integration System (SICA)

2004: Central American and Dominican Republic Free Trade Agreement (CAFTA-DR)

2015: Trial of Rios Montt

2019: Safe Country agreement

1

Enduring

Throughout my time in Guatemala, in interviews and informal chats, women repeatedly told me, "La vida de la mujer es aguantar" (The destiny of women is to endure).[1] Women, young and old, used the saying in a variety of situations. When sitting with family around the hearth, "aguantar" was used humorously as the punchline to jokes about having to get up to get someone more coffee. I also heard the phrase empathetically whispered as wives privately recounted stories of their husbands' cheating and sexual violence. The appropriateness of the adage in a variety of situations reflects the range of the connotations of the word *aguantar*. It can mean "to endure" but also "to put up with" or "to tolerate." Whatever the connotation, aguantar is linked to the idea that, in Guatemala, there are limited options available to Indigenous women. For some Kaqchikel women, enduring was the constant refrain in their daily lives.

Despite improvements in structural indicators of gender equality (education, literacy, age at marriage, physical autonomy, etc.), patriarchal gender relations continue to characterize daily life in Guatemala. Along these indicators, Indigenous women fare worse than their ladino counterparts. Scholars have questioned the extent to which these patriarchal dynamics originate in Maya communities, where traditional subsistence patterns require interdependent gendered divisions of labor for family survival.[2] They suggest the integration of Maya communities into the capitalist market as the impetus for the diminishing importance of this interdependent labor.[3] Although perhaps originating in colonial and later ladino gender ideologies as well as market logics, patriarchal gender norms are now firmly entrenched in Tecpán, regardless of ethnic identity. Kaqchikel women are doubly or triply marginalized in Guatemalan society as poor, Indigenous, and women. Men's and women's work is not equally valued.[4] Women of all ages complained about machismo (exaggerated sense of male ego; sexism) or *machista* (chauvinistic; sexist) attitudes that have limited their opportunities for education, employment, and autonomy.[5]

Patriarchal gender norms correspond to a gendered public-private divide where men head the family and are the ultimate authority figures in the household. Men's primary duties include providing for the family's economic wellbeing and protecting their wives and children. Conversely, women occupy private spaces and are responsible for maintaining the home and the affective labor of raising children.[6] As such, Kaqchikel women's movements outside the home tend to be circumscribed, both by the burden of their care work and by gendered expectations. Tracy Ehlers notes that into the 1990s, Maya women were discouraged from expressing an interest in the outside world because of its inherent dangerous and corrupting nature.[7] For generations, women's restriction to domestic spaces offered protection from the forces that marginalized Maya peoples. Despite its protective intentions, contemporary Tecpanecas found the expectation to primarily occupy domestic spaces as overly restrictive and unrealistic, especially given that most families' economic survival relies—at least to some extent—on women's ability to earn money.

This chapter presents ethnographic perspectives of what it means to be a Kaqchikel woman—what it means to endure.[8] I follow the example set by Kaqchikel anthropologist Emma Delfina Chirix García, who emphasizes the role of social institutions in the defining of personhood.[9] These institutions and ideologies that define what is means to be a woman in Tecpán shape the spaces of women's agency, especially for migrants' wives.

FAMILY AND ELDERS

Children begin learning ideal gender norms at home. It is Kaqchikel mothers and fathers who most contribute to gender socialization and the designation of "correct" gender roles.[10] Milpa farming provides the often-cited model of ideal Kaqchikel masculinity and femininity, instructing girls and boys about gendered expectations of work both within and beyond the home. In milpa production, boys and men are responsible for growing and harvesting corn while girls and women process the corn into food to sustain the family.[11] Integration into capitalist markets has transformed milpa logic, positioning men as the economic providers; Maya men work outside the home earning money for the family. Conversely, Maya women take on the domestic tasks associated with raising children. This shift has diminished women's authority and autonomy, placing Maya women in economically and socially precarious positions.[12]

In Tecpán's urban center, a movement away from subsistence agriculture has reduced the responsibilities of sons. The converse cannot be said for daughters, who are still expected to help with domestic chores. Women who had no or few daughters lamented that they had no one to help them as sons simply could not be expected to contribute to such activities. These women usually described cooking and cleaning as "women's work" and noted that sons were busy with school. Similarly, men who helped in the kitchen, sometimes merely making their own cup of coffee or reheating tortillas, were heralded as "collaborative." From an early age families prepare sons to fulfill their role as economic providers by encouraging their sons to study. It is assumed the sons will complete enough education to pursue a profession. Daughters are expected to help their mothers with domestic chores, even if they attend school. Intergenerational households, often comprised of three or even four generations, may place additional pressure on girls to fulfill "traditional" roles, prioritizing household chores. The implicit message is that sons' studies are an investment while daughters' studies are a diversion. Older Tecpanecos, especially those in aldeas, continue to see educating girls as a "waste" of resources. Such gender socialization prepares girls for the "real" duties of Kaqchikel womanhood: reproductive and domestic tasks. Men described other duties, like managing money, as beyond the abilities or capacity of women.[13] I often heard grandparents and aunts and uncles criticizing women's pursuit of education, especially for women in their twenties. Locally, many continued to see motherhood as the most appropriate pursuit for women.

COURTSHIP AND MARRIAGE

Marriage is integral to the construction of identity in Guatemala and a key institution that defines personhood locally. It is through marriage that Maya men and women become full members of the community. The Kaqchikel language reflects this conception of personhood. Women are referred to as *xtani* (girls) until they marry. Upon marriage, xtani' become *ixoqi'* (women). Similarly, *alab'oni'* (boys) become *ach'ia'* (men) upon marriage. This importance is not merely a linguistic artifact. The father of a transnational migrant told me that his son would return to Guatemala to marry and have children and thus become "a complete man." While it is through marriage that both sexes enter into full personhood, marriage does more to legitimize women's identities, especially those of rural women, because Kaqchikel women are primarily defined by their reproductive roles and their relationships with men.

Courtship

Campesino principles of femininity and masculinity perpetuate traditions of early marriage, early motherhood, extensive care work, and power dynamics that constrain Kaqchikel women's agency, especially young women's. In previous generations Kaqchikeles wed early, usually by age sixteen, and marriages were largely arranged. In such marriages there was little "courtship." Questions about courtship and marriage revealed that women over fifty were more likely to not have experienced courtship, marrying partners picked by parents. Although some of these women described their arranged marriage as one that was filled with love, more often women described these marriages in a way that matched descriptions of the patriarchal bargain where junior women accept some level of subservience to their husbands and mothers-in-law for economic security and the possibility of eventually finding small spaces of autonomy.[14] Early marriage and unavailability of birth control meant that couples had many children. By the early 1980s, these dynamics had already begun to change in the city center and they were beginning to change in Tecpán's aldeas by the 1990s.

In Chimaltenango, the department where Tecpán is located, the average age at first marriage was 20.2 (22.0 years for men) in 2015.[15] In addition to individuals marrying later, women are also more likely to pick spouses for themselves, marrying for romantic rather than purely economic reasons.[16] However, for many women the economic potential of their boyfriends still figured prominently in their selection of romantic partners. Even women who married for love often described economic stability as the quality that most attracted them to their spouse. A thirty-year-old aldea resident commented that she knew she wanted to marry her husband because he "always had money." Another woman, forty-three, described picking her husband because his family had land. Still, despite the persistence of financial considerations in selection of husbands, ideas of romantic love and intimacy are of growing importance in Tecpán.

A sign of the growing importance of romantic love ideals is that women often have multiple boyfriends before marriage—something that was uncommon in the arranged marriages of the past.[17] Most middle-aged women I interviewed had one or two boyfriends before marriage. Irma, a forty-one-year-old teacher from the city, described how important it is for couples to "be on the same path." She cited not being on the same path as the reason she did not marry her first boyfriend. Similarly, Dolores, age thirty-five, had two boyfriends before she married her husband. Her first boyfriend was much older than her and she was "too young" to understand love. Her second boyfriend was "nice" and her parents "liked him because he had land and could provide for me," but the relationship ultimately ended because Dolores did not love him.

Those women dating before marriage met their boyfriends in various ways. Most described meeting the men by happenstance as they completed errands or when attending school or working. After that first meeting, men sought out ways of being in touch. Before the spread of cell phones, romantic communications often took place in the public spaces of the market or town square when couples "happened" to run into one another. Some couples reported first noticing each other at school or church. The possibility for romantic encounters was one reason parents gave for why they preferred their teenage daughter to not be out "paseando" (walking around). While teens were excited about the possibility of seeing their crush while running errands, they were aware of the potential that either some family member was watching and would report on their activities or that they could become the subject of local gossip.

After cell phones became more widely available, men often sought out a woman's phone number to send romantic messages and talk to her. A forty-year-old Kaqchikel man told me how he spent weeks trying to find out the cell phone number of a woman he had seen working in a local restaurant. He described asking everyone if they knew her phone number. Once he found it he called and texted her multiple times a day complimenting her looks in the hopes of starting a relationship. He eventually married this woman. Months after he told me the story of how his courtship started, I shared a meal with his family. We all laughed about the lengths he had gone to meet his wife. His wife explained that his persistence and all the sweet things he had told her made him attractive to her. Smiling, she said, "Well, men fall in love with their eyes and women with their ears."

Several women described the importance of romantic words during their courtships. Middle-aged women described their courtship as taking place in both Kaqchikel and Spanish, with much dialogue about their hopes for the future. Zoraida, age forty-six, described how language impacted the discourse of romance in her courtship, and that of her sisters. In Kaqchikel, courtship phrases included discussion of buying land and having animals, while images typically more associated with romantic love were discussed in Spanish. The few men I talked to about their courtships often mentioned noticing how attractive women were, especially in their traje. Sometimes these men used the Kaqchikel to comment on women's looks. These phrases included referring to the young woman as "jeb'ël q'opoj" (beautiful unmarried young woman) or commenting how the woman was "ruya'al q'antazula'" (a juicy mango).[18]

Today, an emphasis on romantic love means that conversations about dating and courtship are a significant part of young people's daily interactions. As in the 1980s, young men often dedicate love songs to their girlfriends on the local radio stations. This was among the most popular public displays of courtship in the early 2010s. Since the expansion of smartphone usage, *novios* (unmarried couples) increasingly use social media to perform similar acts of dedication, which are usually performed using the "stories" feature of Facebook. Stories offer the ability to link images and videos with music in brief vignettes that are only visible for twenty-four hours. Numerous Facebook stories, created by both young men and women, feature a picture of the couple with a popular Spanish-language love song playing in the background. In the course of my research, I found that when made by men, these Facebook stories and their messages often commented on women's beauty. Women's versions of these Facebook stories often referred to how lucky they were to have the love of their boyfriend. There are also countless WhatsApp messages sent as part of courtship. Usually, these messages describe the woman's beauty, but they also often include images of red roses, as a means of sending a virtual bouquet of flowers. Today these romantic conversations almost always happen in Spanish, similar to the situation of Tzotzil Maya courtship patterns described by Lourdes de León in her work in Chiapas, Mexico.[19]

During my longest period of fieldwork, I volunteered as an English tutor for a group of teenage girls attending a private Catholic school in the city center. Many of the girls were from rural aldeas, living at the school during the week and returning home on the weekends. Although they did not participate in formal interviews, my time with them made me privy to their near constant conversations about love and courtship of Kaqchikel teens (ages eleven to eighteen). Their primary interest in English lessons was how to say phrases such as "You're sexy," "I think you're handsome," "Will you be my boyfriend?" and "I love you." This was especially true in the days leading up to Valentine's Day. The girls also talked about buying and receiving Valentine's Day gifts. Stationary stores in the city center sold valentines appropriate for friends or novios, a marked shift from previous years' celebrations, in which valentines primarily targeted the caring relationship between close friends. These celebrations of Valentine's Day have accompanied the growing importance romantic love and companionate marriage in the city of Tecpán. Several aldea residents and one store owner noted that Valentine's Day was not the holiday it was in the city. The store owner suspected he would sell more of the artificial roses and stuffed animals on his shelf if his store was in the city, not an aldea.

The growth of images and practices typically associated with romantic love has not reduced the importance of premarital chastity for women. Female virginity remains a highly valued form of feminine capital and expected until marriage.[20] A daughter's virginity reflects positively on her parents. Some mothers also suggested that their daughter's virginity could protect her from having to marry an "abusive" or sexist man. There was not the same expectation for Kaqchikel sons. While most mothers hoped their sons did not engage in risky or a lot of premarital sex, a son's virginity did not necessarily reflect positively on his parents or impact his status as a potential husband. One Catholic woman commented that she hoped her son did not visit a prostitute in the neighboring city of Chimaltenango. In contrast, she told me that she hoped her daughters did not have sex before marriage.

While sexual desire is understood to be natural and expected, the value placed on female chastity means that physical expressions of intimacy often happen just outside public view. It is not unusual to see young couples kissing, often intensely, in alleys or at the edges of cornfields. In the city center it is common to see young couples making out between the vehicles parked on side streets, away from the eyes of passersby. I was aware of several such locations known as *puntitas de amor* (little love places) where young, unmarried couples went *hacer el tururú* (to make love; have sex).[21] A broken-down commercial pickup truck parked on a side street was used as a puntita de amor in August of 2021. This specific puntita de amor, located in front of the local Catholic school, was the subject a series of interactions on Tecpán's municipal Facebook page, drawing my attention to its existence even though I was not living in Tecpán at the time.

On August 15, 2021, a private individual posted a video to Tecpán's official municipal Facebook page. The video showed a couple in their early twenties having sex between two parked vehicles. The poster uploaded the video to condemn such behavior and point out that there is always someone watching.[22] The video was removed the same day it was posted, but it prompted a series of posts that I followed from the United States.

The next day another individual posted a screen shot of the young couple with additional commentary cautioning young women to not let men seduce them into such bad behavior. Notably, there was no commentary on the young man's behavior from the female poster. Some of the comments on the video and later screen shot lamented such behavior among youth. At the same time, there were several comments, usually from men, that joked about the pleasures of such interactions.

Within three days of the original post, another community member had posted a picture of the broken-down pickup, with the school and statue of the Virgin Mary in the background. Most of the ninety-six comments on this Facebook post were humorous. One young woman joked that the Virgin Mary statue made any sex had there "safe sex." In another comment, a man jokingly asked if anyone could send him a copy of the original video for review.

Community awareness of this puntita de amor resulted in the municipal government placing a security guard in front of the pickup until it could be removed. Another Tecpaneco posted a picture of the security guard with the caption "Ya pusieron segruidad en el puntito de amor ya no habrá más tururú ahi" (They put security at the point of love don't make love there anymore). Many of the comments on this post were also humorous in content. For example, "☹que los sentimos por los guerreros que pasaron sus mejores momentos en ese lugar, un minuto de silencio" (☹ we feel for the warriors who spent their best moments in this place, a moment of silence.)

Premarital sex occurs in Tecpán, as evidenced not only by Facebook posts about punitas de amor but also by unplanned pregnancies. Nationally, many women still report knowing little about sexual and reproductive health before their first sexual encounter.[23] In interviews, women told me that their mothers and grandmothers had not talked to them about their bodies or sex because they worried that talking about such topics would awaken sexual desire in their daughters. Instead, most women described learning about sex from whispers from older cousins or siblings. In 2001, Congress passed the Ley de desarollo social (Law of Social Development), which mandated the creation of a sex education curriculum, including reproductive health, for public schools. However, the programs have focused on increasing the self-esteem of adolescent girls and eliminating "bullying" based on gender. A twenty-two-year-old woman who had gone through the school's sexual education program laughed at the idea that what the public school taught was sexual education.

Raquel, a thirty-three-year-old single mother from the city center, praised school programming about gender equality and self-esteem but lamented that it did not go further to include actual sexual education. Raquel explained, "I am very straightforward when I talk to Angelica [her daughter, aged ten]. Girls need to know about their periods, about their bodies. If they know these things, then they will be able to make decisions. They won't end up being single mothers." Raquel acknowledged that not all mothers are like her. In fact, she suspected that "most girls don't know anything about sex because mothers don't ever talk about it." She commented that when families do not talk about sexual education, young people are forced to learn "from whispers." She also pointed out that in the absence of sexual education, young men (though not young women) will learn about their bodies and sex by watching pornography or visiting a prostitute in Chimaltenango. Yet, while Raquel favored school programming on gender issues, including sexual education, as a way to improve the lives of Kaqchikel women, her opinion was not widespread. Many more Tecpanecos with whom I talked feared that sexual education would encourage earlier and more premarital sexual experiences.[24]

While talk of (premarital) sex was taboo, I observed sexual joking during my time in Tecpán. Innocent joking, including sexual innuendos among close friends and family, was common, even in mixed company. For example, members of my host family gathered to see the recently purchased car of a cousin. One woman in her late thirties complimented the car saying, "Está grande su trasero" (the trunk is big/roomy). With a mischievous smile, the male owner replied, "Pues . . . asi me gustan" (well . . . that's how I like them). His play on liking cars with a roomy trunk and women with large butts elicited laughter from everyone present, young and old.

Much of the sexual joking I was privy to took place in female-only spaces, for example, conversations had around the pila while washing clothes or around the hearth while making tortillas. Women's health clinics also created the space for talking and joking about sex. Elder women were more likely to speak frankly or make jokes about sex in these clinics. In these spaces, I saw and heard numerous jokes about male anatomy, especially during condom use demonstrations. Elder women joked about how sex became "just for fun" when women used birth control or after menopause. One woman in her early forties explained that since her hysterectomy, "Ahora solo es parque de diversión" (Now it is just an amusement park). I suspect that the older women enjoyed "surprising" younger, less experienced women with their jokes just as much as they found their jokes funny.

There were also jokes about women's sexual desires, which were rarely talked about outside the intimacy of women-only spaces. I helped work a cervical cancer screening clinic in one of Tecpán's more remote aldeas. During the presentation, which described unusual vaginal discharge as a symptom of cervical cancer, a sixty-seven-year-old Kaqchikel woman leaned over and half under her breath told me it was not unusual to have vaginal discharge "when you're with your husband." An anthropologist friend reported a similar interaction in her work with K'iche' Maya women. A woman of about forty came to a women's health clinic complaining of burning sensation during urination. She told the health worker, "Como me arde" (it burns). Changing to a more seductive tone of voice, she jokingly repeated, "me arde" referring the "burning/stinging" of sexual arousal.

Marriage

As Tecpanecas talked about their marriages, it was easier for them to remember courtship and the initial stages of marriage. Some described being surprised by men's expectation to be the head of household. Cecilia, age forty-three, described how her life changed when she got married: "It surprised me. I was accustomed to going out whenever I wanted. But when I got married, I realized that my husband expected me to be home all the time." The rhythm of the daily life as marriage progressed was harder to articulate. Women and men both described coming to know how to be a husband or a wife "little by little." Some women referenced learning how to be a wife from the explicit teachings of their mothers-in-law. Other women described learning from watching the dynamics of their natal families.

While images and language of romantic love in courtship have grown in importance in Tecpán, discussions and interviews about the characteristics of good and bad spouses revealed that many women still primarily conceived of marriage as an institution in which men and women fulfilled particular roles: men taking care of the family economically and women devoting themselves to their husband and children in the domestic realm. Several women described knowing that they had wanted to marry the men who would become their husbands because of their economic status (having land or a full-time job). And while economic security was especially valued as an ideal characteristic for husbands, the ideal characteristics of wives included selfless dedication to children. For example, María Elena, a thirty-one-year-old woman living in Tecpán's city center, told me that good wives "dedicate themselves to their children" and "do not have many friends." She described women with too many friends as bad wives because they were "always chatting in the street instead of caring for their homes and children." Local expectations are that women should occupy the private spaces of domestic life rather than the public spaces of "the street."[25]

In Kaqchikel marriages, it is not only the couple's expectations of one another that is important; husbands and wives are also subject to the expectations of other family members, given couples' postmarital residence patterns. Upon marriage, a couple establishes a new home. This residence may be on the husband's plot of land—bought or inherited—or may be within his family compound. Given the increasing cost of land both in the city center and in the surrounding aldeas, it may take years for men to establish a home for themselves. In the meantime, couples often live in the husband's family compound or even within the same physical building. In this period, the new wife is incorporated into the daily domestic activities of her husband's household, primarily spending her days with her mother- and sisters-in-law. The new wife is expected to prepare food and wash clothes for her husband and to help with the domestic needs of the extended family. Some women described encouraging their husbands to establish their own households more quickly so they could have more privacy and so that they would have the additional autonomy of being in control of their own kitchens.

Patrilocality is still common today, especially in rural communities. Still, there are numerous variations seen throughout the municipality. In the city center, I observed that families of higher socioeconomic status established their own home quickly, sometimes even before marrying. These families still spent the first weekend after marriage with the husband's family in a symbolic patrilocal residence pattern. In such situations the couple usually moved out at night, to protect the man's family from local gossip. The pressures exerted by mothers-in-law (detailed in chapter 4) and the increased independence of women mean that young women try to avoid living with their in-laws. A young, newly engaged woman from Tecpán told me that she did not want to live with her in-laws because she could not tolerate being "treated like a slave." A friend working for an NGO in a neighboring Kaqchikel town told me that many of the young girls she worked with described fearing marriage because they feared having a bad mother-in-law.

A lunch discussion with Raquel revealed how husbands' families evaluate new wives. Over soup and toasted tortillas, we chatted about the situation of Raquel's brother, Miguel, and his wife who—after only two years of marriage—had recently left him. Raquel characterized her sister-in-law as "lazy," saying, "All she wanted to do was watch TV. And when she did wash clothes, she only washed her clothes and the baby's clothes. She never washed *his* clothes." Instead of taking on the domestic duties expected of a wife, she left the washing of her husband's clothes and preparation of his meals to Miguel's sisters and mother. As the conversation continued, Raquel pointed out that her sister-in-law had no reason for such behavior; Miguel had a "good job." That is, he always fulfilled his half of the marital contract by providing economically for the family. Raquel suggested that her sister-in-law's friends compounded the martial problems between her brother and sister-in-law: "She was always at her friend's house. And this friend is not good. She [the friend] was always saying that he wasn't good enough for her [the wife] and how she should leave him and just come live with her."

Marital Dissatisfaction and Infidelities

Fights and dissatisfaction happen in most marriages. Men shared their frustrations with me less frequently, because I did not have the opportunity to have such conversations and because I was primarily friends with their wives. Both men and women described frustrations stemming from the lack of communication. For example, one man described how everyday disagreements compounded because of a lack of communication, especially about intimacy. Taboos about sex sometimes continued into marriage, with husbands and wives not openly communicating about sex. The man, age fifty, explained that husbands and wives would do better to just talk openly about sex. He used the example of his own relationship, commenting that sometimes his wife rejected his sexual advances. He explained that these rejections no longer caused fights because he learned that it mostly happened when she was menstruating. He pointed out that failure to openly communicate this meant that they spent years fighting over something that was easily understood.

Women's dissatisfaction with their husbands was a theme permeating my interviews.[26] Several women commented on the difference between courtship and marriage, noting that courtship was all fun and romance, but marriage was about responsibilities, many of which fell on women. A woman in her forties noted that "when you're dating, it is all hugs and kisses. There aren't responsibilities. In marriage everything changes." Some women described feeling like they carried too heavy a burden associated with childcare and domestic activities.

A key reason for marital dissatisfaction was husbands' failure to provide economically for their family. Women described bad husbands as those men who were "not providing for household expenses," "not being responsible," "hitting," and "being aggressive." They also described those men who are "always out in the street" as bad husbands. This was one of the few times that the phrase "always out in the street" critiqued men's behavior; the phrase was most often used locally to critique and curtail women's behavior and/or mobility. Women's launching of this critique related to their perception that men who were "always in the streets" were dedicating their resources, namely money, to drinking and not their families.

Indeed, women often complained about their men's drinking and wasting money. Frustrations with husbands' behavior generally coincided with men's marital infidelities, which were common and expected as part of marriage. It was only when men failed to fulfill their economic duties that men's infidelities were seen as problematic. When describing how men's sexual infidelities were an accepted reality, a nurse from Tecpán told me the story of how her husband wanted to take her for a coffee at El Cafetalito when their family was visiting Guatemala City. She explained that at first she did not want to go because she thought it was better to spend the fifty quetzales ($6.44 USD) to feed their children. She continued, "But then my sister-in-law scolded me and told me I needed to go with my husband. She reminded me that if I said no he would just spend the fifty quetzales on another woman who did want to go get a coffee." Even if expected, men's infidelities were still disappointing to wives. Xuana, a thirty-one-year-old unmarried woman from an aldea, reflected on the realities of marriage in Tecpán: "In what I've seen, husbands are bad and look for another woman . . . Sometimes in another village, sometimes here. It makes the life of women very hard. There are many women who are single mothers because their husbands found another woman and they are left with the children." She added, "Men only deceive women." Reflecting these dynamics is the local saying that "a good man, like a good avocado, is a hard to find."

While women saw infidelities as unavoidable, they sill lamented the loss of love these caused. Rosa, forty-three, recounted how her marriage had suffered in the years leading up to her husband's migration. She described how the constant cheating of her husband had impacted their relationship: "Once distrust has entered into a relationship it is hard to ever get the trust back. Distrust entered into our marriage before he left [migrated]. He had seen other women for at least ten years, but I never knew. I suspected, but I didn't know. I discovered that he didn't have just one, but lots, of other girlfriends. Instead of coming home, he'd stay out late and drink. . . . This went on and on for years. And so our marriage continued this way. I got pregnant again and again. By the time I discovered that he had other girlfriends, I already had four children with him. There was no way to leave. . . . I know it changed me. Everything that I had once felt for him was gone. The light that we had had was turned off."

Rosa's heartfelt description of the changes in her marriage demonstrate the importance of romance, trust, and intimacy in marriage even in a local context that continues to place importance on the social obligations of the institution.

Domestic Violence

Like other forms of violence in the long durée of Guatemalan history, domestic violence remains commonplace. Historically, it was expected that a Guatemalan woman's pious suffering included mistreatment at the hand of her husband. In her history of marital relationships in eighteenth- and nineteenth-century Guatemala, historian Beatriz Palomo de Lewin points out that a woman could only separate from her abusive husband when she legitimately feared for her life.[27] However, such cases of separation were rare, as the Catholic Church and the state encouraged, or even forced, women to remain in physically abusive marriages. Today, the Guatemalan state does little to punish, much less prevent, violence against women. Rather, as David Carey and M. Gabriela Torres describe, "violence against women in Guatemala has become a constitutive—rather than aberrant—feature of the social fabric."[28] In the 2014–2015 national survey on child and maternal health, 30 percent of Guatemalan women reported experiencing intimate partner violence.[29]

In Tecpán, many continue to see physical violence as a feature of marriage that must simply be tolerated. Indigenous customary law recognizes a man's right to hit his wife to "control" her, promoting the image of a good Maya wife as subservient to her husband. Women themselves suggested that "valid" reason for intimate partner violence included a wife's lack of care for the house, an absence of ready food at meal time, and (rumors of) her flirting with other men. Those women who felt comfortable discussing the topic described domestic violence as a "big problem" in Tecpán. In aldeas, it was possible to hear men yelling at and hitting their wives at night. The urban noise of Tecpán made it harder to hear instances of intimate partner violence, but it continued to occur frequently. Alcohol is often faulted as exacerbating the situation. One woman quietly revealed to me that "yes, my husband has hit me. If he has money, he goes and drinks. He returns to the house, late, drunk. He hits me because he doesn't like dinner or his clothes aren't clean. My mother-in-law tries to help me, to make sure that everything in the house is right. But when he is drunk, well . . . [looking away]."

Regardless of the physical violence and frustrations associated with marriage, Kaqchikel women overwhelmingly marry. The institution is connected to full personhood and is simply another thing for Kaqchikel women to "endure."

Birth and Parenthood

Marriage and parenthood are nearly synonymous in Guatemala. Most Tecpanecos have their first child within two years of marrying. Frederico, a twenty-three-year-old professional from the city center, commented, "In Guatemala, we get married to have children. If we don't want children yet, we don't marry. It isn't like the United States where people marry and sometimes never have children. We don't have that way of thinking." Throughout my doctoral fieldwork, my—at the time—childless marriage was often the topic of conversation among both men and women. They expressed their concern over my lack of children with refrains of "¡Primero Dios!" or "¡Kaketa!" (God wills it!). One elderly woman assumed that I had made a mistake in my Kaqchikel because she could not imagine that it was possible for me to not have children:

> Nan: Are you married?
> Meghan: Yes, I'm a married woman. I've been married eight years.
> . . .
> Nan: How many children do you have?
> Meghan: None
> Nan: No children. So, you got married eight months ago, not years.

It was incomprehensible for this monolingual Kaqchikel woman in her nineties that I could have been married for eight years without having a child.

Despite my repeated correction that I had been married for years, not months, it made more sense to her that I spoke bad Kaqchikel, rather than living in a childless marriage for eight years.

Upon learning of my lack of children, women—old and young, rural and urban alike—would earnestly ask whether my husband was looking for another wife, demonstrating the important role birth has in cementing the bonds of marriage.[30] When I replied that he was not, women commented how wonderful my husband was to stay married to me. Kaqchikel women saw it as my husband's right to look for another wife because I had failed to fulfill the main duty of women within a marriage: providing children. My husband's status increased; he was labeled "a good man" because he did not abandon me, despite my "failures" as a wife. Their concern revealed not only the value of children within Kaqchikel marriage but also my vulnerability in the marriage if it were childless.

Rural Indigenous Guatemala has the highest fertility rate in Central America. In 2015, the total fertility rate for the country was 3.1 children per woman (in rural areas: 3.7 children per woman; in urban areas: 2.5 children per woman).[31] Lower rates of education for females and a tradition of large families result in higher fertility rates in rural Indigenous communities. In Guatemala, rural women's average age at first birth is 20.6 years.[32] Among my interviewees, the average age at first was 20.5. Among those women I interviewed, the average number of children per women was 4.5. Such high levels of fertility reflect both the importance of child bearing for full personhood in Kaqchikel communities and a lack of consistently accessible contraception in rural areas. Overall, fecundity rates have declined in Guatemala due in large part to increased awareness of and interest in long-acting reversible contraceptives such as implants and intrauterine devices (IUDs).[33]

Those people whom I formally interviewed and casually chatted with (my work with a local medical NGO meant that I often had health-themed conversations with friends and acquaintances as we ate or traveled together) often cited the same reasons people were suspicious of using contraception. Rumors, augmented by the Catholic and evangelical churches, about the abortive or carcinogenic qualities of birth control were the most often discussed. A midwife from an aldea in Tecpán's more remote northern sector told me that "sometimes women ask me about birth control pills. I cannot recommend them. They harm the uterus. They cause cancer [because they prevent menstruation]." Continuing, the midwife reported that the one woman she knew who had used birth control pills experienced amenorrhea. Her period returned when she stopped taking birth control pills, but the midwife reported that her period was "choj carbón" (pure carbon). Here, the midwife connected birth control pills with necrosis in the uterus. Similarly, a middle-aged professional woman in the city center pushed back against my advocation of contraceptives, telling me, "One way or another, they [birth control pills] do cause cancer."

Regardless, men and women expressed interest in limiting the number of births, within and outside of marriage.[34] The primary time I saw marked disagreements over the use of contraceptives was when husbands were preparing to migrate. Removal of IUDs was often part of the preparations for becoming a transnational household. Husbands did not want their wives to have access to birth control, especially a long-acting reversible contraceptive, when they were away. Migrant men saw such access to contraceptives as facilitating women's infidelities. They were especially suspicious of wives who did not want to have their IUDs removed, saying that such protests demonstrated that they were already planning on cheating. Attitudes toward contraceptive use was one area in which local perceptions of acceptable behavior changed in a transnational context. These situations, discussed more in chapter 4, almost always meant that wives' freedom and agency were constrained.

CATHOLIC AND EVANGELICAL CHURCHES

Guatemala is an extremely religious country. Almost 90 percent of the country's inhabitants identify as Christians (45 percent Catholic; 43 percent evangelical).[35] Religious activities and the religious calendar organize the passage of time in local communities. Tecpán's *feria* (town fair) happens in October leading up to St. Francis of Assisi's feast day. At the same time, in concert with Catholic and Evangelical religious traditions, many Maya Tecpanecos continue to look to Maya spirituality. Many Catholics I knew consulted both priests and *ajq'ij* (day keepers) when making significant life decisions, such as about migrating.[36] Just as the use of day keepers remains vibrant, so does participation in *cofradías* (religious fraternities). Despite their predicted decline, elders and middle-aged community members continue to participate in them.[37] Middle-aged (and middle-class) participants see their participation in cofradías as a means of establishing themselves in the community. In addition to creating a sense of community and shared cultural traditions, religious institutions exert significant influence on the construction of local femininities. Throughout the year women actively participate in their church community, attending mass at least one time a week and, when possible, serving on "women's committees."

Churches actively promote traditional images of women, emphasizing their reproductive and domestic roles, but church attendance also created spaces of possibility and agency for Kaqchikel women in Tecpán. Attending church, with or without other family members, is a culturally appropriate ways of socializing. Church attendance, no matter how often, rarely results in local gossip. Therefore, most women attend services multiple times a week. Regular church attendance also corresponds with participation in women's committees, including cofradías. The Catholic women I knew regularly attended church, usually multiple days a week. Several commented that church attendance was a social enterprise that was deemed acceptable for "good women." Tecpanecas also described enjoying participating in women's groups and the space this afforded them to help their fellow (female) community members (fig. 1.1). While all I spoke to highlighted the importance of these committees, some women whom I knew commented that they found participation in the women's committees burdensome given their already high burden of domestic chores. In the nearby Kaqchikel town of Santa Catarina Palapó, anthropologist Joyce N. Bennett describes how these organizations provide Kaqchikel women an avenue for building self-improvement, solidarity, and personal satisfaction. However, as in the case of Tecpán, women's organizations do not necessarily translate to increased gender equality. Indeed, the organizations may serve to elevate the status of *male* parishioners and church leadership.[38]

Figure 1.1. Wives of cofradía members wearing the traditional traje of Tecpán, Palm Sunday, 2014. Photo by Meghan Farley Webb.

A key trope of Kaqchikel femininity taught by the Catholic Church is that of women as self-sacrificing mothers. The Catholic Church teaches that children are, as many women said, "a gift from God" or "a destiny decided by God." In much the same way that Mary accepted the blessing of being Jesus's mother, so too Catholic women must accept the blessings of children. In fact, Stevens's trope of marianismo uses Mary as the model of self-sacrificing motherhood and moral superiority, in contrast to men's machismo.[39] Scholars critique this simplified image of Latin American women and diminished women's subordination under patriarchal relations. Locally, women had never heard the term marianismo but thought that the description of self-sacrifice, especially when it comes to enduring multiple, sometimes unwanted, pregnancies, was accurate.[40]

In Guatemala, almost all Protestants identify as *evangelicos* (evangelicals). Since the 1970s, Protestant movements have spread rapidly across Latin America, especially in Guatemala.[41] In Guatemala, evangelical churches membership has been seen as a means of self-improvement among lower socioeconomic classes.[42] In Tecpán, evangelical churches are popular among women because of evangelical churches' stricter policies on the consumption of alcohol. Women especially sought this out given the association of men's drunkenness with physical abuse. And finally, Guatemalan women have found evangelical churches' emphasis on individual salvation to be empowering.[43]

EDUCATION

Like churches, schools are another institution that presents ideal versions of Indigenous womanhood. Education is important to the making of citizens, a process that in Latin America has meant transforming "Indians" into "citizens."[44] As recently as the 1980s, formal education was considered important primarily for boys, who would eventually engage in formal wage labor. Destined to be in the domestic sphere and already undertaking essential household tasks, girls were discouraged from attending school and consequently much less likely to learn Spanish. Sebastian, a seventy-six-year-old farmer explained to me that "long ago women didn't go to school. We didn't see it as necessary . . . Long ago women didn't need school. But now we educate girls. Now women focus on their studies and families are smaller." In previous years lower levels of education corresponded with lower levels of Spanish fluency. Being monolingually Kaqchikel (or unpracticed in Spanish) severely constrained women's interactions with the world outside the village. Compounding matters, Kaqchikel parents throughout the region saw education as a gateway to the potentially morally corrupting outside world.[45]

Educational opportunities have improved across Guatemala; however, Guatemalan girls continue to receive less education than their male counterparts. The 2014–2015 national survey revealed that 14 percent of Guatemalan women complete primary school (compared with 16 percent of men) and 22 percent are "without education" (compared with 16 percent of men).[46] In Tecpán, the education of girls is now more widespread, but both rural and urban women continue to be dissatisfied with the level of schooling they are able to complete. Reyna, age thirty-two, said, "I wanted to go to school longer. But my father didn't want to spend the money on my school supplies. . . . He said, 'Why pay for you to attend school, you'll just get married.'" Universally, female interviewees above the age of thirty reported that their parents had taken them out of school because of a lack of money. Sometimes, parents diverted money from older children, especially older girls, to free up money for younger siblings to attend school. For example, Wilma, a thirty-five-year-old vegetable vendor in Tecpán, revealed that she had wanted to study more but was forced to leave school to help her widowed mother sell in the market.[47] As she was the oldest child, her labor in the market ensured that her younger sisters could complete high school.

Feelings of losing out on a formal education inspired some of the women I interviewed to take on debt to ensure that their daughters completed more school than they did. The idea that education and "achieving a profession" were the ultimate ways out of poverty was a prominent theme in my interviews with women in the Tecpán area. They saw education as an "inheritance" for their children—boys or girls. However, mothers of girls particularly emphasized the importance of education for their daughters. They saw their daughters' education as a means of not "having to endure women's problems" of poverty and gender inequality. Conversely, male relatives often continue to see educating women as a waste of time and resources. For example, Luisa, age twenty-two, told me her uncles constantly ridiculed her for continuing her education. This was true even though Luisa had sought out scholarships and worked to pay the quotas associated with her studies on her own.[48] Her uncles implored her mother to stop encouraging Luisa's education, as he felt she should be dedicating herself to more important things like taking care of her younger brothers and sisters and looking for a husband. But women like Luisa understand that more education results in more economic opportunities. In private, Luisa's mother supported her daughter's decision, but she found it difficult to stand up for it in front of her own brothers.

ECONOMICS

Guatemalan women must endure the labor of daily life, which they categorize as "bien sufrido" (miserable). Positioned as natural caretakers, Kaqchikel women are expected to spend most of their time at home, cooking, cleaning, and caring for children and elderly relatives. This leaves very little time for employment outside the home. None of the women I interviewed from aldeas described themselves as anything other than "homemaker" or "working in the home." The one exception was a midwife who described herself as both a homemaker and midwife. Such foregrounding was true even for those women I knew to occasionally work with NGOs, in the weekly market, and/or seasonally harvesting crops. Instead, women in aldeas saw harvesting coffee or working occasionally for an NGO as a means of earning a "few extra cents" to supplement their husbands' earnings or to purchase goods that were normally beyond the family's means. In the city center it was more common for women to have formal employment, especially educated women and those of higher socioeconomic status. Residence in the city center also made it easier for women to seek out opportunities for informal employment. Women of lower socioeconomic levels often took jobs cleaning or washing clothes in homes. Women of all economic backgrounds sought ways to make extra money. Often these strategies involved selling food items like quesadillas, chocobananas, or cooked peaches.

Neoliberal economic restructuring since the 1990s has decreased social spending and contributed to the need for women to work outside the home for the family to survive. Today, Kaqchikel men experience widespread un(der) employment. Many men struggle to provide economically for their families. Increasingly, Kaqchikel families have had to embrace a variety of economic strategies that include taking on debt, selling belongings, migrating, and women entering the workforce. While women's work outside the home is now critical to familial survival, it remains undervalued. Often, women's work is not seen as "providing for the family," even if it is the family's sole source of income. This undervaluing prompts anthropologist Tracy Ehlers to categorize Maya women as "providers of last resort."[49] In Tecpán, this manifests itself in various ways. Flora explained that "many women have to work. But they [men] discriminate against women . . . They think that women should only do the jobs in the house."

Women's Employment outside the Home

In my research, I found that rurality greatly influenced whether a woman worked outside the home. Those living in the city center were much more likely to work outside the home than their counterparts in aldeas. Educated women from the city center often worked as teachers, lawyers, and secretaries in the city center, the department capital of Chimaltenango, or even the national capital, Guatemala City. Tecpanecas with little education tended to work as maids. These women's work was usually in the informal sector—allowing for the flexibility needed to simultaneously complete domestic tasks such as caring for children or ill family members.[50] In Tecpán, it is not uncommon for poor women to seek out part-time work cooking and cleaning in others' homes. Young, unmarried women without children are the most desired employee for this type of employment. However, married women and single mothers seek out these jobs as well, which necessitates leaving young children at be home to be cared for by other women in the household.

Susi is a twenty-four-year-old widow for whom informal labor enabled the survival of her two young children. After months of illness, Susi's much older husband died from a condition related to his alcoholism. Because they were renting the house they lived in, Susi had very few options. She was able to return to her parents' home to live but needed to seek out a source of income, which she found working as a maid for a family in Tecpán's city center. Susi's domestic work required her to work from seven in the morning to four in the afternoon Monday through Saturday. This schedule meant that Susi's children stayed with their grandmother while Susi worked. Informal-sector work, like Susi's, provides support for households, especially in cases where husbands are not able to earn enough money to meet their needs. The "extra" money from women's work is critical to the functioning of many Maya households; however, this strategy is specific to urban areas. In Tecpán's aldeas, where there is significant need for extra money, there are few opportunities to take on extra domestic chores. One aldea resident explained, "I can't take in wash here. No one has the money to pay for another woman to do their work."

As educational opportunities for Maya have expanded, more women are completing the education necessary to become teachers, nurses, secretaries, accountants, lawyers, and more. Irma, Susi's boss, is one of many professional women in Tecpán. As a child, Irma loved school. Her mother, a war widow, encouraged Irma to pursue her studies past elementary school. However, she could not afford to help Irma with the costs of her studies. Undeterred, Irma sought out scholarships and took a job as a maid in a "big house" in Guatemala City to pay for her books and supplies. Irma explained, "I wanted to be a doctor. I even went to the first year of school to become a doctor, but the books were too expensive. I couldn't continue. It was then that I returned to Tecpán and became a teacher." Irma's framed degree is proudly hung in the family's sitting room next to their altar to the Virgin Mary. She fondly remembered her first years as a teacher, traveling with her fellow teachers to the rural aldeas to teach. Like many women, Irma began her working as a single woman. However, unlike a majority of other Maya women, Irma continued working outside the home after marrying and having children.

Irma is able to continue working after marriage largely because she is educated and of higher socioeconomic status.[51] Her family can afford to pay Susi to help around the house. Even with Susi's help, Irma feels the burden of the "doble jornada" (double shift) required of her as both a teacher and a mother and wife. Irma's typical day starts around five o'clock, "unless I have grading I didn't finish the night before." Irma wakes and lights the stove to heat water for coffee while she dresses. She then makes breakfast for those who have to leave the house the earliest: herself, her eldest son, and husband. Irma's mother arrives to help with the younger children, getting them dressed for school and preparing their food. Susi arrives by seven, gets brief instructions from Irma as she leaves the house, and begins cleaning. During the day, Irma's mother oversees Susi's work, assigning her tasks, which include washing dishes, going to the market, cleaning the house and patio, washing clothes, and—under the close supervision of Irma's mother—preparing lunch. Susi does the physical labor associated with domestic work, while Irma's youngest children play with her mother.

Irma returns home at lunchtime. After the family eats, Irma watches the news on a TV in the bedroom and plays with her two youngest children. With her baby on her back, Irma completes the tasks that Susi was unable to finish. Irma also goes to visit her elderly grandmother in the afternoons, helping to clean her kitchen and wash her traje. Irma always washes her own clothes. She told me that she does this to ensure that the job is done well, but I suspect that she does this work to counter potential criticisms. In addition to completing these tasks, Irma often takes her grandmother extra tamales or soup. When I asked whether it was hard to find the time for this she replied, "Yes, but there is no other way." In the evenings, Irma prepares for her next day at school and supervises her children's homework. These tasks are generally done in tandem with her preparing and serving dinner.

Working outside the home did not excuse Irma from domestic chores. Despite her duties as a mother and wife and her job as a teacher, Irma enjoyed being active in the local Catholic church. She tried to attend mass at least twice a week. The exhausting schedule required of those women working outside the home is a reason that formal employment is seen as impractical for married women and often shunned by elders and men. Irma is respected in Tecpán. She is a well-known teacher. Her husband, who is also a professional, is proud of her. Their collaborative efforts have enabled them to send their children to school and create a successful household. However, not all Tecpanecos share their point of view. I found, in my fieldwork, that many households shunned women's work outside the home following marriage.

A conversation with Katarina, a twenty-year-old nurse from an aldea working in Tecpán, revealed that nearly all of the young women in her class were excited to be nurses but were nervous about whether they would be able to continue with their careers after marriage. Katarina said, "One of the girls got married right after we graduated. She said that she was going to work after she got married; she said that her husband wanted her to continue working. But once she got married, he made her quit . . . I don't understand it, all that school. That is why I am not getting married for a long time." Within two years of this conversation, Katarina had married and within six months of her marriage she had stopped working. Though she was not pregnant, her husband and his family had encouraged Katarina to quit working as it was "inappropriate" for married women to work outside the home.

As Katarina's experience demonstrates, women's participation in both formal and informal labor markets is often conditional and constrained by male expectations.[52] Before marriage, fathers define appropriate work for their daughters. A twenty-five-year-old married woman explained, "Before I got married I worked at a business in Chimal[tenango]. There were several of us who did. . . . My father was very nervous about it. He almost didn't let me work there. I always had to be home right after work. He basically never let me leave the house." After marriage, it is a woman's husband—sometimes in consultation with his parents—who determines whether women can work outside the house. This phenomenon is not merely a local tradition: until 1998, Guatemalan law gave men the authority to deny their wives the permission to work outside the home.[53] Wilma's story demonstrates how husbands constrain their wives' ability to work outside the home.

Specifically, Wilma described to me how she had to constantly get permission from her husband to sell in the market: "I have to fight with my husband for him to let me go sell in the market. And I am always with my mother. If she didn't accompany me, I wouldn't be able to sell [in the market]." Wilma continued, "No, Meghan, Guatemalan men are not like American men; they don't let you go anywhere. My husband would never let me travel to another country without him."

CONCLUSION

Concerted efforts by the Guatemalan government and numerous NGOs have resulted in improvements in major indicators of gender equity in the country. Total fecundity rates have declined (5.6 average number of births in 1987 compared with 3.1 average births in 2014–2015).[54] Maternal mortality rates have improved as more individuals have greater access to medical care and women have increased access to contraception. Women's educational opportunities have also increased. However, rural (often Indigenous) women have less access to education and complete fewer years of schooling than their urban counterparts and rural men. Despite these promising data, biological and cultural reproductive roles continue to feature prominently in local definitions of womanhood. The emphasis on parenthood translates into the centrality of marriage, a local prerequisite for full personhood. Within marriage women described enduring infidelities and general marital dissatisfaction. Religious institutions define women as mothers, requiring pious dedication to their children. Increased educational opportunities translate into greater financial freedom, at least before marriage and children. However, Kaqchikel women often find their involvement in such enterprises constrained by the desires of men. Work outside the home is generally considered appropriate for women before the birth of children.

Despite increases in autonomy and agency, Kaqchikel women must continue to endure gender inequality as communities look to traditional gender dynamics and expectations of behavior to prevent cultural loss. More and more Kaqchikel men from Tecpán are foregoing years of domestic migration, instead seeking to achieve something of the good life through transnational migration. In such contexts, traditional gender dynamics often have increasing importance. For the wives of migrants, their husband's migration—the crushing debt, the years apart, the fear of abandonment—is yet another thing to be endured. The idea of enduring is often tied to the realities experienced in transnational households as women stay behind in Guatemala. Transnational migration offers one of the few options for achieving something more or the good life; the only option is enduring.

These gender dynamics, which are informed by larger economic, political, and social processes, shape Kaqchikel personhood. The institutions discussed in this chapter define the space of agency and how Kaqchikel women can negotiate power, intimacy, and identity within their families and the larger community. Yet, as discussed in the following chapter, today, digital information and communication technologies influence Kaqchikel women's ability to negotiate new forms of personhood, new intimacies, and potentially new family dynamics associated with men's transnational migration.

2

Mediated Lives

Raúl called Flora one morning while she and I walked around the remote aldea she where lived. I was conducting interviews with other migrants' wives whom she knew. Flora paused to answer her husband's call, telling me, "It is Raúl." Raúl was calling from New Jersey, where he had been for two years at the time. To give Flora some privacy, I stepped off the road and looked across the valley, lush from the winter's daily rains.[1] As I watched the clouds cast their shadows on fields of broccoli and milpa, I heard Flora explain that she was out walking with me, helping me conduct interviews. After a pause where I assume Raúl asked where we had gone, Flora told Raúl who we had visited and where we were going next.[2] Just as quickly as it had started, the conversation was over; Flora walked to the edge of mountain where I was standing. I confirmed that her helping me was not causing her problems with Raúl. Flora put her smartphone in the pocket of her apron and quickly brushed aside my worries, saying that Raúl just wanted to know who she was out with. After a quiet moment walking down the dirt road, I teased Flora that people were talking about her walking around town with that strange white lady. Laughing, Flora nodded and responded, "Exactly."

Cell phones have come to mediate all relationships in rural Indigenous Guatemala. As Flora, the twenty-nine-year-old wife of a transnational migrant, has experienced, technology now shapes the dynamics of her relationship with her husband, with her community, and with herself. Broadly, mediation is the dynamic processes in which social orders produce and reproduce themselves through particular forms of media.[3] Discussions of mediation tend to focus on the most recent technologies, often referred to as "new technologies" in the academic literature.[4] However, mediation is not limited to these digital technologies. As Tiffany Creegan Miller points out, Maya peoples, like other Indigenous peoples, have long used a variety of media to encode their knowledge and identities.[5] Newspapers, books, and letters mediate daily life. There are other less expected forms of mediation in daily life as well. For example, in Guatemala, women wear forms of mediation on their bodies in the form of town-specific huipiles.[6] Understanding these messages requires the cultural knowledge and technological and functional literacy to "read" them.

This chapter traces the trajectory of mediated relationships in the recent lives of Tecpanecos, exploring how daily life has gone from minimal technological mediation in the 1990s to full digital mediation in the 2020s. It pays special attention to the mediation in transnational households. The physical separation experienced by transnational families requires the mediation of relationships, making members of transnational households early adopters of communication technologies.[7]

Something as old as letters or newspapers or as recent as smartphones both mediate daily life in Tecpán. Regardless of the format of the mediators—traje, letters, or smartphones—these objects are shaping how humans experience and perceive the world around them. They redefine the limits and possibilities of relationships. Today, the cell phone is the primary technology shaping relationships around the world, including the municipio of Tecpán. Smartphones are everywhere, even in remote aldeas like the one Flora and Raúl lived in before his migration. New media connect the municipio of Tecpán to the Unites States in ways that were never possible before.

The World Bank, which uses cell phone ownership as an indicator of development, reports that there were roughly 114 cell phone subscriptions for every 100 people in Guatemala in 2020.[8] In Chimaltenango, the department where Tecpán is located, more than 315,000 individuals over the age of seven reported using a cell phone in the 2018 national census. This almost three times as high as those who reported using a computer (~104,000).[9] But cell phones are not merely indicators of development or "modernity." They shape Guatemalan society. Local *tienditas* (corner stores) are painted Tigo blue or Claro red.[10] Cell phones also shape the spaces of personhood and expand the boundaries of the municipio.

For the purposes of this chapter, I divide Tecpán's transnational migrants into three generations based on the available technologies: first generation (1990–2005), second generation (2005–2015), and third generation (2015–today).[11] These technological generations are specific to Tecpán and roughly correspond to divisions ascribed by transnational households to themselves. Their categorizations emphasized communication as the salient difference between the experiences of the different waves of migrants.[12] The first technological generation emerged from an absence of a significant telephone culture in Guatemala. Payphones dominated this period. The second technological generation was characterized by the use of cell phones in both the United States and Guatemala. However, it was equally marked by a digital divide. The third, current technological generation is associated with the widespread availability of smartphones and various social media platforms. Throughout the chapter I consider forms of media separately; however, media never operate independently of each other. New technologies are always emerging in already media-rich contexts.[13] These influence local forms of mediation, opening and closing different topics of conversations and intimacies.

SE AQUILA TELÉFONO: THE FIRST GENERATION (1990–2005)

The first wave of transnational economic migration from Tecpán began in earnest in the 1990s.[14] Much of the information communication technology usage in this wave of migration concerned the logistics of daily life. Migrants who left and their families who remained in Guatemala were unintegrated into a mediated world, although mediation did exist. Carol Hendrickson and Edward Fischer's ethnography of Tecpán in the 1990s describes the presence of newspapers, local community radio stations, televisions, and public TV parlors. However, news stories from the main newspapers *Nuestro Diaro* or *Prensa Libre* (in addition to not being read by the majority of Tecpanecos) had little impact on the intimate relationships of families.[15] Similarly, the TV parlors showing a variety of movies ranging from children's programming to soft-core pornography described by Hendrickson and Fischer were not universally mediating daily life.[16] The most widely mediating technology was the radio.

There was not a tradition of phone usage in Tecpán at the time. Cell phone service was just beginning to arrive to the Western Highlands in the late 1990s, but few individuals had them.[17] Before the proliferation of cell phones, those wishing to use the phone had to "rent" the use of a landline at a local store or street-facing room of a house.[18] Most larger tienditas displayed a handwritten sign saying "Se aquila teléfono" (phone for rent).[19] Renting a phone at a tiendita offered little privacy and usually required standing just inside or outside to use the phone. With luck there was a plastic stool to sit on or maybe even a plywood "phone booth" erected for some privacy. Regardless of the phone booth's configuration, privacy was largely an illusion; it was nearly impossible to have fully private phone conversations. Half the conversation could be heard by store owners, clients, and passersby. If such conversations were had in local communities, there was a high likelihood that neighbors or relatives could easily eavesdrop on phone calls. Consequently, domestically, chatting, courtship, or gossiping rarely took place on public rented phones. Those interactions were much easier to have face-to-face. Instead, individuals rented a phone with a specific task in mind, often related to (men's) economic enterprises, coordinating various logistics, or the health of a family member. Those in Tecpán noted that the exception was that families used public phones to talk to family members who were living or studying in the capital. However, these individuals described waiting to discuss sensitive or delicate topics until family members were at home and matters could be discussed face-to-face.

Transnational Phone Calls on "Payphones"

Like their family members in Guatemala, the first generation of migrants were dissatisfied using publicly rented phones. These individuals undertook their migrations in a media and technology context that did not have a strong culture of talking on telephones. Tecpanecos used telephones out of necessity, not for making small talk. However, for transnational households catching up on the mundane aspects of life was the necessity; small talk *was* the objective. This was especially true for transnational couples who had few ways to connect with their spouse. Phone calls on public phones was the only synchronous form of communication available to such families at the time. It took transnational households some time to establish patterns that facilitated good communication.

Using public phones presented a series of logistical hurdles. Most notable was the coordination of calls. Transnational families had to navigate different time zones and different rhythms of life. For example, in Tecpán the intimate spaces of families is found sitting around the hearth after dinner. Having to a use a public phone (in the United States or Guatemala) reduced the couple's ability to replicate this space, especially temporally. Families described not wanting to leave their homes following dinner to walk to a public phone. It is possible that doing so was easier in Guatemala, where using a payphone meant going to a close tiendita, often at a neighboring house. In the United States, using a payphone required going to the nearest gas station or standing on the street. Most often, payphones in the United States were outside; using them required standing in the elements, something that migrants did not want to do in New Jersey winters. The time difference between New Jersey and Guatemala also frustrated transnational families.

Once the difficulties of scheduling calls was worked out, members of transnational households still had to navigate the lack of privacy, which affected actual conversations as well as news of receiving phone calls. For example, if a tendita received a phone call intended for a member of a transnational household, the store owner would send a family member—often an older child—to run to the neighbor's house to tell them that they had a phone call. Locally, this spread the news of a communicative moment throughout the neighborhood. Indeed, it could prompt some nosy family members or neighbors to "serendipitously" visit the corner store for a purchase at just the right time to overhear conversations. Even if a couple did and managed to duplicate the temporal aspects of shared conversations after dinner, the intimacy of the hearth could not be so easily duplicated.

I spoke with several families of returned migrants from the 1990s, and they all reported the lack of privacy as the primary difficulty associated with communicating on rented phones. Issues of privacy were especially noticeable for migrants' wives. They described not feeling comfortable having conversations with their husbands in front of their in-laws or neighbors. The logistics of using a public phone in Guatemala meant that whole families often went to the store to talk at a time. There was very little privacy for conversations just between husbands and wives. For those wives who arranged to speak with their husbands when they were alone, there was always the potential that store owners were listening to their half of the conversation. In aldeas, these workers were almost always known to wives, and often related to them. The women characterized this a significant problem; they had to choose between gossip and intimacy.

Eduardo, age thirty-nine, had just returned from working in Canada when I interviewed him in 2013. I spoke with Eduardo on the front steps of his house while his wife moved around the courtyard completing her daily chores. She stopped in now and then to add to the conversation. His recent return from Canada prompted discussion about his experiences as an undocumented migrant to Dallas, Texas, during the first technological generation and his experiences migrating with a work visa.

Eduardo's first experience as a transitional migrant was in the late 1990s. At the time the first cell phones were just beginning to be available in Tecpán, but no one in Eduardo's family had one. Instead, his family walked down the street to a neighboring tiendita to rent a phone. In the United States, cell phones were readily available in the late 1990s, but international calling on them was extremely expensive. Eduardo, like other migrants, called Guatemala using international calling cards through a landline. Both Eduardo and his wife noted that there were issues with privacy and the coordination of calls. After some experimenting, they set times when Eduardo called her every week. They described these calls as somewhat dissatisfying as both had to remember the topics that they wanted to talk about over the course of the whole week. They complained that this reduced the spontaneity of their conversations. Ultimately, they figured out a strategy that worked for them as they bonded over their shared frustrations.

In comparing his experiences as an undocumented migrant in the United States (in the 1990s) and as a visa-holding migrant in Canada (in the 2010s), Eduardo highlighted the differences in communication technologies and how they mediated daily life, especially messages of connection and intimacy with his wife and children.[20] He explained, "It was harder to communicate with her [his wife] and my parents in that time. You see, it was before there were cell phones. To call I had to use a card at the payphone. And they had to go to a store where they rented the telephone . . . No, it [communication] was hard. With cell phones, it is very easy now."

Similar forms of technology mediated the communication of Eduardo and his wife. Both used public phones, Eduardo a payphone and his wife a rented phone. However, Eduardo's payphone offered more privacy than did the rented phone used by his wife. The phone Eduardo used was on the side of a gas station, where no one listened to his conversation. The rented phone his wife used was in the front room of their neighbor's house. She described being conscious of not saying too much and noting who could be listening to their conversation. While Eduardo's wife had little to no way of initiating a conversation with him, they experienced the same frustrations with the payphone technology and the limitations that mediation presented. This is something that would not be true for the second generation of transnational migrants and their families.

Transnational Letters

Even though using payphones was frustrating and required transnational family members to have conversations in public, former migrants and their families described them as more helpful and rewarding than sending letters, which was the one of the few communication options available to transnational households in the first technological generation. While the first generation of transnational migrants who left Tecpán in the 1990s relied widely on this method of communication, mailing letters was precarious; numerous migrants described how letters were unlikely to arrive. If letters sent through the mail did arrive, the process generally took two to three weeks. It was more reliable for letters to be carried by hand, but this meant that members of transnational households were dependent on individuals who might be traveling back and forth.

Men described letters as particularly unsatisfying means of communicating love and intimacy. Some described how issues of literacy impacted the writing and reading of letters. An older man pointed out that his wife had not completed school and therefore had to have someone else, usually his brother, read his letters to her. He asked me to imagine having to have someone else read me a love letter from my husband, quickly pointing out that such an experience would be highly unsatisfying.[21] Women in Tecpán expressed different frustrations. They found letters inadequate for addressing immediate concerns of daily life.[22] For example, several women complained that letters could not help them discuss financial decisions with their husbands. This difficulty was a pressing issue for those women whose in-laws received all the money sent home by their sons and then distributed remittances to their daughters-in-law.

Members of transnational households established their own culture of phone use and letter writing where one had not previously been established. In this first technological generation, "payphones" and letters were the technologies that mediated daily communication. A lack of privacy and lack of immediacy characterized the mediations during this time. Talking only at an arranged time, often once every seven to fifteen days, meant there was little spontaneity of conversation. Additionally, the cost of international calling was notable; each word had the weight of its economic and symbolic cost.[23] The lack of privacy prevented some family members from being able to adequately express their emotions, and it was hard to have meaningful exchanges that kept couples "united." However, some return migrants noted that genuine moments of connection came from the shared experience of frustration with the limitations of available technologies and the possible mediations. This changed with the second generation of transnational migrants.

CELL PHONES, NOT SMARTPHONES: THE SECOND GENERATION (2005–2015)

The expansion of cell phone service in Tecpán characterizes the second technological generation. While cell phones arrived in Guatemala in the late 1990s, they remained expensive and inaccessible to the average Guatemalan until the mid-2000s.[24] So when the second generation migrated to New Jersey, it moved from a place with a nascent cell phone culture to one where the technology was well-established. As in other similar communities, the cell phone became the "social glue" of the second generation of Kaqchikel transnational communities in Tecpán.[25] Widespread usage created rapid communication as well as a virtual co-presence, facilitating intimacy. Community members valued regularly talking on the phone, which remained the primary mode of synchronous communication. Issues of privacy were more easily navigated given that both parties had cell phones.

At the same time, while both those in New Jersey and Tecpán had cell phones, the digital divide that existed between migrants in New Jersey and their family members in Guatemala greatly influenced how transnational intimacies played out. Various levels of connectivity, phone sharing, and economic limitations constrained the quality and intimacy that cell phone communication offered before 2015.[26] Indeed, the digital divide that characterized the second generation's communication strategies was influenced by different cultures of cell phone usage as well as the features and availability of different types of phones.

Depending on their family's socioeconomic status, migrants may have owned a cell phone before migrating. It is likely that at least one person in the household owned a phone and a cell phone culture specific to rural Indigenous Guatemala was developing during these years. For example, device sharing within households meant that cell phones often stayed in homes and were used more like landlines. Deborah Rodman's description of cell phone use in eastern Guatemala parallels what I observed in Tecpán. In both contexts, cell phones were primarily used for receiving calls, especially among families of low socioeconomic status.[27] Receiving calls was free, but placing calls required the purchase of minutes. Most individuals did not keep *saldo* (a balance of money to be used for making phone calls or sending text messages) on their phones, only buying minutes when they needed to make a call or send a text message.

During the second technological generation, which corresponded with my longest period of continuous fieldwork, the cheapest and most popular cell phone available in the municipality was known as the *frijolito* (little bean) because of its resemblance to a black bean. The frijolito was available new for 130 quetzales ($16.72 USD).[28] This price included the phone, its accessories, a SIM card, and promotional saldo. These prices could be expensive for the average individual, but there were other means of acquiring cell phones. The most economical was to purchase a second-hand device from a friend or neighbor or at the market. Those who reported purchasing phones this way described simply buying a new SIM card to avoid unwanted or extortive calls on the old number.[29] At the time new SIM cards could be purchased for roughly 50 quetzales ($6.43 USD), including a promotional saldo of 30 quetzales ($3.86 USD). At this time almost everyone used prepaid cell phones and individuals made sure to maximize their saldo purchases. For example, whenever possible, people waited to purchase saldo on triple saldo days.

In contrast, in the United States there was a well-established cell phone culture. Readily available WiFi and relatively cheap data plans meant that nearly all migrants, regardless of socioeconomic status, had access to their own smartphones. At the time most cell phone plans offered free long-distance calls on nights and weekends. Still, most international plans did not include calls to Guatemala. As such, migrants' continued use of international phone cards made calling Guatemala economical, and cheaper than calling the United States from Guatemala. International texting was more economical than calling; again, texts originating in the United States were cheaper to send than those originating in Guatemala. The free messaging option of iMessage, available on Apple's iPhone, was launched in 2011, toward the end of the second technological generation. Yet, even after 2011, iMessaging was not an option for transnational families, because family members in Guatemala did not have the required Apple devices. Thus, the distinct cell phone cultures in the United States and Guatemala impacted communication in transnational households.

From 2009 to 2015 the typical communication pattern, reflecting both logistical and economic concerns, between the United States and Guatemala was that migrants called their family members once a week. From a logistical standpoint, migrants called so as to accommodate their work schedules. One wife explained, "He works hard at a bakery. He has to be there early and goes to sleep early. He calls on his day off." A return migrant who had worked in construction told a similar story: "In that time we worked long hours. Not like here, where we take breaks for coffee or for a festival. . . . No, in the United States the point is to work, not just waste time. . . . For this reason it was sometimes hard to find the time to call my family."

Patterns of communication were also influenced by socialization. The model of migrants calling once a week, on their day off, was established by the previous technological generation of migrants. Upon their arrival to the United States, migrants from Tecpán were socialized by other migrants that calling once a week was the "right" way to stay in communication with family members. Here, the previous media context defined the usage of the next-generation technology.

Furthermore, migrants called Guatemala because their families did not have sufficient saldo to place international calls. Given the economic constraints that the majority of transnational households faced, especially in the initial years following a migrant's departure, many migrants' wives saw cell phones as merely a means of receiving calls, resigning themselves to talking primarily when their husbands initiated communication. This communication pattern constrained intimacy. Quick calls or messages to share happiness or struggles were virtually nonexistent. Instead, weekly phone calls often involved the recounting of what had happened in the week, what needs the household was experiencing, and directions on how to spend, but mostly save, remittances that had been sent home. Descriptions of these conversations made them feel perfunctory and removed from the events the couple would have shared with each other had all their communication not been digitally mediated.

During the second generation, texting via SMS messages was largely a domestic practice; international texting was uncommon among the transnational household members I interviewed.[30] Wives described using text messages only for emergencies. In such instances wives would send their husbands un *mensajito de cobro* (a collect text). The message of this text was not important as the messages were rarely, if ever, read. Instead, Guatemalan cell phone etiquette—both nationally and transnationally—dictated that receiving a collect text message from a known number was an indication both of a need to communicate and a lack of saldo. Instead of accepting the charges and reading the message, it was common practice to simply call the number back. For the majority of wives, this was the only time they texted their migrant husbands.

A few wives reported sending a message of *hola* (hello) or "TKM" (*te quiero mucho*; I love you a lot) if they received a packet of promotional text messages to the United States. Cell phone companies typically offered promotional calling or text messages to the United States for those numbers whose owners made new saldo purchases. For example, Tigo sent text messages informing me that by entering a code I could receive twelve hours of discounted calls to the United States. Importantly, Tigo offered such promotions only in connection to purchasing saldo. Those who did not purchase saldo, as was common among rural and poorer families, did not have access to discounted calls or text messages to the United States. Outside of such promotional times, sending international text messages was seen as a "mismanagement of money." As I have described elsewhere, because of the severity of the critiques levied against migrants' wives, women did not spend money on texts to their husbands.[31] The price of international calls made such critiques even more salient when it came to women calling their migrant spouses.

WhatsApp (launched in 2009) existed during this technological generation, but it was not widely used in Tecpán. Using WhatsApp required a smartphone. During this second wave of migration, most transnational families in the municipio did not have a smartphone, meaning that WhatsApp was not a "workaround" for free messaging.[32] This precluded the growth of transnational texting as an economical means of contacting migrant family members.

While the pattern of migrants calling their loved ones in Guatemala once a week may have started for economic and logistical reasons, it facilitated the monitoring of women who remained in Guatemala. Unlike the rented phones used by the previous generation of migrants, cell phone technology meant that family members in Guatemala, especially wives, had to always be "on call," ready to answer a phone call from their migrant relative at any time. Indeed, while migrants still mostly called once a week, cell phones created the ability for migrants to call anytime. If a migrant became suspicious of his wife's behavior, he could monitor her whereabouts by calling her at any time of day or night. This practice was simply not feasible before the proliferation of cell phones. The digital divide, coupled with wives' lack of saldo, meant that in Guatemala cell phones were primarily experienced as one-way surveillance, extending the husband's gaze transnationally.[33]

Nery, a thirty-four-year-old return migrant from the city center, told me the story of how a local man tried to take advantage of Nery's migration to seduce his wife. According to Nery, this man searched out the cell phone number of Nery's wife, repeatedly asking friends and family members to share her number with him. Once he got the number, the man began calling her "constantly." Transnational gossip quickly spread. Some versions of the gossip chastised the man for his "abusive" calling. Others chastised Nery's wife for somehow inviting the man's flirtations, suggesting that Nery's wife was not a good woman; she was out in the streets, not at home. Nery explained, "There was gossip that my wife was going around with another man while I was in the United States. I was away but my heart was here with her. I thought, 'But I love her why would she do this?'" Nery doubted the transnational gossip, but the persistence of the rumors made him unsure what to believe.

Nery employed the same technologies that had so quickly spread transnational rumors and gossip to verify that his wife was telling him the truth about spending her days at home. He explained his strategy for doing so. Nery would call his wife at random, unexpected times and ask if she was at home. He informally triangulated his wife's location by calling other family members to inquire about and confirm his wife's whereabouts. Nery told me, "So I called my mom and asked, 'Where is my wife?' She responded, 'In the [garment] workshop [located in their home] working with your brother.' I then called my brother and asked him, 'Where is my wife?' He said, 'Here in the house.'" Nery explained how he then had his brother pass the telephone to her wife so he could talk to her. For Nery, this was the ultimate confirmation that his wife and family were not lying to him and that he need not believe the transnational gossip suggesting that his wife had been unfaithful.

This pattern of calling various family members to confirm the physical location of one's wife seems extreme, but it was common throughout the municipio. Indeed, Dinah Hannaford described a similar transnational triangulation among Senegalese migrants and their families. Hannaford notes that migrants working in Italy call various family members in Senegal to ensure that their wives are telling the truth. Migrants often employed these strategies if they heard "suspicious" sounds in the backgrounds of calls.[34] In Tecpán, migrants described sometimes asking children to participate in this monitoring because they deemed children to be the least likely to lie to cover a wife's "bad" or "improper" behavior. Ultimately, these calling patterns allowed migrant husbands like Nery to triangulate the location of their wives in much the same way that family members in the Global North might use a "find my phone" feature. The surveillance strategy Nery pursued confirmed that the information he received from his family was not false. Cell phone technology allowed migrants like Nery to determine the location of their wives, circumventing their potential mobility.

While cell phones enabled the surveillance of wives, they also created the conditions under which such surveillance was deemed necessary. As cell phones enabled easy and frequent communication, greater privacy and ease of communication increased satisfaction and came closer to recreating the intimacy of conversations around the hearth. However, this also meant the growth of a transnational gossip network—one that had a far greater reach than those facilitated by payphones. Additionally, such rumors became more believable given that cell phones offered potential for more private, even secret conversations. In the case of Nery's family, there was the potential for secret conversations between his wife and local men, as cell phones could allow such conversations to happen even if she was home.

Tecpán's second wave of transnational migration saw a gradual decrease in the divide between the technologies available to male migrants living in North Jersey and their wives living in Tecpán. In 2012, Tigo began a campaign for Guatemalans to *desfrijolízarte* (un-bean yourself), or upgrade to a smartphone (with a monthly calling and data plan). The ads from the time featured three black beans turning into black smartphones with the words "No hay excusas" (there aren't any excuses [to not upgrade your phone]). The only other text in the ad communicated the prices of the phones, which ranged from 399 to 549 quetzales ($51.42–70.75 USD).[35] The campaign suggested that with these more affordable options, it would be possible for anyone to purchase a smartphone, not just those who could afford an iPhone or a Blackberry.

The desfrijolízarte campaign proved most successful in urban settings, like Guatemala City. In Tecpán's city center, young and middle-aged professionals (who often worked in the capital) purchased smartphones, but the campaign had little success in rural areas. The cost of even the cheapest smartphone (399 quetzales) made them unattainable for nearly all rural Indigenous families in the aldeas surrounding Tecpán. For those of lower socioeconomic status, the frijolito and similar phones remained the most popular cell phone during this second generation of transnational migration.

Because of their expense, smartphones were a sign of social status at the time of migration. The status associated with smartphones, like the iPhone or BlackBerry, made cheaper "quasi" smartphones described in the *desfrijolízarte* ad desirable. These phones resembled their more expensive counterparts but lacked all the features of smartphones. For example, I purchased an Alcatel "BlackBerry" that had a full keypad, WiFi capabilities, and a limited number of applications, including Facebook.[36] WiFi compatibility was only of interest to those individuals living in the city center as aldeas did not generally have access to WiFi. Instead, almost everyone accessed the internet by going to an internet café or through USB modems used with a personal laptop. There was no ability for the average Tecpaneco to take advantage of the WiFi capabilities of their "quasi" smartphone. For those who purchased such a device, the phone came with a promotional month of text messages and data, aimed at encouraging customers to purchase a data contract. However, like most rural Guatemalans I knew, I did not purchase the data plan at the end of the promotional period. Instead, I used this "smartphone" in much the same way that I used my frijolito. The only exception was that I had a full keyboard for sending text messages, a vast improvement over T-9 texting using the number keypad on my frijolito.[37]

When They Were Not Early Adopters

Tecpán's transnational households were usually early adopters of new technologies, placing them at the forefront of digital mediation in the daily life of nearly all Tecpanecos. Facebook presents an instance in which it was youth, not transnational families, who were early adopters of a technology that would become central to the life of the community. Members of transnational families in the second generation of migrants did not use Facebook or Skype to communicate across national borders. At the time these technologies were effectively computer-based, placing them outside the realm of "easy" communication strategies as most families did not have personal computers in their homes. I only knew of three transnational households that had computers, and all lived in the city center. Only one of these had internet and this was because the family ran an internet café out of the front room of their intergenerational household. Even this transnational couple did not regularly use computer-based technologies like Facebook and Skype to stay in touch. At this time, almost everyone who had a personal computer, regardless of transnational household status, accessed the internet through the expensive and frustratingly slow means of a USB modem. Even though I had my own laptop and a modem, I preferred to go to an internet café to do anything more than send quick emails. These realities meant that Facebook and Skype were only used in local internet cafés.

While such cafés were widespread and did not present a significant hourly cost, using Facebook in these locations made it a very public form of communication. Not only might posts be viewed by fellow community members but, more importantly, people would see that women were spending time in internet cafés. As such, using Facebook became associated with the drawbacks of public phones, namely their public nature. While messaging was not audible—and therefore more private—people continued to be wary of communication that took place in public where others might be monitoring their conversations. The local culture of internet cafés also limited migrants' wives using them, as the spaces were dominated by young people. A middle-aged woman sitting in a café Skyping or chatting on Facebook would have seemed out of place. Spending time and money at an internet café would have been interpreted as wasteful, opening the woman up to local and transnational critiques. Additionally, the rhythms of daily work meant that the time when women were most likely to have a lull in their domestic work corresponded to times that their husbands were working in the United States. In the evenings, when husbands were the mostly likely to have time to chat on Facebook or Skype, the wives would not have time to chat. Additionally, going to an internet café at night would be deemed inappropriate and/or dangerous by many Tecpanecos. Ironically, in most communities, including the city center, the danger of visiting an internet café came from the gossip rather than crime.

Differences in the available technologies influenced calling patterns and how cell phones mediated relationships between members of transnational families in the second generation of transnational migrants. Guatemalan's lack of access to smartphones prevented their use of the messaging app WhatsApp. It also meant that platforms like Skype and Facebook remained computer-based.

Encomiendas: Slow-Moving Mediations

Despite the exponential advances in communication technologies experienced by the second generation of migrants, sending care packages, which included letters and photographs, remained important. In fact, this practice expanded during this technological generation. Instead of sending items through the public mail system or international shipping companies like DHL, the average transnational family sent items through private Guatemalan-owned shipping companies known as *encomiendas*. Unlike a national mail system, encomiendas serve specific communities. For example, there were specific encomiendas for sending items from north New Jersey and Tecpán. Different encomiendas connected the Atlanta area with the town of Comalapa near Tecpán. To use an encomienda, clients provide the name and phone number of the recipient; the sender is then given an approximate date of delivery and told the price (based on weight and size). Once the items arrive, the recipient is contacted and comes to the local office to pick up the items, making it difficult to send packages to individuals who do not live near the local offices.[38]

By the time the second wave of migrants had left Tecpán for New Jersey, encomiendas were well established and widely used. During this time there were three encomienda services operating in Tecpán.[39] Guzmán, the father of my host family, worked for the most popular of the three. My room was across the patio from the street-facing room that served as the encomienda "office" in Tecpán, giving me the opportunity to observe many aspects of the encomienda process. Families came to the house, usually on Thursday's market day, bringing items they wanted to send to their relatives in New Jersey. They sent food and photographs they took at special occasions, including weddings, birthdays, and Tecpán's celebration of its patron saint, St. Francis of Assisi. Physical photographs sent between Guatemala and the United States were highly prized in these households. Recently returned migrants often commented that they liked receiving the photographs their families sent. Guzmán, who sometimes used his visa to carry photos and videos to migrants in New Jersey, explained how happy migrants were to get "remembrances" from home. I also saw families arrive to pick up packages sent from the United States. Fathers and sons in New Jersey sent packages that contained toys, clothing, and the occasional laptop. Guzmán sometimes arranged to deliver larger items, relating that the largest item he had ever delivered as part of an encomendia was a piano keyboard.

One week, I had the occasion to accompany Guzmán when he went to Chimaltenango to deliver and pick up encomienda items. As we drove, Guzmán explained the process to me: "This family [in Chimaltenango] takes things to and from Guatemala City. That is where the boxes arrive . . . unless it is a big package then they come by ship." That day Guzmán picked up a small box intended for someone in Tecpán, but he explained that if it had been for a family from an aldea, he would call them and keep the package at his house until they could come to Tecpán and retrieve it. Guzmán described how the sending and receiving packages ebbed and flowed, telling me that families sent the most packages to the United States "so they arrive during Holy Week or for Day of the Dead" and that migrants sent more packages home in November for Christmas. Guzmán characterized Christmas as the busiest time for packages traveling both north and south.

Families held the items shipped via encomiendas dear to them; they often showed them to me when I visited. These things were especially prized in aldea homes, given that families in rural areas were less likely to have access to such items. For example, Angela, the twenty-seven-year-old wife of a migrant, showed me the printer that her husband had sent from New York. As she removed the woven cloth protecting the printer from the dust of the dry season, Angela revealed that she was having trouble finding the printer cords she needed in Tecpán and asked if I could help. She casually, though timidly suggested, maybe I could bring the right cord the next time I traveled to Guatemala City or the United States. Angela smiled proudly when I remarked that her printer was nicer than the one I owned in the United States; she commented that her husband had sent the printer to make sure her children did well in their studies, saying, "He is a responsible father." Similarly, Zoraida praised the laptop her husband sent to help their teenage son with his studies. The printers and laptops, like so many items shipped via encomiendas, served as tangible and visible proof of men's continued contributions to their families. They were tangible and offered an immediate reward for the struggles of migration. The items demonstrated not only the success of migrant husbands but also the couple's ongoing togetherness.

Transnational packages provided a means of maintaining ties and doing kinwork from afar. Previous studies describe how items sent in transnational packages are especially important in transnational parenting, noting that gifts attempt to compensate for the physical absence of the migrant parent.[40] Among Kaqchikel transnational families, gifts like Angela's printer or Zoraida's laptop were an important way for migrants to demonstrate their dedication to their family members who remained in Guatemala. These gifts did not assuage the profound sadness children felt due to their fathers' physical absence, but they were held up as evidence of the love and sacrifice of their fathers. Furthermore, much as in the case of letters in other migrant contexts, Kaqchikel families enjoyed the tangible aspect of gifts sent via transnational packages.[41] Items in transnational packages were a form of affective work and a means of increasing intimacy. In addition to gifts, photographs and videos were an especially important part of encomiendas.

Ricardo, a forty-two-year-old return migrant, showed me the house he had built using remittances. As we toured the house, with the rest of the family trailing behind us, I noticed several photographs from his time in the United States. In a hall, on the unpainted cinderblock wall, hung a simple 8 by 10 picture frame that held several pictures of Ricardo in the United States. He explained, "I sent these to my wife when I was gone." Ricardo's wife shyly smiled when I asked her about the photos. She explained that she had bought the frame to protect the pictures and how, with the help of Ricardo's family, she had hung the pictures up where all could see them as they walked to and from the courtyard.

All the transnational families that had received photographs of their husbands and sons proudly displayed them. Most often photographs showed the men at parks, on the balconies of their apartments, and at local tourist attractions, like the Statue of Liberty or Times Square. Migrants posing in the snow was another common picture I saw. Indeed, many family members in Guatemala asked me about snow and winter because of the photographs their relatives sent. Additionally, the permanence of a photograph, unlike a phone conversation, proved to be an important comfort to families in times of sadness or loneliness. The tangibility of items sent via encomiendas increased the significance of these items given that, in transnational households, so many interactions taking place were virtual and fleeting.

While pictures were a means of maintaining communication and doing the affective labor of families in the extended absence of undocumented transnational migration, they were also testimony of good health and good behavior. The visual images of photographs told the truth in ways that text messages and phone conversations alone could not. In the context of the United States, Ila Gershon notes that photographs give the potential for truth.[42] In the Guatemalan context, pictures of healthy migrants showed that they were working hard and had not "fallen into vices." Family members used the phrases "see[ing] how he is" or "see[ing] that he is ok" to describe what they enjoyed about getting photographs of their migrant sons and/or husbands. Conversely, pictures of a "skinny" migrant revealed a migrant who was struggling and needed emotional support and prayers.

Similarly, return migrants reported enjoying seeing pictures of how their children had grown while they were away. These served as evidence that remittances were being managed well. I took lots of pictures and short videos of building projects and new business enterprises.[43] Families then asked that I burn DVDs of these videos and physically send the DVD or photographs to their relative once I returned to the United States. Some families preferred that I print the photos or burn the DVD and give them to the families so they could include them in an encomienda package.

The testimony provided by photographs sent via encomiendas was especially important because of the digital divide experienced by transnational households in the second technological generation of migrations. Technological limitations combined with local gender dynamics to constrain the strategies wives had for monitoring the behavior of their migrant husbands. Generally, wives could not make multiple international calls to other migrants to verify what their husbands told them in the same way that Nery had when trying to distinguish between reality and gossip about his wife's behavior. Photographs were the best evidence, as they offered the potential to reveal the truth.

Enselmo, thirty-eight, described how he had been in New Jersey for approximately a year and a half when he began hearing rumors of his wife's infidelity. These rumors originated in their rural aldea to the United States in calls between family members and quickly spread among Kaqchikel migrants in North Jersey, especially as migrants teased each other while working. Enselmo told me that at first he did not give much credence to these rumors, given the intense rivalries within his aldea and the community's propensity for false gossip. However, gossip of his young wife's infidelity continued and took on another element—his wife's pregnancy. To discover the truth, Enselmo called his widowed mother, with whom his wife was living (see chapter 4 for a discussion of mothers-in-law as agents of surveillance). However, whenever Enselmo broached the subject of the gossip, his mother denied the rumors and changed the subject. Juanita, Enselmo's wife, always replied that the gossip was only idle talk. Convinced more by the persistence of the gossip than by their responses, Enselmo called Jervin, a recently returned migrant friend who lived in the city center.

Enselmo knew Jervin from the time that they had overlapped in New Jersey. He knew that Jervin had purchased a digital camera before returning to Guatemala. Enselmo called Jervin and asked him to go take pictures of his wife. Jervin explained, "He [Enselmo] didn't believe his mother or his wife, so he called me. Enselmo asked me to take photographs of his wife for him. He used it as a threat to force Juanita tell him the truth." After making arrangements with Jervin, Enselmo called his wife to tell her that a friend was coming to take a picture of her for him. He did not reveal to Juanita that he wanted to verify what she was saying. Instead, he claimed that Jervin was coming to take photographs because he missed her. Enselmo quickly pointed out to me that he did miss his wife, so this was not exactly a lie, but it was not the sole reason for taking the photographs. The threat of pictures—where she could not hide her pregnancy—prompted Juanita to reveal the truth to Enselmo. She was in fact pregnant by another man. After Juanita admitted to her infidelities, Enselmo contacted Jervin to tell him that he did not need to take photographs of his wife.

The second technological generation was characterized by the emergence of cell phones as the "social glue" of transnational families. These technologies facilitated regular and often more effervescent conversation. That these conversations took place at home rather than at a public phone also contributed to families characterizing these communications as more rewarding. However, the drawback to this easier communication was that it allowed for greater movement of transnational gossip. Freely circulating gossip, combined with women's inability to initiate phone calls, means that much of the technology served as surveillance of wives. In addition to phone-based mediations photos, videos, and gifts sent via encomiendas also mediated relationships. Photographs and videos especially served as testimony in ways that phone conversations did not. Finally, an absence of smartphones in Tecpán meant that other platforms like Facebook and Skype were not used by transnational households as a communication technology; as such they did not mediate daily life.

FACE AND WATS: THE THIRD GENERATION (2015–PRESENT)

The span of my years working in Tecpán saw a significant reduction in the digital divide between the Global North and the Global South. Today, cell phones rival the radio for the most pervasive information communication technology across Guatemala. Not only are cell phones more widespread, following 2015 it was much more likely that those phones that families possess were smartphones. Today, it is hard to note the difference between the technologies used by transnational and nontransnational households; this is in marked contrast to the first two technological generations, where members of transnational household were early adopters of technologies and were among the first to experience the mediation of daily life. Full mediation is no longer the domain of transnational households. Now, most residents of Tecpán and the Tecpán diaspora experience mediation in multiple parts of their lives. All relationships are much more likely to be digitally mediated. Transnational migration no longer presents the first time a couple's intimacy is mediated through technology. Migrants do not have to learn how to use media to increase intimacy and maintain the unity of their marriage. Indeed, it is likely that couples' courtship included the use of cell phones.

Technological changes have impacted how transnational families use encomiendas. It might seem as though the proliferation of new media would render encomiendas obsolete. However, they remain popular. Indeed, Guzmán has started his own encomienda business with his friends in New Jersey. He now goes to the capital every week, on Wednesdays, to transport packages sent between North Jersey and Tecpán. Guzmán's starting a new business suggests that he still sees the ongoing potential of encomiendas.

While encomiendas remain important, the contents of the packages have changed. Letters, which were popular among the first and second generation of transnational migrants, are now nearly obsolete because WhatsApp has rendered this mediation redundant. Likewise, families no longer send physical photographs back and forth as they did during the second technological generation. Despite these changes, encomiendas remain important for transnational households. Gifts and foods are still sent back and forth as a means of affirming love and demonstrating ongoing participation in familial partnerships. Laptops and tablets have become key items sent back to Guatemala. The trend increased during the COVID-19 pandemic. For example, Guzmán noted that everyone needed all the technology they could get so the children could go to school online. While encomiendas continue to be valued for their ability to demonstrate men's economic dedication and provide a venue for them to perform kinwork from afar, it is digital mediations through WhatsApp and Facebook that most influence daily life in transnational households.

As they were in the second generation of migrants, cell phones continue to be the social glue of transnational families; however, now they are also the social glue of Tecpanecan society more broadly. Today, the most popular phones are Samsung and Huawei smartphones, which are desired because they have good cameras and are affordable. These smartphones come equipped with WhatsApp (locally referred to as Wats) and Facebook (locally referred to as Face). These two platforms are widely used and mediate nearly all aspects of life.

In 2016, cell phone service providers Claro and Tigo altered their plans; Facebook and WhatsApp no longer required data that users had to pay for. This change expanded their usage dramatically. Today, people of all ages send numerous WhatsApp messages a day. Businesses use WhatsApp to send receipts. This simple change has altered the media landscape of Tecpán, creating new forms of intimacy, friendship, and support.[44] For example, a young Kaqchikel man, originally from the city center and now living in Guatemala City, noted how smartphones and WhatsApp messaging in particular have allowed him to stay in close contact with his family who still lives in Tecpán. He also described how the mediation of daily life has enabled his younger siblings to talk more with their father who often travels for his work as van driver. He explained, "Listen, Meghan, they have a much closer relationship because they can communicate frequently on WhatsApp." When he was young, his dad's travel felt like an absence in a way that they do not given the connection allowed by WhatsApp.

Messages and photographs shared via WhatsApp help to cement social bonds between family and friends. At times the app even creates the opportunity to become friends, as the example of Alicia demonstrates. I first came to know Alicia in 2012 when she participated in a scholarship program I sponsored in her remote aldea. During her participation in the program, she learned to do decorative machine embroidery. She hoped that doing so would add to her already existing weaving abilities, to help earn enough money to achieve her goal of earning a college degree. At this time, I knew Alicia in name only. When the original program ended, she contacted me through a mutual Facebook friend to ask if I would continue sponsoring her studies. After much discussion, sometimes in person, but mostly via WhatsApp messages, she told me she wanted to pursue a law degree, which would take at least five years to finish. We created a plan for our mutual contributions to her studies, with me finding the funds to cover those expenses she cannot manage. Alicia is grateful for the money but has repeatedly described the friendship and *ánimo* (courage; emotional support) as the biggest help as she pursues her studies, especially when older male family members question her decision to delay marriage as she works toward this goal. It is the messages we share on Facebook and WhatsApp that have given her the emotional strength to continue her studies.

While my sponsorship of Alicia's studies created a need for us to stay in touch, a true friendship developed. We send each other messages of encouragement and ask about one another's families. We regularly exchange photographs and videos. Alicia sometimes sends me photographs of new weavings and embroidery projects as she works on them. I send her photographs of my garden, cross-stitch, or child. WhatsApp messages have also allowed Alicia to be better connected to my daughter and husband, who do not read Spanish. Alicia sent my daughter (who was too young to read at the time) a video of her harvesting coffee. Both my husband and daughter were excited to see the process and Alicia was excited that she was able to teach them something about Guatemala.

Several scholars have pointed out the importance of personal relationships with foreigners to navigating the precarious conditions of daily life in Guatemala.[45] In addition to the messages of friendship, WhatsApp also maintains Alicia's connection to me that facilitates the various advantages that come from relationships with foreigners. Alicia benefits from the various Guatemalan networks I operate in that she as a young, unmarried Kaqchikel woman from an aldea does not have access to. For example, during the pandemic, Alicia felt very sick and was having trouble breathing. She messaged Guzmán, the father of my host family and a mutual contact, to ask if he knew what to do or would mind contacting me. Guzmán and I helped put her in contact with local medical NGO providing care via telehealth. When the initial treatment did not alleviate her chest pains, she again contacted Guzmán who contacted me in confidence. After talking with Guzmán, I got in touch with Alicia to check on her. This conversation created an opportunity for her to ask for help without feeling as though she was taking advantage of me. It was understood by both of us that I would not have called had I not been willing to help. I used the information shared in our conversations to put Alicia in contact with another group able to provide more robust care. Alicia ultimately recovered from what was most likely COVID. Both her studies and the medical attention she received during the pandemic would not have been available to her without her pursuit of a network of support and ultimately our friendship.

Creating and maintaining networks of support are a key use of cell phones in rural Indigenous Guatemala. As cell phones allow for a much wider network of support to be created, a network is no longer dependent on face-to-face interaction. Furthermore, connecting with a network through phone messages allows for a more conscientious construction of a network rather than relying on sheer serendipity.[46] WhatsApp messages served a means of ensuring the stability of one's support network, which is important in rural Guatemala where so much of one's ability to get services (medical, educational, etc.) depends on mobilizing extensive but precarious networks.[47]

WhatsApp allows people to send more photographs than was possible using encomiendas, thus enabling children to participate in messaging and transgress the literacy divide that accompanies so many digital communication technologies. I occasionally received pictures from the children in my host family, but I never received typed messages from them. For example, in 2021 the family's middle child, Cristian, sent me a photo of a picture he painted for me to wish me happy birthday (fig. 2.1). His father later sent me a photo of Cristian painting the picture for me. The exchange brought me a lot of joy and created a greater connection than a text message alone would have. Later, when I chatted with the family, we all lamented that a photo of the painting was not the same as being able to have the actual painting but were glad to have had the exchange facilitated by WhatsApp.

Despite the popularity and rapid growth of WhatsApp, Facebook continues to be slightly more popular than WhatsApp. Today, the use of Facebook largely happens via cell phones. Accessing Facebook no longer requires going to an internet café or having a personal modem; it is no longer conceived of as "computer-based" technology as it was in the second generation of migrants. It is now part of daily life and there are now locally specific ways of using Facebook.

Collages and inspirational posts are common in Guatemalan Facebook usage. Digital collages are rarely built within Facebook itself; its platform focuses more on filters to be applied while taking photographs. Instead, individuals use various apps to add overlays and stickers to existing photographs. The collages are created in the app, saved to the picture roll of the maker's phone, and then uploaded to Facebook (and sometimes sent directly to an individual via a messaging service). In addition to stickers, users may put a background

Figure 2.1. Photograph of Cristian, sent via WhatsApp. Photograph courtesy of Florencio Cali.

behind multiple photographs, creating a digital photo album or scrapbook. The creation of such collages, which almost always incorporate bright colors, is analogous to creating scrapbook pages. These collages are usually made by girls and women to enhance photos of themselves together with their closest girlfriends and/or significant other.[48] However, the enhancement does not parallel how users in the United States typically enhance photos, where enhancing a photograph usually means making the subjects more physically attractive.

In Guatemala, collages are much more about commemorating a special event, like weddings, baptisms, and other family gatherings than about producing an "Instagram-worthy" photograph. For example, Blanca enhanced a picture of a daytrip she made with her husband to Lake Atitlán. The photograph is not particularly clear, and Blanca's face does not show. Indeed, the frame or border is more prominent and colorful than the picture itself (fig. 2.2). The fact that Blanca made it her Facebook profile picture demonstrates the value she places on the picture and the memories it evokes.

Figure 2.2. Blanca's Facebook profile picture. Photograph courtesy of Blanca.

My pictures have also found their way into Facebook photo collages. Alicia made a collage from the photographs she took when came to visit me and my daughter in Antigua one last time as we prepared to return to the United States. By all criteria the picture is not great: none of us is looking at the camera, my daughter is crying, and the intense sunlight bleaches out the upper half the photo, including our faces. However, Alicia still created a collage using only this photo. She added two stickers to the photograph (within WhatsApp): a heart next to a smiling cup of coffee and chocolate chip cookie. The collage is a testament to our friendship and the opportunity we had to squeeze in one more coffee and chat before I returned to the United States. She sent me the photograph in WhatsApp and told me that she had shown it to her family.

This is the context of technology use for the third technological generation of migrants from Tecpán.

WhatsApp

WhatsApp, locally known as Wats, is now the preferred way to send messages, audio files, and photographs across Guatemala, especially in transnational contexts.[49] One wife of a migrant explained that "with Wats we can talk every day. Without Wats calling everyday would only be wasting money." Indeed, the most often described benefit of using WhatsApp to stay in contact is that it allows families to always be in touch replicating and sometimes even improving the level of communication between household members.

Members of transnational household also described the benefits of using audio messages. Santiago, a fifty-four-year-old migrant who has been in New Jersey for eight years, described using WhatsApp messages to communicate with his wife and children. He had several ways of communicating with them: SMS, Facebook, and WhatsApp messages. However, WhatsApp audio messages enabled him to talk to his elderly parents who were less literate (especially in Kaqchikel, a primarily spoken language). The practice of using WhatsApp audio messages resulted in a meme that spread among my Kaqchikel friends from Patzún, a neighboring town. The meme, shared on Facebook, featured the image of Mexican comedian Roberto Gomez dressed in his signature role as El Chapulín Colorado. Written under his face were the words "Kaqchikeles: se mandan audios y mensajes en Kaqchikel . . . Los de WhatsApp: #kotzijonpakaqchikel" (Kaqchikeles: sending voice and text messages in Kaqchikel . . . WhatsApp: #Letschatinkaqchikel). WhatsApp's voice messaging allows users to bypass issues of literacy that underlie most information communication technology usage, allowing the oldest and youngest people to participate. Migrants who were in their mid-twenties especially commented on how much they used this feature to leave messages for their very young children.[50]

The free nature of WhatsApp allowed migrants' family members in Guatemala to initiate communication, something that was not feasible using SMS text messages. Wives, especially those whose husband's migration spanned the second and third technological generation, celebrated being able to send a quick message, photograph, or even audio message whenever they wanted. They described this as more like "actual conversation." They described how using WhatsApp let them contact their husbands; they did not have to wait for a weekly call initiated by their husbands to talk.

WhatsApp also proved to be more empowering for migrants' wives because now they had the ability to initiate conversations. Previously, text messages and calls primarily originated from migrant husbands, making cell phones instruments of surveillance. The expansion of smartphone technology and use of WhatsApp disrupted this tendency. Women heralded their ability to initiate messages and calls to their migrant husbands from Guatemala. WhatsApp made the surveilling potential of cell phones work both ways. Yet, WhatsApp did not completely disrupt the culture of surveillance that developed during that time. In fact, the constancy of contact exacerbated some gossip and created a new space for monitoring.

In 2015, during a brief trip to Tecpán, I met with Jervin and asked him about some of our mutual acquaintances from transnational families. The brevity of the trip precluded me visiting everyone and I hoped that Jervin had some news he could share with me. His usually animated face grew quite solemn, and he spoke in a low tone: "Look, Meghan. I am glad we are alone because I am afraid Dolores has fallen into vices. . . . No, things are very bad." He had become aware of this change because of her new picture on WhatsApp. As he described the photo, which featured a heavily made-up face, Jervin lamented these changes because Dolores "has young children." Aware of Jervin's tendency to exaggerate, I purposely let the gossip about Dolores wane.

As our chat meandered through updates on various acquaintances, Jervin again returned to his concern for Dolores. This time I asked if I could see the picture. He reluctantly replied that he would show it to me but warned me it was "delicate." Given the build up, I had imagined Dolores's new profile picture to be a photo of her in heavy eyeliner and or bright lipstick, rarities for rural middle-aged Kaqchikel women. I had also imagined that Dolores might be wearing "scandalous" clothing—corte that was too short, perhaps. Such things would be consistent with local critiques of women's behavior, especially in the context of transnational households. However, I was genuinely surprised to see the new picture on Dolores's WhatsApp profile was a of a clown, obviously from a movie or TV show. With Jervin's emphasis on "lots of makeup" and his hushed tones, I had expected some sort of policing of Dolores's sexuality. Instead, it was a different policing of Dolores, perhaps rooted in Jervin's charismatic Catholicism. Jervin linked the clown picture to demons and moving away from Christian behavior. Although I did find the choice of an angry clown an odd picture for Dolores, I did not interpret it as a sign that she was in moral trouble. I thought it far more likely that her son, age seven at the time, had changed the picture. Ultimately, who changed the profile picture and their motivation matter less than how the new picture was locally received and that WhatsApp, while increasing intimacy, also created a new space for monitoring and (mis)interpretation.

Facebook and Hometown Pages

As already indicated, before the mid-2010s Facebook was considered a computer-based technology. This made it the domain primarily of young people and the professional class (both Maya and ladino) living in the city center. In the early 2000s Tecpán's municipal government had a Facebook page that enumerated local events and provided photographic evidence of its good work. For some administrations these photo ops were their key achievements. Conversations at the pila or at lunch regularly critiqued mayors for going around the municipio and taking photos but doing little else. Here, the Facebook posts became a place for critique of the municipal and national government, especially its poor administration of funds. The permanence and visibility of these posts elevated these critiques and perhaps initiated change.[51] Tecpán's municipal Facebook page offered no migrant-specific content. Most of the latter was produced by migrants themselves who would occasionally comment on a picture about how much they missed Tecpán.

Before 2015, I found no hometown pages for Tecpán and its aldeas. Hometown pages have proven to be important aspects of the transnational process and the mediation of life in other transnational contexts.[52] Since 2015, notably, there has been a growth of hometown Facebook pages used by local and transnational members of the community. Twenty-one of Tecpán's thirty-four aldeas have community Facebook pages and seven aldeas have multiple pages, usually run by young men in the home community with the goal of keeping viewers up-to-date on local happenings. While these pages are not specifically for migrants, there is a lot of migration-related content among the posts about local events. In the course of my research, I found that these community pages occasionally featured posts about individuals who were held up as models of "honorable work."

Current migrants described using their smartphones to visit hometown Facebook pages to see what was happening. Martín, a recent migrant currently living in New Jersey, revealed how he enjoyed seeing videos and photographs of festivals and parties. He also commented that his aldea had posted a video of someone driving from the city center to the aldea. Martín noted that it was one of his favorite posts, which he watched whenever he missed the sights of home. Santiago, a fifty-four-year-old migrant, also described enjoying seeing posts on hometown pages. However, he noted that he had seen problems affecting young couples who used Facebook. Santiago explained that "you use Face to look at posts, pictures from birthday parties and weddings. I also can get news from the villages, a lot of things . . . but there is a lot of gossip that causes problems for them [young families]. For example, they upload photos from some party or they make a post just to cause problems." Here, Santiago was referring to the group of community members who always created trouble. Facebook offered them a new means of creating gossip and stirring up local rivalries.

Use of community Facebook pages was particularly noticeable during the COVID-19 pandemic when stay at home orders in Guatemala and the United States meant everyone had more time to be online. This was also a time in which people more actively sought out a sense of community. In the initial stages of the pandemic, two community Facebook pages from Tecpán's aldeas created posts as tributes to migrants working in the United States. One town's page had a video of a group of migrant workers building a deck in what appeared to be the eastern United States. None of the individuals was identified, but the video ostensibly featured at least one community member. The caption referenced how hard migrants work in the United States, praising their sacrifices. Similar posts spoke to the sacrifice of the migrants and served as a testimony to the roles they played, providing economically for their families. These sentiments were often expressed and shared privately but became more publicly visible during the pandemic. In contrast, I have never seen any corollary posts highlighting the sacrifice of women who remain at home; this sacrifice goes largely unnoticed. Women I spoke to suspected that this was largely because their work is similarly invisible.

As the pandemic continued, Facebook posts about Kaqchikel migrants working in the United Sates showed migrants undertaking new jobs. One video showed a migrant man in personal protective equipment spraying disinfectant in an office building in New York. The caption to the post emphasized migrants' sacrifice. The community page of one of Tecpán's aldeas framed the sacrifice of the community's migrants in a slightly different way. It showed the image of a young man wrapped in the Guatemalan flag standing on railroad tracks. Over the image the creator had written "Dios te bendiga a ti amigo y hermano guatemalteco que hoy te toca sufrir también en un País extranjero" (May God bless you Guatemalan friend and brother who is now suffering in a foreign country). Below the text block were two smaller circles: one featuring a crying face emoji and the other featuring an American flag.

In 2020, when New York and New Jersey were hotspots for COVID-19 infections, the Facebook posts on hometown pages focused on decidedly more somber topics. Several pages posted images of those who had fallen ill or died from COVID-19 while in the United States. Often these posts sought to identify the individuals and their families. They usually featured a picture of the migrant when they were healthy. The pictures were captioned with the migrant's first name, where they were living in the United States, and some general information about their hometown in Guatemala. The captions usually also included the phone number of one of their acquaintances in the United States so that the family could be in contact with them and find out about their sick loved one. These posts were widely shared, even if the migrant in question was not from the area. For example, in April 2020 alone I saw four such posts on the Facebook page of one of Tecpán's aldeas. One migrant pictured was from Huehuetenango, roughly four hours drive from Tecpán, but the posts were still shared on Tecpán pages. Some of these posts asked for donations to help support the family while the migrant was sick and unable to work or to help pay the migrant's medical expenses. There were also posts asking for donations to help families repatriate the bodies of those who had died. Such requests are common in migrant communities in Latin markets and restaurants in the United States, where one often sees a picture of a migrant in need of help next to a can for donations. Here Facebook offered a new format for already-existing traditions.

CONCLUSION

Today, residents of Tecpán, like so many around the world, are living fully mediated lives. Despite popular conceptions of Indigenous peoples as existing in the natural rather than the technological world, transnational families have been at the forefront of mediation for more than thirty years. In Tecpán, such households were often early adopters of the newest communication technologies. But as technologies change so do the mediations migrants and their families experience. The first generation of economic migrants left Tecpán in the 1990s; these migrants relied primarily on payphones and letters (1990–2005). In the second generation (2005–2015), a digital divide gave migrant husbands significantly more power to initiate communication with their family members. It also saw a rise in the use of encomiendas. The third generation (2015 to the present) has been characterized by the expansion of smartphone technologies and the use of social media platforms. In transnational households, WhatsApp has become especially popular because it allows couples to send private messages and photos, resolving many of the complaints of previous generous of migrants and their families.

Given the features of WhatsApp and the increased accessibility to the platform, it is surprising that Facebook continues to be the most widely used social media platform in Guatemala, including among transnational households who use the platform to post videos, photo collages, and inspirational posts on each other's walls and to send private messages via Facebook messenger.[53] The ability to have synchronous, private, in-depth conversations via text messages raises the question of why Facebook has become a space in which couples exchange (publicly visible) messages, a topic I take up in the next chapter.

3

Doing Family on Face

Nohemy, the twenty-nine-year-old wife of a migrant, sometimes creates "family photographs" by combining pictures she has taken in Guatemala with those Francis, her husband, has taken in New Jersey. She makes these photo collages on her sleek, black Huawei smartphone when she is not busy with her daily domestic tasks. Once the photo collage is complete, she posts it on her Facebook wall. One such photo collage featured three hearts on a bright-pink ombre background. The three hearts, each with a different floral frame, contain pictures of her family members. In the upper left-hand of the image there is a selfie that Francis took in his room in the apartment he shares with three other migrants. Just below his image is a selfie of Nohemy in front of a cornfield. Diagonally and back to the left is a heart that contains a picture of the couple's child in its dress clothes. A cinderblock house, built using remittances, is visible behind the child. In the past two years, Nohemy has posted six such collages on her Facebook wall. Sometimes these posts commemorate special occasions, and sometimes there is no discernible special reason.

Over a series of WhatsApp messages, I asked Nohemy to clarify how she stayed in touch with her migrant husband, who had been in New Jersey for the past four years. She described how they sent each other messages and called each other through WhatsApp. Notably, she did *not* mention the Facebook posts the couple shared on each other's walls. Yet, Nohemy was one of the most active Facebook users I knew. In addition to posting "family photographs," she also posted pictures and inspirational posts and shared various migration-related posts from community Facebook pages. Given the activity I saw on her Facebook wall I imagined that she had to be using Facebook to stay in contact with Francis. I probed, "You don't use Facebook to stay in touch? But you post things on each other's Facebook pages?" Nohemy quickly replied, explaining, "Facebook is just for entertainment."

Nohemy and Francis, like so many Kaqchikel transnational couples in Tecpán, live digital lives. In the previous chapter I described the ways relationships are mediated in the daily lives of Tecpanecos and how these mediations have changed over the past fifteen years. The decreasing digital divide means that Tecpanecos now have access to platforms like Facebook and WhatsApp on their personal smartphones. Despite the popularity of WhatsApp and its ability to allow couples to regularly send each other private messages and call each other without additional costs, Facebook remains extremely popular among transnational couples because it offers them a public, "private" space.

Facebook is the world's most used social medial site.[1] On the platform, users create personal profiles where they share photos, videos, and news on their wall. Users' friends can then comment on these posts or react to them using one of seven emoticons. While the ways people use Facebook reflects individual preferences, typically in Tecpán, people's "Facebook friends" include friends, acquaintances, neighbors, and other community members. Unless otherwise specified by the user, profile pictures and posts are visible to all the user's Facebook friends. As such, Facebook represents a space where individuals perform their social roles and do the affective labor of kinship.[2] In transnational households in particular, Facebook posts are a means of publicly performing the appropriate duties of husbands and wives. Such public performances are especially important for women who remain in Guatemala, often living in the household of their in-laws.

Nohemy did not see her use of the platform as communication. For her it was solely entertainment. In both anonymous surveys and interviews, Tecpanecos described Facebook as *entrenimiento* (entertainment) or a *pasatiempo* (hobby). Some described their interactions with the social media platform as "a way to distract myself while I watch videos or look at memes." However, no matter how entertaining social media platforms are, they are always something more. Paralleling the work of anthropologist Baird Campbell, I suggest that Facebook posts are performances of gendered and locally relevant images of self (described in chapter 1).[3] Furthermore, Facebook posts are simultaneously curations of images of the good life. Among Kaqchikel transnational households, Facebook is a place to "do family," craft identities, and bolster a partnership in the physical absence but virtual presence of migrants. Couples' curation of Facebook posts serves as a public performance of intimacy and its intersection with ideas of Kaqchikel masculinities and femininities. In short, Facebook posts are a critical part of making a life that is livable now and in the future.

In transnational families, Facebook posts are a way to "do family" across geographic distance. In much the same way that scholars use the concept of "doing gender" to explore the individual and institutional aspects of gender performance, they have mobilized the analogy of "doing family" to describe the contextually specific interplay between individuals and society in the construction of families.[4] Scholars primarily explore "doing family" in Western contexts, but the examples in this chapter will demonstrate that in Kaqchikel families—where transnational migration simultaneously challenges and reifies traditional gender role and family dynamics—"doing family" is about the (re)assigning of culturally appropriate duties. Social media posts are an excellent place to examine these dynamics, as posts are individually relevant but also structured by family, community, and societal expectations.[5] Facebook becomes a place where familial monitoring can take place, a site that can be assessed by all, despite geographic separation. Ultimately, "doing family" whether done online or in person, involves monitoring one's own and others' performances.

Tied to the project of "doing family" is the crafting of identities. Anthropologists Baird Campbell and Nell Haynes describe how social media posts allow individuals to construct their gendered and sexual selves. Posts allow individuals to perform their values, desires, and tastes.[6] In the case of Kaqchikel transnational families, these constructions of digital selves are important for migrants' wives. Women use Facebook posts to create a visual vocabulary of ideal Kaqchikel femininities as they imagine new, and affirm existing, identities for themselves in the physical absence of their migrant husbands.

Despite increased levels of education and formal employment, Kaqchikel women's status and identities continue to be tied to their relationships with men—first their father and then their husbands.[7] This creates an unlikely parallel between the experiences of migrants' wives and that of civil war widows. Guatemalanists have documented the crisis of identity rural Indigenous women have felt following the loss of their husbands.[8] Judith Zur suggests that the loss of a husband results in "a sharp break in the [widow's] social and personal identity." Similarly, my previous research suggests that the long-term absence of husbands calls into question women's place and status in families and makes community members suspicious of their actions.[9] In the extended absence of migrant husbands, it is important that migrants' wives have a means to confirm that they are virtuous, "good women."[10] Facebook offers them a strategy for living in a "particular way," a way for them to do family.[11] Doing family, like doing gender, is about performances of "appropriate" types of behaviors like devotion to children, making food, and weaving. These duties of good women are often less visible to the community at large because they are performed in domestic spaces. Facebook provides a way around this obstacle.

Finally, in transnational households doing family is also about imagining a future that is not filled with the problems and frustrations associated with undocumented transnational migration. Facebook provides an outlet to imagine what "the good life" will look like after migration.[12] It becomes a space in which both men and women in transnational households can create a life, sometimes real and sometime fantasy, for themselves and others to consume. In her ethnography of Walter Reed Hospital, anthropologist Zoë Wool describes the "intimate work of making life in the present that might sustain life in the future" undertaken by veterans and their families.[13] Although in a different context, the affective labor done by migrants' wives on Facebook parallels that described by Wool. Facebook posts, used in concert with other communication technologies, allow families to image a future that is livable, where they are all together.

Given the history of Facebook's usage in Tecpán and its perception among Kaqchikel women, it is surprising that Facebook has become a place for doing family, imagining the good life, and defining new identities. Facebook has transformed expressions of intimacy among its users in rural Indigenous Guatemala, especially the intimacy expressed within families. To understand the weight of the current usage of Facebook in Kaqchikel transnational marriages it is necessary to first understand how Facebook has transformed as an intimate space.

WHAT FACEBOOK USED TO BE

In the early 2010s, Facebook was firmly a computer-based technology in Tecpán.[14] During this time (which corresponded to the second technological generation described in the previous chapter), most households did not have an internet connection in their homes; using Facebook required going to an internet café and paying an hourly fee to log on. In 2014, the cost of using an internet café in Tecpán was six to eight quetzales an hour ($0.77–$1.03 USD). This expense did not represent an exorbitant cost to the average family living in the city center, but those families who were of lower socioeconomic status and/or trying to pay off interest on money they had borrowed to send a family member to the United States sometimes found it difficult to justify spending money on something "nonessential." Additionally, more remote aldeas did not have reliable internet cafés; residents wanting to use the internet would have to travel to Tecpán or a neighboring aldea to do so. The cost to go from Tecpán's furthest aldea to the city center ranged in cost from 6Q ($0.77 USD) on the bus to 200Q ($25.82 USD) in a private car and required around two hours of travel time. Therefore, in the 2010s, Facebook was simply not a viable form of communication for transnational families. It was likewise not a widespread form of entertainment outside the city center.

Before 2015, Facebook users in Tecpán were primarily teens. Parents rarely accompanied their children to internet cafés. Teens were old enough to go do their schoolwork on their own and both parents were busy working (either inside or outside the home). These dynamics had several consequences. Teens went to internet cafés to do their schoolwork but spent most of their time chatting and looking at each other's Facebook pages. The unsupervised nature of internet cafés meant that for many Kaqchikel teenage boys, "completing their schoolwork" involved exploring their sexuality in these locales, usually by looking at soft-core pornography.

Men were the other users of Facebook in the early 2010s. During this time Kaqchikel women shunned the platform because they perceived it as a place where men sought out extramarital affairs. This perception was tied to men's and women's differential access to the medium. Although the gendered public-private divide has declined in Guatemala as more women pursue education and professional employment, men continue to be more likely to work outside the home (especially after the births of children). Men's occupation of public spheres presented them with more opportunities to visit internet cafés, which was the primary way of accessing Facebook in the 2010s. Men were also more likely to have some "extra" money to get on the internet.[15] Conversely, women, who typically devote themselves to domestic work, had fewer reasons to visit internet cafés and therefore fewer opportunities to log into Facebook (or email). Even those women who worked outside the home were still responsible for domestic duties, cutting into their leisure time. These patterns of usage left Kaqchikel women, especially rural women, outside the influence of Facebook. It also made women highly suspicious of men's use of the platform. Most women understood that Facebook simply offered a new, and harder to monitor, place for womanizing.

More specifically, Kaqchikel women saw Facebook as presenting men with a new way to flirt with impressionable young women. Tecpanecas described that such men sought to take advantage of the naivete of teenage girls. Kaqchikel women saw this as particularly dangerous because such behaviors happened beyond the gaze of (female) community members who might report men's questionable actions to their wives. Similarly, women remarked that men who might otherwise not engage in such behavior felt safe to flirt digitally with women because of the lack of consequences. Importantly, these qualities that made Facebook a place for flirting were also true of cell phones, but it was only Facebook that locals perceived this way. I knew of more flirting and (potential) cheating that took place via text messages than via Facebook. However, women did not perceive cell phones and Facebook equally. Tecpanecas accepted that cell phones were an essential component of daily life. Additionally, the cost of texting during this time period and the materiality of the phone resulted in different perceptions. The ephemeral quality of Facebook, where one could create a false identity, further complicated local Facebook usage. Despite being publicly visible, Facebook was a space that was beyond the gaze of the community, where locals could not ensure men's good behavior. In much the same way that women's sexual naivete "necessitates" the monitoring of women, men's predisposition to infidelities and womanizing meant that their use of Facebook could not be trusted.[16]

In 2013, Ixb'ätz, a thirty-six-year-old single mother from the outskirts Tecpán, tried to clarify the local perceptions and dynamics of Facebook for me: "Facebook is not good for Guatemalan men. Maybe in the United States, they [men] can use it, but in Guatemala it is not a good idea. Guatemalan men are not responsible." Ixb'ätz had seen the problems Facebook had caused women she knew, as their husbands became fixated on a virtual world where there was always the potential to interact with women. Ixb'ätz saw such (potential) infidelities as rooted in men's use of Facebook, although she noted that these same men were often "womanizers" who sought out affairs offline as well.

Ixb'ätz viewed Facebook as problematic for all Guatemalan men, but particularly problematic for migrants who were more likely to abandon their families. Ixb'ätz based this opinion on her own experiences with a migrant who attempted to begin a relationship with her. She explained that "this guy in New Jersey started emailing me. He sent me emails saying he had seen pictures of me weaving on Face[book]. They were pictures that Deborah [a Peace Corps volunteer] took. He liked that I could weave. So he called all his friends until he found out what my email address was. He sent me so many emails!" Ixb'ätz had no intention of migrating; she assumed the migrant hoped to engage her in a long-distance, digitally mediated relationship while he was in the United States that would lead to a physical relationship when he returned to Guatemala.

Ixb'ätz continued describing the migrant's attempt to engage her in flirtatious emails. "He talked about how his wife couldn't understand him but that I could because I had friends like you [from the United States]. I never replied, but he just kept sending me emails, many emails. That is why I don't use my Hotmail account anymore. I got Gmail. I know his family by name; he abandoned them. He doesn't send them money. And he wants to talk to me, like boyfriend and girlfriend? No! I know his type. No. I told him, 'Go back to your wife and kids.' And it is for this reason that I don't think Facebook is good for Guatemalan men. . . . They only use it to look for girlfriends and abandon their families."

Ixb'ätz used this example to describe the problems Kaqchikel men had with Facebook even though the migrant used multiple forms of technology to contact and try to "court" her. In fact, the migrant's attempts to flirt with Ixb'ätz happened through email. However, for Ixb'ätz, the interaction would not have happened had it not been for Facebook. The migrant saw pictures of Ixb'ätz weaving that a Peace Corps volunteer had posted to their own Facebook page. Ixb'ätz did not know whether finding these pictures was happenstance or intentional. She wanted to believe that the migrant was looking through various Facebook posts of friends from Tecpán, probably because he missed home. However, she noted that it was completely possible that the migrant was actively seeking out photographs of women in Tecpán with whom he could interact online. While the migrant transferred a courtship strategy—persistence—to a digital platform, the costs and effort involved to do so from another country made Ixb'ätz suspicious.

As we continued talking, Ixb'ätz commented that Guatemalan men are always looking for opportunities to cheat on their wives, but Facebook provided a more efficient means of seeking these opportunities out. Furthermore, philandering men could seek out encerrada women, locally perceived to be pious and desirable. This would suggest that women's suspicions about Facebook may have also been tied to the platform's ability to jeopardize even good women's reputations. For example, even though Ixb'ätz was not "out in the streets," she found herself caught up in some man's scheme to cheat, potentially making her the subject of gossip. This shows the precarity of being a "good" woman.

Seeing Facebook as a space for infidelities meant members of transnational households did not conceive of the platform as a valid means of staying in touch during migrants' extended absences in the 2010s. The threat of infidelity was usually just below the surface of discussions about conversations about abandonment. Santos, a return migrant, explained, "In most cases the men send money back for a couple of months, maybe a year, but then they make a new life there [in the United States] and they slowly quit sending money." A migrant's sister was more explicit: "The men say, 'Wait for me.' And they never return. They always look for [other] women. They deceive their poor wives. They send money to cover basic needs of the house and look for another woman there [in the United States]. Worse, the wives are left all alone. They remain here struggling. Single men, married men, it doesn't matter. They always look for another. . . . A couple has to be very strong . . . [Women] have to be ready for what may happen." Women saw infidelities as the first step on the path to abandonment. Husbands also did not see using Facebook as a means of staying in touch with their wives. Often men did not want to admit to using Facebook or having Facebook profiles.

Thus, while families cited lack of internet access as the reason that they did not use Facebook to keep in touch with each other, it was not merely access to reliable internet that precluded the use of Facebook. María, a thirty-four-year-old woman living in the city center of Tecpán, had both with a reliable internet connection in her home and access to a personal laptop (which her husband had sent his family from the United States). However, she and her husband did not use Facebook to stay in contact. Instead, they occasionally used Skype. Before 2015, only two of the more than one hundred individuals (representing more than forty transnational households) I interviewed used Facebook to stay in touch with their migrant family members. In both instances, it was men who used Facebook to stay in touch with other men.

Daniel was an upwardly mobile thirty-two-year-old aldea resident. I met Daniel by happenstance; I was perusing a *variedades* store in one of Tecpán's aldeas while waiting to conduct an interview. Daniel quit playing games on his smartphone to talk, probably because it was novel to see an American in the remote aldea. As I described my research, Daniel knowingly nodded and told me his younger brother was in the United States. Daniel described how both had wanted to find a way to *salir adelante*. Daniel's method for doing so had been education. He studied in Chimaltenango and Guatemala City, parlaying his studies into managing his family's stores in two different aldeas. His brother, in contrast, had pursued transnational migration as his means of providing for his family. The two brothers used Facebook to keep in touch, posting photos and sending messages to one another. However, Daniel noted that "those that use it [Facebook] are few. What they [other transnational households] use more is telephones. In the past there was only the telephone but now there are other ways. With Face[book] you can see him, how he is. . . . Using Face[book] has helped significantly." Daniel acknowledged that his family's use of Facebook was uncommon and most likely came about because Daniel had studied in the cities of Chimaltenango and Guatemala City. In 2014, Daniel was the only Kaqchikel person I knew who used Facebook to keep in touch with their migrant family member.

In the early 2010s, the only other family among those I interviewed who used Facebook to communicate with their migrant family member in the United States was Tomás's. He was a sixty-eight-year-old retired social worker.

A self-identified "mestizo," Tomás enjoyed using Facebook to communicate with his migrant son in California.[17] His son, Rolando, was a young, single man when he migrated to the United States in 2004. Rolando saw migration as a way to pay off his mother's medical bills. No one expected Rolando to still be in the United States more than a decade later; however, Rolando made a life for himself in California and is currently dating a woman from the United States. Tomás has resigned himself to the fact that his son will never return to Guatemala. Tomás was saddened that Rolando had missed out on so many things in Tecpán: weddings, births of nieces and nephews, and even his mother's funeral. However, he was grateful for his financial support and proud of Rolando. Laughing, Tomás said that he had really enjoyed learning about the "real" United States from his son.

Every two weeks Rolando calls Tomás and his unmarried sister to chat. These calls provide Rolando the opportunity to stay in touch with his family and keep abreast of events in Tecpán. At the same time, Tomás also uses Facebook to remain in contact with his son. Tomás described riding his bike to a local internet café to access Facebook where he can "see pictures and wish his son and his girlfriend happy birthday." He told me that he likes using Facebook because Rolando's girlfriend "doesn't speak Spanish. But we can use Facebook to say hello to each other. It is a way for me to get to know her because she can't talk to me on the phone. But on Face[book] we can say a few phrases to each other." While the family occasionally used Facebook messenger for real-time communication, most often on birthdays, the logistics of coordinating times to be on the computer proved difficult. Therefore, Tomás and his son primarily used Facebook asynchronously, posting pictures on each other's walls and sending brief messages in messenger.

Despite minor frustrations associated with having to go to an internet café, Tomás enjoyed using Facebook to stay in touch. The usually asynchronous nature of their communication left both Tomás and Rolando's girlfriend with enough time to translate, process, and respond to messages. Facebook gave Tomás a way to communicate with his son's girlfriend, letting him access a part of his son's life that would otherwise be inaccessible.

When Tomás went to a local internet café to send messages to Rolando, he did not include his daughter or granddaughter in these conversations, even though he lived with them. Their exclusion was partly tied to logistics and convenience; taking his young granddaughter would have complicated a trip to the internet café. However, Tomás never stayed with his granddaughter to facilitate his daughter's conversations with her brother via this medium, suggesting an understanding that this form of communication was somehow inappropriate.[18]

WHAT FACEBOOK IS NOW

The digital inequities that previously characterized transnational households' engagement with Facebook are decreasing. It is easier and cheaper for anyone—not just men—to access media-rich platforms like Facebook from their personal smartphones. More access to the platform means that Facebook usage is now widespread across generations in the Tecpán area. As such, the platform has become a place for getting information and staying in touch with friends. Increased access means that Facebook is no longer perceived as a place for men to pursue extramarital affairs. Unlike previous generations of transnational migrants, the current wave of migrants and their families are using Facebook to stay in touch, do family, and (re)imagine themselves and their futures.

Today, members of transnational families use Facebook in much the same way that everyone in Guatemala does, for "entertainment." Current migrants described using the platform to see pictures of things happening in town, especially local celebrations and parties. They also liked using Facebook to stay in touch with acquaintances, even if one might not have their phone number. Likewise, just as Tomás described, family members in Guatemala enjoy getting to see the real United States in posts made by migrants. Videos of migrants working in the United States are always popular posts on hometown Facebook pages. In my interviews, most people's descriptions of how they used Facebook focused on its entertainment value; however, social media usage is a way of creating solidarity, defining who is and is not part of circles of friends and family, and, in the case of transnational families, establishing and enforcing connection and enduring patterns of behavior. Facebook is where transnational couples do the digital affective labor of marriage and family.[19] Family members post photographs, collages, and inspirational posts and comment on the posts of their friends. The visibility of these posts, and their accompanying comments, become increasingly important as transnational families live out their shared lives in the disparate spaces of Guatemala and North Jersey.

DOING FAMILY

While members of transnational households saw Facebook as a means of staying informed of local happenings, these "entertainment" aspects occurred alongside more specific ways that transnational couples used Facebook to "do family." For example, Oswaldo, a forty-two-year-old migrant currently living in Massachusetts, posted on his wife's Facebook wall for her birthday. The post said "Happy birthday my love" in Spanish. Couples typically share such messages directly on WhatsApp, as discussed in the previous chapter. Oswaldo did wish his wife happy birthday when he called her privately; the Facebook post was both about sending birthday wishes and receiving credit from friends and family who viewed the post for being an attentive husband. The benefit of friends' and family's consumption of Facebook posts is especially evident in couples' use of photo collages and inspirational posts.

Photo Collages

Photo collages often memorialize special occasions. Sometimes they are created and shared for no discernible reason. Maybe the woman had some extra time and made the collage "just for fun." Regardless of the motivation, the digital and shareable "scrapbooks pages" are an important part of doing family among Kaqchikel transnational households. Digital collages create "family photographs" in the years of separation when taking an actual family photograph is a physical impossibility. In this way current migrants can "participate" in everyday and important events even when they are not physically present. Indeed, migrants may *actually* participate in important events through a video call or by watching videos of the event that are shared with them.[20] But such participation is ephemeral. Photo collages allow for men's presence in the permanent records of the event—photographs shared on social media platforms.

Despite the years of physical separation, technology has enabled members of transnational households to replicate the experience of copresence, including in the creation of "family" photographs. Ixkanul, age thirty, lives in an aldea north of Tecpán. At night, from the comfort of her modest cinderblock home, she creates photo collages that serve as family photographs. Made at the same time that wives formerly talked with their spouses around the hearth, these photo collages become places of intimacy and unity. For example, Ixkanul created a collage to commemorate the graduation of the couple's eldest child from primary school. This collage features two photographs. One features Ixkanul's migrant husband: it is a selfie in which he is wearing a button-down shirt, and his hair is carefully gelled. The other is a photograph of Ixkanul and their children at the graduation ceremony. In the background are pine needles on the concrete floor of the school and a ribbon of balloons. The eldest child proudly holds his diploma and each of the family members is almost smiling. Magenta frames surround each photograph, making them stand out against the white background. Overlaid around the photos are three magenta orchids. The collage allows Ixkanul's husband to be present. It is a tribute to his sacrifices and financial contributions that have enabled their child to complete primary school. The collage is also a testimony that the couple is still together. After Ixkanul posted the photograph, it received likes from thirteen of her seventy-two friends. The only comment on the post is an animated sticker of a puppy blowing kisses that was made by her husband, Gaspar.[21]

As described at the beginning of this chapter, Nohemy, age twenty-nine, was an active creator of photo collages while her husband Francis was in the United States. One photo collage of the couple included three images: one of her, one of Francis, and a larger image (underneath) of a bouquet of roses that says "Love is forever" in English, a language Nohemy does not speak. Nohemy added two lines of text in Spanish that reads "I love you, Love" and "I love you sweetheart." In my research, I found that the premade templates women used to create photo collages on Facebook were universally written in Spanish or English. There were never any in Kaqchikel. Although it is unsurprising that there were no readily available templates in Kaqchikel, none of the transnational families I knew personalized their romantic posts to include Kaqchikel, instead using Spanish when personalizing templates and posts.

These collages present the visual unity of the family and serve to remind those viewing the posts that the couple is united in their construction of a better future. Nohemy and Francis are wearing their nice clothes, as they would be if they were together in Guatemala for a special occasion. Nohemy is wearing colorful traje and Francis is wearing a button-down shirt. Francis's photograph is an obvious selfie taken on a cell phone while Nohemy's picture is a medium shot taken by another person against a pretty background featuring mountains and plants. The other "couple's picture" that Nohemy posted to her Facebook page is similar, featuring individual medium shots of both her and her husband. He stands in a suit in front of a fireplace in a building that is obviously in the United States, presumably New Jersey. She wears traje that is nice, but not her finest, and stands in front of trees on her in-law's property. These two pictures are layered on top of a bright background of hearts with the addition of stickers that include two love birds and a yellow "post-it" note that says "love" in English.

Such mediations are changing the language and visuals of love. As Ixkanul's mother explained to me, "Courtship in Kaqchikel was about making a life together. The phrases of courtship were about having land and buying a cow . . . young people now have courtship about flowers and hearts, you know the things they hear in [Spanish language] songs." Similar to the realities of courtship in Maya communities in Mexico, in Tecpán romantic messages are primarily delivered in Spanish, not Mayan languages.[22] This is regardless of the ethnic identity of the couple.

Facebook produces photographic evidence of familial dedication and unity. In these collages the family remains a visually cohesive unit. This is evidence to each other and to other members of the family and the community that the couple is in love, despite the extended separation of transnational migration. The posts use a visual vocabulary of love that is locally relevant: portraying men as providing economically for the family and women as caring for children. Facebook becomes a medium for performing that love in a place that is visible in ways that private phone calls and WhatsApp messages are not. Such public performances of love are similar to song dedications played on the radio or Facebook stories described in chapter 1. However, unlike public performances that take place on the radio, it is women who are making collages and posting them.

Digital collages that present the family as a visually cohesive unit are important for migrants' wives, influencing how the community perceives and ultimately treats the family. Publicly documenting the unity of the family may provide migrants' wives ammunition against the potentially intense monitoring of their mothers-in-law. It also protects wives from local men who may try to take advantage of husbands' absences. Within the couple, these posts create reminders of a shared life before migration and suggest the possibilities of their lives together after the separation of migration ends. Women see this as a way to potentially prevent husband's infidelities and abandonment. Thus the collages serve as public performances of feminine ideals, given that other feminine ideals such as being encerrada are not easily visible and having children, another key element of good Kaqchikel womanhood, is not possible in a situation of separation.

Inspirational Posts

Transnational households also do family through the use of inspirational posts, which are much more popular than photo collages. I found that both men and women posted premade inspirational posts on their Facebook walls. Overwhelmingly the images came from one of several websites featuring images for use on social media. The two sites I most often saw used were Cartas de Amor y Pasion (Letters of Love and Passion) and Imagines de Amor Gratis (Free Love Images). Both websites gave users the ability to search for images based on theme. Cartas de Amor had thematic groupings that included greetings, absence, kisses, birthday, deception, happiness, cheating, passion, respect, distance, and missing one another. Many of the images focus on ideas of romantic love, but there were also images that focused on other forms of love including love of self, love of God, friendships, and a mother's love.

All the individuals who created family photos via digital collages and posted them on Facebook also posted inspirational posts. Generally, these dealt with romantic love, but occasionally some focused on faith. For example, there were posts about not needing luck because "I have God in my heart" or posts asking for God's support in difficult times. Other inspirational posts shared by migrants include Bible verses overlaid on picturesque landscapes. However, unlike posts from those not in transnational households, in transnational households many inspirational posts dealt with love and romance.

For example, Sonia posted a close-up of two light-skinned hands clasped together. The wedding rings suggested that these hands belong to a married couple. The text imposed on top of the hands reads "Gracias for todo el amor que me demuestras siempre ocupas el lugar importante en mi ❤" (Thanks for all the love you show me you always occupy a special place in my ❤). Four people, all Sonia's (female) friends, had liked the post. The only comment came from Joel, her migrant husband, who posted a similar picture of a couple's hands with text below that said "TE PROMETO que estaré contigo en las buenas y en las malas . . . y no dejaré que nada te suceda . . . Te quiero mucho :) ❤" (I PROMISE YOU that I will be with you through the good and bad . . . that I won't let anything happen to you . . . I love you a lot :) ❤). This example demonstrates the way that some transnational Kaqchikel couples use inspirational posts to communicate with each other, to do family, and to affirm their love for one another. The posting of such messages of Facebook, rather than Sonia and Joel sending these images privately, suggests the local consumption of such communications is important.

On another occasion, Sonia posted a black-and-white image of joined hands with interlaced fingers. Immediately below the image of the couple holding hands was large white text that read "LA DISTANCIA" (THE DISTANCE). Just beneath "la distancia," in slightly smaller text, is the phrase "No importa cuando el amor es veradero los corazones están juntos" (Doesn't matter when it is true love hearts are together). The post has been liked by four people, including both Sonia and Joel. Joel was the first to comment on the image, with a Facebook animated sticker of a puppy blowing a kiss under a red heart. Within hours Sonia had replied to Joel with another animated sticker of a woman blowing a kiss, also under a red heart. There was only one other comment on the post, by a male community member who posted an animated sticker of two hands clapping. These posts create a space for the couple to remember the love and romance the two share despite the difficulties of physical separation. They are about the consumption of these sentiments.

Most of inspirational posts posted by women described ideas of romantic love but some suggested ideas of sexual desire or longing for husbands. For example, Nohemy made a black-and-white image of sensual kissing her profile picture (fig. 3.1). This evokes a sense of sexual desire, one that is not often publicly asserted by Kaqchikel women. It is remarkable that Nohemy made such a statement of sexuality on Facebook, a platform that is visible to community members, given that women's sexuality is often locally understood as "dangerous." Locally, the sexuality of certain women—unmarried women and women whose husbands are away—is seen as especially dangerous, even more so when these women are in their late teens and early twenties.

Figure 3.1. Nohemy's Facebook profile picture. Picture from Imagines de Amor Gratis website.

While the photograph evokes female sexuality and sexual longing, the text of the image serves to temper these sentiments. Initially the text is strong, saying, "I need one of your kisses." But then the second line of the text less intensely says, "for the pain I have in my heart." The second line moves the desiring into the realm of romantic love as located in the heart, versus the corporality of "needing" sensual kisses. The image was visible on Nohemy's profile picture for approximately one month. As a profile picture it also remained more visible because it did not "disappear" on her timeline as other posts moved it down.

This post is a message for her husband, but one that was made on Facebook, not through a private WhatsApp message. This strategy is notable given that public displays of affection between couples do not typically happen outside of courtship.[23] It is even stranger given that women's sexuality is seen as dangerous, corrupting, and in need of regulation.[24]

Men also made Facebook posts about missing their wives. For example, Ramos, a thirty-one-year-old migrant, created an inspirational post in which he added his wife's name to the bottom of a photograph that he found online. I do not know where Ramos found the image, but I found it, minus his wife's name, on a website filled with saying and quotations about love and passion.[25] The post has the image of a maple tree with red leaves in the mist. Some of the leaves have fallen and are strewn across the sidewalk and road. The picture appears to have been taken in the United States and would be familiar to Ramos and other migrants from Tecpán who migrate to New Jersey. The words "Amar no es mirarse el uno al otro, sino mirar juntos en la misma dirección" (Love isn't looking at one another, but rather looking in the same direction together) are superimposed over the image of the maple tree. This message, an approximate translation of the famous Antoine de Saint-Exupéry quotation, feels especially powerful for transnational couples.[26] Living in separate countries prevents the couple from gazing into each other's eyes for years on end. However, just as the quotation suggests, the transnational couples' looking together in the same direction keeps them "on the same path." Such a post reminds them, and the consumers of the post, that there is hope.

Just as inspirational posts can demonstrate a couple's unity, they can also be evidence of martial frictions or problems. In the course of my research, I found that inspirational posts were sometimes cryptic and prompted local and transnational gossip. For example, a migrant posted a picture of two hands holding a red heart with the text in Spanish, "Do you see this? It is called a heart . . . and you use it to love not to play." The post had three likes, none of which were by his wife or her family members. I never spoke with the migrant or his wife about this specific post, but it is clear, even from the United Sates, that the couple was experiencing difficulties. Facebook usage means it is possible to know who is fighting transnationally; it is not just neighbors who might hear an argument who know when couples are going through a hard time.

Several months after this post the migrant's wife told me it was important to be careful with personal information that one posts on Facebook. This comment as well as Nohemy's management of her profile pictures, namely removing the post about physical desires, demonstrate that Kaqchikel women consciously manage their online image. Through these images a couple can craft their own identity and their identity as a couple. Inspirational posts shared on Facebook create a space in which migrants' wives can preserve their identities as wives and "good women" while their husbands are away.

CONCLUSION

Since 2015, Facebook usage in Guatemala has greatly expanded. It is now the most-widely used social media platform in the country. Kaqchikel transnational families use posts to define self and demonstrate adherence or resistance to local expectations of gender dynamics. Posts become a place for migrants' wives especially to do the affective labor of family and marriage. Sociologists Margaret Nelson and Anita Garey point out that "doing family" means monitoring and policing family members' behaviors.[27] Situations that involve gender and sexuality are particularly prone to familial surveillance based on how individuals should behave.[28] It is through this familial monitoring that rights and privileges are assigned.[29] The way in which people curate their images is driven by the "strong notions people have about what a family should be and what family members should do."[30] It is also affected by how much individuals want to comply or push back against local expectations.

The use of Facebook to do family is a precarious enterprise. Can the performance of love and family on Facebook protect women from gossip? Many hope so as the often malicious gossip that circulates locally and transnationally often focuses on women's behavior. In the case of transnational households, perceptions of migrants' wives' behavior are particularly fraught, as the following chapter explores.

4

Suegra Surveillance

Dolores, age thirty-five, lives in a small cinderblock house—built using remittances—with her four children. Five years ago, Dolores and her migrant husband, Edwin, separated. While informal, this separation is known throughout town with many, including Edwin's father, describing him as "single." This is an interesting description given that Dolores and her children still live in a house that sits just across the pressed-earth patio from his parents' house. Despite the small tree Dolores planted in the patio, her life plays out in front of her in-laws. The tree's narrow branches, dotted with delicate flowers, do little to block the view of Dolores's turquoise cement pila. Day after day Dolores stands at her pila—now weathered and faded—washing clothes and dishes, under the watchful eyes of her mother-in-law. This serves as a constant reminder that Dolores lives at the mercy of her in-laws.

One afternoon as Dolores and I chatted at the pila, she remarked that her mother-in-law was "always preoccupied about where I am, what I am doing." Another day, as Dolores and I sat talking, this time in the privacy of her own two-room house, we returned to the topic of the monitoring women experience. Dolores, like other Tecpanecas, was aware of surveillance that happened virtually, like when people suspected a fall into vices from WhatsApp photographs, and the surveillance that occurred at the hands of their in-laws. For Dolores, the monitoring that most impacted her daily life was that from her mother-in-law. I asked Dolores how she perceived the actions of her mother-in-law, inquiring whether she felt like the woman was trying to protect her or simply "vigilarla" (surveil you). Dolores quickly and unequivocally replied, "Fue vigilancia" (It was surveillance).

Surveillance—the "focused, systematic, and routine attention to personal details for the purposes of influence, management, protection, or direction"—permeates the lives of Kaqchikel women.[1] The monitoring takes place in the public spaces of town squares, weekly markets, and church gatherings. It also takes place at home, especially for those women living in multigenerational households. As men's transnational migration alters daily life and family dynamics in Tecpán, migrants' wives often find themselves subject to increasing familial surveillance. This chapter examines the intensive monitoring of women's behavior that migrants' wives face in the extended absence of their husbands.

Two contradictions characterize the worlds of migrants' wives. First, while the monitoring that women experience in the context of transnational migration is intended as protection, it is also disciplinary.[2] In the response to public gossip and private surveillance, migrants' wives become encerrada in hyper-feminine displays of seclusion and to avoid the panoptic gaze of the community. This choice—that women sometimes undertake willingly and more often are coerced into making—places them squarely under another gaze, that of their *suegra* (mother-in-law). It is other women—namely mothers-in-law—who are the primary agents of the disciplinary control experienced by migrants' wives. At the same time, women's expanding virtual worlds sit in direct contrast to their shrinking physical worlds. As should be clear from the preceding chapters, in the context of transnational migration, increasing access to smartphones, and free messaging software like WhatsApp, allow family members unprecedented access to each other. This access has facilitated greater connections, especially for couples whose marriages often play out on Facebook, but it also amplifies the power of gossip, allowing it to reach more people and traverse the distance between Guatemala and North Jersey almost instantaneously.

GOSSIP AND SOCIAL CONTROL

Gossip is not just "idle talk"; it is a powerful form of social control in contemporary Kaqchikel society.[3] Tecpán, like other Maya communities, demonstrates a preference for conformity, with locals placing a high degree of importance on reputation. The importance of reputation and the fact that most people know, at least by name, members of their local community—regularly interacting at church, in the market, and so forth—mean that behavior is always under intense scrutiny. Today, as in the past, gossip is a powerful force demanding "correct" behavior.

Tecpanecos know that gossip has significant and real consequences. During Guatemala's thirty-six-year genocidal civil war, gossip created a "climate of suspicion."[4] Cursory participation of all males aged eighteen to sixty in Civil Defense Patrols blurred the lines between enemies and friends, creating a sense of mistrust in the countryside.[5] During *la violencia*, mere rumors that a person was a "communist" or subversive resulted in disappearances and massacres of entire villages. In Tecpán, men associated with the military murdered the local priest and several leaders of the Indigenous youth group Círculo Cultural Ixmukane.[6] The government also carried out massacres of entire aldeas seen as colluding with the "enemy." These events, which occurred in 1981, are part of the town's collective memory, reminding Tecpanecos of the very real consequences of rumors and gossip.

More recently, Tecpanecos have again seen the importance of conformity and compliance to avoid unwanted gossip, envy, and extrajudicial forms of "justice."[7] In 2013 and 2014, several stores were robbed in the city center. Among the stores burglarized over the course of three months were a thread distributor, a shoe store, and a clothing store. As expected, local gossip centered on the exact methods the criminals used to break into the stores, the potential suspects, and the probable complicity of local police. However, as locals tried to make sense of these crimes, another theme emerged: that the shop owners themselves had invited the robberies because they were known to flaunt their wealth.[8] In Tecpán, as elsewhere in the Maya area, rumors and gossip not only have tangible impacts but also a moralizing element. In the case of the robberies, the thread distributor had flaunted his wealth and failed to share his good fortune, demonstrating the dangers of inequality and inconformity.[9]

Gossip is important in transnational contexts, and smartphones have altered the gossip landscape in Tecpán. Before 2015, sharing gossip on cell phones required that the gossipers had minutes on their prepaid phones. Only the most compelling gossip was worthy of spending the money to share. Other, more mundane, or obviously false gossip continued to be shared in face-to-face interactions, but these interactions were constrained. Today, gossiping is no longer relegated to face-to-face sharing of information in chance encounters. With the expansion of smartphones with access to WhatsApp, gossip does not even have to be "juicy" to merit sharing. WhatsApp eliminates the calculation of whether the information is "worth" sharing; a furtive glance is enough. The immediacy of sharing gossip through WhatsApp and similar platforms also expands the amount of gossip circulating. Gossip now—more than ever—readily circulates between the mountains of Guatemala and Kaqchikel migrant enclaves in the United States.

Throughout my time in Guatemala I often heard, or was asked to confirm or deny, migration-related gossip. Migrants' wives were almost always at the center of this gossip: how they saved or spent money, who they talked to, what they wore, and how their kids behave. Women's behaviors were gossiped about because of the uncertainty transnational that migration creates, bringing expectations women have for themselves and others have for them into conflict. Kaqchikel women are locally seen as (sexually) naive and needing protection from the outside world and themselves.[10] Men's extended absences leaves their wives dangerously "unattached."

As I sat enjoying the sunshine of the patio—a rarity in the rainy season—and playing "tuk-tuk" with the children of my homestay family, I listened to the maids, Sabina and Marcela, gossiping. While they washed, one dishes and the other clothing, they discussed the local happenings around town:

> Sabina: Lili [a neighbor] is looking for another man.
>
> Marcela: Which one is she?
>
> Sabina: The sister of Doña Emilia. She is looking for another man while her husband is in the United Sates. Well, that is what people say.
>
> Marcela: Well, I heard that her husband got sick up there.
>
> Sabina: Yes! He has sent money, though, for her children. One is the husband's, the other who knows . . .
>
> Marcela: Yes, her husband sends money. But it is always that way. The woman does that [cheats] or the man does. That's why my husband didn't go.

The interaction between Sabina and Marcela was characteristic of one type of ever-present migration gossip—talk of infidelities. Rumors of both men's and women's infidelities were rampant. However, as this brief conversation demonstrates, the transgressive nature of these infidelities is perceived differently. It is not the migrant's infidelities that make the information gossip-worthy. Men's infidelities are expected and largely tolerated both locally and transnationally. Furthermore, the women excuse the migrant's assumed infidelities because he "sent money" for his children. Lili—the woman whose behavior is at the heart of the gossip—is not afforded this luxury. Her labor involving the day-to-day care of their children did nothing to mitigate any potential infidelities. Here it becomes obvious the extent to which traditional gender dynamics inform gossip and how gossip reinforces these same dynamics. The gossip exchanged by Marcela and Sabina is relatively benign. Indeed, Marcela, who is in her thirties, gave Sabina's gossip very little attention. But that is not always the case. Sometimes equally mundane pieces of gossip capture local attention.

Sitting in the front room of her newly constructed house, Glenda, thirty-five, described the gossip she experienced as the wife of a migrant. Glenda and her husband have managed their remittances well and constructed a home that is admired in the community. Though sparsely furnished, Glenda's house has a ceramic tile floor and a gas stove in the kitchen; these features are uncommon in aldea homes. While Glenda's home is admired and held up locally as an example of the good life that is possible through migration, her family's successes also make her a target of gossip. Glenda explained that "two years ago I had severe stomach pains. My stomach really, really hurt. Magdalena [her mother-in-law] called the midwife. When she arrived, we went into the *tuj* (sweat bath). She massaged my stomach and gave me herbs. But the gossip was that I had gotten pregnant while my husband was gone and was having an abortion. These are the problems with gossip that women must endure."

The gossip that circulated throughout her aldea, a community of roughly two thousand people, quickly made its way to New Jersey. The gossip suggested that Glenda had participated in two of the most egregious acts for married women in Guatemala: being unfaithful to her husband and having an abortion.[11] Glenda suspected that the gossip about her was related to jealousy and local rivalries. She commented, "People like to talk here. They talk about me because they are jealous, but they don't understand my sacrifice." Glenda's husband did understand her sacrifice as well as the community's propensity for gossip. However, he could not fully believe Glenda until he called his mother. Glenda explained, "He called his mother and asked if it was true that the midwife had come to see me. She said, 'Yes. Glenda was sick.' My mother-in-law defended me against the gossip."

The constant co-presence of mothers-in-law protects women whose husbands have migrated from malicious gossip. In many instances, it is the only source of protection they have. Migrants' wives are acutely aware of this. Every community has their own "Glenda," a woman who has adhered to all expectations of good behavior and yet still finds herself at the heart of salacious gossip. The fear that what happened to Glenda could happen to them is what prompts women in Tecpán to spend much of their time within the confines of their homes, at rates much higher than their counterparts in nonmigrant households.

GOOD WIVES AVOID GOSSIP

The prevalence of gossip about members of transnational households altered the physical environments that migrants' wives occupy. Almost universally, women reported altering how they navigated their communities following the departure of their migrant husbands. Some described not attending church or reducing their trips to the market. They implemented these restrictions because these spaces were "too public." It did not matter that both were considered "approved" spaces for women. For migrants' wives, it was better to be encerrada in intergenerational households. The primary piece of advice that women offered to other migrants' wives was "Don't be in the streets so people don't talk about you." This recommendation mobilizes the well-established expectation that "good" women stay at home.[12] The advice suggests that women should not be walking aimlessly; a good Kaqchikel woman runs her errands and returns home to protect herself from malicious gossip.

Hilda, the forty-one-year-old wife of a migrant, was among the many women who altered her movements outside her home upon the departure of her husband. Hilda stopped working after marriage. Before her husband migrated, she maintained a significant life outside her home, participating in several women's groups at her church. After her husband's migration Hilda no longer participated in these activities. Instead, she found running errands stressful, not enjoyable. Hilda also abandoned her volunteer work in the church. Hilda did not feel pressured by her husband or her in-laws to be encerrada. It was her neighbors' propensity for gossip that drove these decisions. Hilda explained, "I don't want them to talk about me like they talk about other women."

While Hilda "chose" to be in the house to avoid gossip, she lamented the resulting feelings of isolation and loneliness. Women's restriction of physical space is simultaneously a restriction of social space and connections to other women in the community. As Hilda, and others like her, removed themselves from the panoptic gaze of the community, she removed herself from key places of women socialize.[13] Hilda's restricted use of space protected her own reputation and that of her marital family. Restricting her movements outside the house made her feel like a "little chicken in a cage. This chicken in the cage has no one to talk to." Hilda found this sacrifice to be worth it since it demonstrated her moral character. Yet, while being at home takes migrants' wives out of the gaze of the community, it subjects them to the constant view of other women in transnational households—suegras.

SUEGRAS AND THEIR CONSTANT CO-PRESENCE

The proximity of mothers- and daughters-in-law in Maya households is notable; many families, especially in aldeas, continue to live in patrilocal intergenerational households until the new couple establishes their own home. This also means that houses are rarely empty, as women spend a substantial amount of time at home busily preparing food. Food preparation that often occurs on (wood-burning) stoves of various levels of efficiency takes up much of the day, even when these responsibilities are spread among several women.[14]

The description of Flora's daily routine demonstrates the sometimes crushing proximity of suegras and *nueras* (daughters-in-law).[15] Flora wakes early, usually around four. The first moments of her day are spent lying next to her toddler son under the heavy wool blankets on their bed. She explained that in the quiet of the early morning "Yimayon yimayon pa ri ch'at" (I worry a lot in the bed). She soon begins the process of cooking breakfast. The first of her daily domestic chores is walking across town with her sister-in-law, to the mill where the *nixtamal* (corn cooked with calcium hydroxide) will be ground into the *masa* (corn flour) for making tortillas. Flora loves these walks across town, valuing the peace she feels watching the sun gradually peak over the corn and pine-covered mountains where her aldea is located. Flora notes that these walks are among the few times in the day that she is away from her mother-in-law, Eugenia.

Eugenia supervises all the domestic activities that take place in the familial compound, whose residents include herself, her husband, and the families of their two migrant sons as well as their two unmarried daughters. Eugenia's status (and power) within the household is most obvious in the home's shared spaces like the kitchen and the courtyard. It is Eugenia who determines what foods will be bought at the weekly market and what foods will be cooked each day.[16]

Flora's "free time" is similarly spent with all the members of the household. In rural areas, women often spend several hours weaving on a backstrap loom while listening to one of Tecpán's Kaqchikel-language radio stations on the household radio or a few songs saved on cell phones. Weaving fills the "lulls" in women's days: after breakfast or lunch had been served and the dishes washed, but before the next meal's preparations begin. One afternoon, Flora and I sat on the patio, her hands quickly and deftly wrapping the brightly colored *sedalina* (silky thread) around the beige warp threads of what would become a huipil. Flora and I joked and gossiped with Eugenia and her sisters-in-law. Today, I was the primary source of their amusement (as I often was). I described my frustrations how the *pa's* (woven belt) I was weaving kept flipping due to the narrowness of the belt and my inexperience as a weaver. Our laughs brought Flora's father-in-law to the pressed-earth patio. He was simultaneously impressed and amused at my "skill" as a weaver. As the laughter waned, he commented on the importance of weaving for his daughters and daughters-in-law: "It is good that [they] can weave . . . It shows that they have good character." Eugenia emphatically nodded her head in agreement as he said this. While the comments were compliments about the good characters of this groups of women, they reveal how even in times of recreation at home, women's behavior is under evaluation.

Suegras have several impulses for monitoring their nueras. First, it is part of the expectations of all Kaqchikel households. Caring for and monitoring their daughters-in-law is an expected part of local family dynamics. Mothers-in-law supervise the incorporation of their daughters-in-law into their family. The time before a couple establishes its own household is an important time for in-laws to evaluate the work ethic and moral virtue of their daughter-in-law.[17] One of the primary roles of suegras is to monitor, evaluate, and sometimes reeducate the new daughter-in-law in the initial period following the son's marriage.[18] As the mother-in-law supervises her daughter-in-law's integration into the family, the new wife is expected to prepare food and wash clothes for her husband and contribute to the domestic needs of the family. It is her husband's family—namely her mother-in-law—who evaluates her performance in these tasks. The hierarchy established during this time continues as long as both suegras and nueras occupy the same household. Daughters-in-law living in their husband's family compound describe how their mothers-in-law often monitor and/or control multiple "female responsibilities," such as food-purchasing decisions.[19]

Second, their sons explicitly ask parents to "watch out for, "care for" and "protect" their families for the roughly five years that the migrant anticipates being in the United States. Eduardo, a thirty-nine-year-old return migrant living in the city center, explained to me, " In that time, I think that we were about the same [as now]. We have always lived in the same house as my parents and, well, it is them who cared for my wife . . . Yes, they protected her because that is the culture here. The parents always live in the same house as their sons, sharing the same patio. . . . So I knew there was always someone here with her. There was always someone available." Thus, intergenerational households mean that someone is always available for migrants' wives, available to support her but also available to monitor her. The monitoring of daughters-in-law is seen as the suegra's responsibility to their migrant sons and their contribution to his success.[20]

The third impulse motivating mothers-in-law's monitoring of their daughters-in-law is the local perception that one can never really trust a daughter-in-law; she is not truly family. In the initial years after marriage there is a level of suspicion of daughters-in-law who have yet to prove themselves. Anthropologist Debra Rodman, working in eastern Guatemala, cites the popularity of the saying "Nuera no era" (a daughter-in-law could never be) to demonstrate that a mother-in-law's loyalties always lie first with her son; a daughter-in-law is not blood and therefore cannot be fully trusted.[21] The same sentiments prevailed in Tecpán. Elvira, a sixty-seven-year-old woman from the city center recounted the instructions her mother-in-law gave to her when her eldest son married: "My mother-in-law told me you don't treat a daughter-in-law like you treat a daughter, you can't love her like a daughter." Surveillance of her daughter-in-law provides a mother-in-law with assurance that all resources, especially remittances, are going to support the household.

Finally, the desire to protect the family's reputation motivates mothers-in-law to surveil their migrant sons' wives. In the context of Tecpán, undocumented transnational migration of men challenges—if only theoretically—conventional gender dynamics, placing women's behavior under increased scrutiny.[22] In this situation, mothers-in-law surveillance extends to their daughters-in-law's sexuality. Such surveillance "protects" their son. But, perhaps more importantly, it protects suegras' own positions in the hierarchy of the household and the community. A suegra's moral correctness is confirmed by her nuera's moral correctness. The status of mothers-in-law increases because they have raised "good" sons who are willing to migrate to care for their families. Monitoring of a daughter-in-law ensures her upright behavior, marking her as a "good" daughter-in-law—one who is dedicated to her husband's family, even in his physical absence, and who is deferential to his family. Thus, suegra surveillance serves to protect the reputation of the family, a reputation that the mother-in-law has helped to establish through years of her own "appropriate" gendered behaviors and performances. If she were to have a daughter-in-law who did not comply with local gender norms, the mother-in-law's reputation might also be questioned.[23]

MALICIOUS MONITORING

María's situation demonstrates the increased control and monitoring that result in migrants' wives circumscribing their world, despite connections to vast virtual worlds. Originally from the outskirts of Tecpán, María now lives in the city center, only a couple blocks from the town square. She lives in a two-story house with her in-laws.[24] The front room of the multistory, multigenerational household boasts a business, a small internet café with four computers. Despite her easy access to both computers and internet, María and her husband do not use Facebook to communicate. In the 2010s they video chatted using Skype, on special occasions. Overwhelmingly María stays in her part of the house.

María's section of the house is a windowless room that she lives in with her three children. The room is dreary. The only source of natural light is a "skylight" made by the insertion of glass tiles in the ceiling. Even on the sunniest days, the room is dark. In the rainy season, María's room is also damp. The few sources of bright color in the room are the ever-present glow from a small flatscreen TV, the children's toys, and the flowers adorning the neck and sleeves of María's huipiles. María spends most of her time in this room, leaving only to wash her family's clothes and eat her meals. She is largely removed from the daily activities of the household, sometimes by choice and sometimes by design. Strife between María and her mother-in-law means that María does not feel comfortable in the shared spaces of the home: the kitchen, the den, and the courtyard.

The house's location near the town square on one of Tecpán's main roads makes it an ideal location for a small business venture. In an effort to earn extra money, the women of the household sell snacks and *atoles* (corn gruel beverages) in the bustle of the early evening. However, María told me that her mother-in-law, who had the ultimate decision-making power in this situation, forbade María from participating in selling snacks and atoles in front of the house with her sisters-in-law. This was a pragmatic decision on the part of her mother-in-law: it prevented the additional gossip that was sure to come from the jovial and sometimes flirtatious María interacting with men as she sold quesadillas. It was probably also meant to punish María for her failure to comply with local standards of behavior. For María, her exclusion from the business venture was emblematic of how she was treated. She did not feel at home in her own home.

When I first met María in 2012 she was using remittances to finish building her kitchen and bathroom; she eagerly looked forward to the increased privacy the completion of the construction would provide her. Privacy became important to her upon the departure of her migrant husband. Since he left for the United States, María felt like her mother-in-law was "always watching" and reporting her every move to her husband. Because of this increased monitoring María did not like sharing a kitchen with her mother-in-law. To avoid spending time in the kitchen María often prepared her children instant soups to eat. When the dynamics of their relationship were better, María tried helping and contributing to making the food eaten by the larger household. But María described how her quality of her relationship with her husband and her overall life had worsened after her husband migrated. For María, the ultimate source of all of her problems was her mother-in-law.

The relationship between María and her suegra was precarious. María said, "She always talks about me." For example, María's mother-in-law reported on María's behavior to her son on his weekly calls to the family. Sometimes this included gossip and rumors of María's infidelities. María's own private conversations with her husband could not convince him otherwise. Instead, he believed what his mother reported to him. Naturally, such news angered him, and he refused to send money to María, sometimes for weeks. When this happened, he sent the "extra" money to his parents. This further marginalized María's ability to be in private contact with her husband as she did not have sufficient money to make international calls. María was dependent on his calling her, giving María's mother-in-law additional power to persuade her son to divert money to away from María and to the larger household.

María attributed the gossip spread by her in-laws to the fact that, unlike most Indigenous women, she is *abierta* (open) and this angers them. She said, "They don't like me because I cut my hair, wear a bra, wear perfume, bathe every day. Indígenas are closed, but I am open. My family is open." It was this openness that first made María attractive to her husband when they met at the factory where they both worked. María was funny and liked making jokes and laughing with her friends. But her openness quickly changed from an attractive quality to a liability once her husband migrated, giving María a reputation as a "bad woman" in Tecpán. Indeed, another woman—after seeing me enter María's house—later cautioned me about being her friend as it could compromise my own reputation in town.

María felt that her mother-in-law's constant gossiping about her was primarily motivated by María's failure to abide by local expectations of good Kaqchikel womanhood. María picked at the sleeve of her beautiful, but now fraying, huipil as she told me about all the problems she has had with her in-laws since her husband left for New Jersey: "They don't love me. They don't like me because I go out [of the house]. If you hug someone then people talk about you. If you say hi to a man in the street, then people say he is your lover." Her mother-in-law's monitoring and critiques were in part motivated by efforts to impose a hyperfeminine (traditional) Kaqchikel identity on María, which would protect the reputation of her affinal kin. Selfless dedication to their husbands and children were key among the possible ways to demonstrate this traditional femininity. Behaviors deemed to be in contrast to these expectations were subject to critique—including hair length, clothing choices, and personality type. María's failure to comply with publicly visible markers of traditional Kaqchikel femininity (i.e., cutting her hair, wearing a bra, being *abierta*) further demonstrated her unwillingness to acquiesce to the demands of her mother-in-law—another aspect of traditional Kaqchikel identity. To her mother-in-law María was a failure as a "good" or "responsible" wife. These failures, and the potential damage they could cause to the family's reputation, increased the monitoring that María experienced.

María's failure to comply with traditional models of behavior likely surprised María's mother-in-law. María is originally from the outskirts of Tecpán. Tecpanecos describe rurality as an attractive and desired quality in wives/daughters-in-law because these women are more likely to be "traditional." Here, traditional meant that aldea women were more likely to weave, be hard workers, and obey to both their husbands and their mothers-in-law. María's mother-in-law may have felt as though she had not gotten the kind of daughter-in-law she expected. María's refusal to conform to traditional models of Kaqchikel femininity could also be a source of local embarrassment to her mother-in-law. Her inability to "control" her daughter-in-law would signal her failures as a mother-in-law, making her the subject of local gossip.

In addition to the desire to protect her own and the family's reputation, María felt that her mother-in-law's surveillance was motivated by greed and envy. María said that her mother-in-law was "unhappy" when she did not receive "sufficient" remittances. In these times María's suegra was very critical of María's behavior. A way of accessing additional funds was to ensure that María and her husband were fighting: "When he is angry he sends his parents more money. They get my part." María claimed that her in-laws did not see her as "deserving" remittances. She was likewise not trusted to carry out the financial desires of her husband, given her failure to comply with his desire for her to simply obey his mother. María's story shows that women's worlds are no longer their own upon the departure of their migrant husbands.

My understandings of the surveillance María experienced comes only from her perspective. I never spoke to María's mother-in-law beyond exchanging pleasantries as I entered or left María's room. This was at the request of María, who felt like me talking to her mother-in-law would be a betrayal of our friendship and trust. Besides, she liked having something—especially an American friend—that was all her own and could not be coopted by her in-laws. Additionally, I got the sense that María's mother-in-law viewed me with suspicion and did not want her daughter-in-law associating with American women, who are sometimes perceived as potentially subversive or of lose morals. That I was in Tecpán alone would have made me a suspicious figure. As such, my impromptu visits to visit María were generally thwarted by María's mother-in-law, who would tell me that María was busy; later, María would tell me that she had not been busy when I stopped by to chat.

In the same conversation in which Dolores disclosed to me that the monitoring she experienced was surveillance (not protection), she admitted that her relationship with her in-laws had been strained from the time she and Edwin married. Dolores, and several of her neighbors, told me that before Edwin left for the United States, her mother-in-law had encouraged him to hit Dolores to establish his manhood and ensure her subservience. His first migration to the

United States provided a break from this physical violence but it was also when Dolores and Edwin's relationship began to deteriorate, in part because of the constant gossiping that her mother-in-law vigorously participated in. During this time Dolores and Edwin were using his remittance to build a modest cinderblock house on the family compound, but it was not yet complete. Dolores lived in the same building as her in-laws, meaning she had very little privacy. Reflecting on this time she said, "I felt like I wasn't able to leave the house" because of the surveillance and constant gossiping of her mother-in-law. Dolores continued, "Mother-in-laws are the worst about gossiping [back to the United States]." Like María, Dolores suspected that her mother-in-law's surveillance was aimed at gaining a larger portion of Edwin's remittances. Dolores described the family's situation with remittances before she and Edwin separated: "He sent money in the name of his father and a little in my name. Each of us managed the amount sent to us. Our goal was to build our own house. To be able to do this I had to save more for the house and less for food. . . . It was hard because the remittances were divided in two, not just for one. It is better if the money is only for one, only for the wife. This would be the case if you already had your own house. Then your husband would send money just to you, not to his parents too." Dolores blamed her mother-in-law's surveillance and gossiping about her as one of the reasons that Edwin began sending less and less money directly to her.[25]

After three years in New Jersey, Edwin returned home. He stayed with Dolores just long enough to impregnate her. Before the baby was born, Edwin abandoned a pregnant Dolores for her younger sister. Initially, Dolores's parents thought that Dolores was "crazy" for saying that she thought that Edwin was "walking around" with her younger sister. Several months later Dolores's sister and Edwin returned to the United States together. After they left for the United States, Dolores's parents apologized for not believing her but could offer her little support besides kind words.

Dolores continued living in the home that she and Edwin had built in part because she had no alternatives. Dolores could not return to her natal house to live with her parents; there were insufficient resources in the household. Dolores also rejected this option as she did not want to leave her children to be raised by her mother-in-law, as is the norm in separations in rural Indigenous Guatemala. She just had to endure. Through tears, Dolores said, "I have very few options. I have to try to find jobs, like harvesting coffee. Weaving here at home doesn't give me enough to buy soap, food, school supplies . . . Sometimes my brother helps me, but he has his own family to support. . . . There is nothing for me to do. Sometimes there aren't even tortillas."

Dolores and her four children continue to live on the property of her ex-husband's family. Furthermore, her in-laws are not sympathetic to Dolores's situation. Her mother-in-law reportedly approved of Edwin's decision to *unirse* (unite, marry) with Dolores's sister because she was younger than Dolores. These comments reflect not only the tumultuous relationship Dolores has with her mother-in-law but also how migration alters status in transnational households. As a return migrant Edwin had increased his status and desirability even as a man locally reputed to be a "manipulative," "bad guy" and one who had already abandoned his wife and children. Conversely, Dolores's reputation was tarnished because of "her failure" as a wife and therefore woman. Maintaining her status in the community and in her in-laws' home is conditioned on her compliance with the ongoing monitoring of her in-laws.

After enduring years of this situation, Dolores has grown accustomed to the constant monitoring of mother-in-law. Dolores admitted that things "have improved a little." In part, this was because she has demonstrated that she is dedicated to her children, the primary marker of being a "good" Kaqchikel woman. However, today, years after separating, Dolores feels like she is still under the control of her in-laws; she always lets them know where she is going. She fears that if she does not comply with her in-laws' desires they will kick her out of her house. Dolores still feels subject to "pressure" and "surveillance" by her mother-in-law. The need to comply with the monitoring and demands of her in-laws compounds Dolores's economic precarity.

SUEGRAS AND THEIR SUPPORT

Diana is also subject to the gaze of her husband's family, especially that of her mother-in-law, but the tone of that surveillance is much different from the surveillance that María and Dolores experienced. Diana, twenty-six, lives in an aldea of Tecpán in an intergenerational household. She expressed no concern about the attention she received from her mother-in-law; rather she appreciated it, since "because she cares for me and knows where I am, people are not able to gossip about me."

When Diana's husband, Victor, requested that I make a video showing improvements to the house, his mother, Silvia wanted to participate. In the video his mother had two messages for Victor, who is currently living in New Jersey: first, that the family is grateful for the financial support that he has provided through his migration, and second, that Diana is a good wife to him. Silvia delivered her first message as I videotaped the store the family built in the front room of their home. As I panned across the bags of chips that hung above a new refrigerator, Silvia thanked Victor for his hard work, saying that his "sacrifice up north" had provided the family with the money needed to build a house, supply their little store, and a buy a truck. Later, I filmed Diana sitting in the cab of the new truck. As the family members teased Victor that Diana would probably be a better driver than he was by the time he returned from the United States, Silvia walked into the frame and interrupted to offer a second testimony of Diana's good behavior, saying, "Thankfully, I am here with my daughter-in-law.... Always during this time that you are there we are here. I am always at the side of my daughter-in-law. I am thankful for your sacrifice.... I am always with her. When she leaves I am with her. She is a good wife. I'm always with her. She is a good wife she doesn't spend money badly." Silvia's messages to her son emphasized her constant monitoring of and co-presence with her daughter-in-law. It provided a validity to her testimony that Diana was a "good" wife. Silvia's constant co-presence served as testimony to Diana's dedication to her husband and children.

Suegras are conscious that they must protect her daughter-in-law through their testimony. Magdalena saw how gossip about Glenda's "abortion" had caused problems for her daughter-in law. Magdalena told me, "I give my daughter-in-law advice. When she wanted to ride the bus to Tecpán by herself I reminded her that people will always talk [gossip]." When Glenda is frustrated by having to be encerrada, Magdalena reminds her of how quickly the unsubstantiated rumors of her unwanted pregnancy and abortion circulated and the limits of protection available to her. Magdalena also tries to bolster Glenda's spirits by finding errands for the two of them to do together. She says that she often talks with Glenda and her migrant son, reminding both that transnational gossip is "only invented words." Suegras like Magdalena and Silvia realize that their co-presence and testimony are the only sources of protection their daughters-in-law have from the onslaught of gossip that cell phones enable.[26]

Constant monitoring and co-presence protect the family from malicious transnational and local gossip and are also perceived to protect daughters-in-law from themselves. Miguel, the fifty-five-year-old father of a migrant, said, "We don't leave her [his daughter-in-law] alone. Usually, my wife is with her. She takes her to church. Since my wife is with her nothing can happen. She won't fall into vices. She won't lose herself." Both falling into vices and losing oneself were local euphemisms for being unfaithful. While migrants' wives' infidelities are uncommon in Tecpán, Miguel acknowledged that it was "natural" for his young daughter-in-law to be lonely and have sexual desires that are unmet because her husband is away. While Miguel more readily acknowledged rather than demonized his daughter-in-law's sexual longing, he did not see her as capable of stopping herself from cheating, primarily because of her youth. Meanwhile, Ixey's monitoring of her daughter-in-law controlled the literal and figurative spaces in which her daughter-in-law operated, preventing her infidelities.

After listening to her husband, Ixey confirmed that she was always with her daughter-in-law: "I have the responsibility to care for her." This couple's remarks speak to the multiple motivations for monitoring their daughter-in-law. Both Miguel and Ixey spoke of their responsibility to their son to ensure the upright behavior of his wife, and to their daughter-in-law to offer protection. Miguel offers more insight about the multiple motivations for monitoring their daughter-in-law. From the outside, the monitoring offered by Miguel and Ixey was about protecting their daughter-in-law from the ill-thought-out mistakes of youth as well as a desire to control her sexuality. As Miguel commented, "We don't want either to make decisions they will regret."

Pabla is the twenty-four-year-old wife a of migrant from the city center. She revealed that when her husband left, she feared staying in Guatemala by herself because she knew that she would become the subject of transnational gossip once her husband left. She said, "He has friends here [in Guatemala] and there [in the United States] saying things that aren't true. People always gossip." As with other wives of migrants, this gossip suggests that Pabla has been unfaithful to her husband. For Pabla, it is being with her mother-in-law that protected her; her mother-in-law's confirmation of her "good behavior" reassured her husband when he called. This is not to say that sometimes Pabla does not have problems with her mother-in-law or her sisters-in-law or that it is easy to live with her in-laws. Pabla readily admitted that they sometimes have "difficulties" and she had to "manage a little bit" their relationship. However, Pabla recognized that the surveillance of her mother-in-law protects her: "More than anyone it is my mother-in-law who protects me because I'm always with her in the house."

Pabla's comments about her mother-in-law's monitoring parallels what many migrants' wives described. While wives were not always happy that they were subject to the constant "pressure" of their mothers-in-law to be at home with them, it was their mothers-in-law who offered the "protection" of familial surveillance. Migrants' wives saw the "difficulties" associated with the increased pressure from their mothers-in-law as a reality of being the wife of a transnational migrant. Tecpanecas preferred to endure the caring or controlling surveillance of their mothers-in-law than face the ramifications of being the subject of gossip.

For a few, the constant co-presence of mothers-in-law offered protection and also emotional support. Alma, age thirty-eight, described how living with her mother-in-law offered her "support" while her husband was away. She said, "It is hard being alone. I am not accustomed to it. We [me and my husband] went everywhere together . . . but my mother-in-law helps me. She is seventy-eight and sick. I spend a lot of time taking care of her. But she is someone to talk to, to share ideas with. I can unburden myself by talking to her." Alma's positive relationship with her mother-in-law provided her with the opportunity to talk about her feelings and frustrations associated with missing her migrant husband. However, Alma's experience is anomalous. As a woman and mother to nearly adult children, Alma was less subject to malicious public gossip. Additionally, Alma and her mother-in-law have had nearly twenty years to navigate the dynamics of their relationship. As an elderly woman in ill health, Alma's mother-in-law was not preoccupied with engaging with gossip. The anomaly of Alma's experience demonstrates the extent to which the public gossip and private surveillance Kaqchikel women experience is informed by traditional models of femininity as well as age.

CONCLUSION

Mothers-in-law monitor their sons' wives for a variety of reasons: local expectations of family, lack of trust, and/or to improve their own reputation and status in the household and community. These motivations are not mutually exclusive. Indeed, scholars of familial surveillance point out that the motivations for the types of monitoring that take place in intimate settings cannot be separated; the situation is always ambiguous.[27] Migrants' wives experience this surveillance differently, some interpreting it as protection and others as control.

Public gossip and private surveillance are among the key forces shaping the worlds of contemporary Kaqchikel women. These parallel forms of social control operate for all Kaqchikel women, but the intersection of men's transnational migration with the increased use of information communication technologies, namely smartphones, results in increased monitoring and enforcement of traditional gender norms. As such, migrants' wives experience more intense monitoring of their femininity and sexuality than their counterparts in nontransnational homes. Suegras emerge as a key actor in the surveilling of migrants' wives, demonstrating that women, especially older women, actively participate in the subjugation of other women. This monitoring can be experienced as caring protection or controlling punishment. Regardless of the women's experience, the escalation of monitoring is disciplinary, constraining the spaces that contemporary Kaqchikel women can assert their agency and define their identities.

Ultimately, the stories of the women presented in this chapter challenge the notion that both technology and migration are universally emancipatory. Intensive monitoring and pressure from mothers-in-law were something that migrants' wives had to endure as they tried to create a livable life in the physical absence but virtual presence of their husbands.

5

Ties That Bond, Ties That Break

Miguel had stopped working at the foot loom when I arrived, but he remained where he had been weaving the pink corte fabric.[1] Miguel, thirty, described the difficulties he had faced as an undocumented migrant: crossing the dessert, working nonstop, and ultimately deportation. His eyes— usually twinkling— were filled with a heaviness as he told me about the abuse and racism he endured at the hands of his Mexican bosses while in the United States. Miguel talked openly about these stories in front of the two younger men who worked at their respective treadle looms in the home workshop.[2] As we began talking about the impacts of migration on his family, Miguel stood up and signaled that we should talk in a more private corner of the patio. We pulled up two blue plastic stools and Miguel told me that as hard as life was for him in the United States, he knew that his wife had endured significant hardships: "It is worse for women [in Guatemala]. They suffer more."

The suffering described by Miguel was not widely recognized in Tecpán. Community members, especially those without family members in the United States, often viewed migrants' wives harshly, critiquing the ways they raised their children and spent remittances.[3] Such sentiments were so widespread that community members often did not understand my research when I tried to explain it. Instead, they suggested that migrants' wives did not experience hardships, specifically because they received remittances.[4] Even within transnational households it was uncommon for there to be significant discussion of women's struggles. It was only the occasional person who acknowledged the depths of changes and struggles that women faced. This is in contrast to much discussion in homes, on social media, and in local and national news about the sacrifice and difficulties that men faced when clandestinely crossing the border and working in the United States. By revisiting the stories of women already introduced in the book, this chapter explores the experiences of women, which Michael Taussig describes as a "public secret" or an "unknown known."[5]

The ways in which the lives of migrant men change as they move to the United States and eventually back to Guatemala are obvious. Community members express concern for how men will cope with these changes. Locally, there is usually not the expectation that women's lives change as they shift from being the wives of local men to members of a transnational household; they continue caring for children and dedicating themselves to their families (in a variety of forms). However, as my conversations with Miguel and nearly every migrant's wife suggests, women's worlds change drastically following the decision that their husbands will migrate.

Some changes take place almost immediately, even before the migrant's departure. Families begin spending less money as they prepare to take out loans to pay "coyotes," to facilitate migration. For women, this often means spending less on household items, including food. Women described this as good practice for the first couple of years that husbands are away, when almost all the money earned is spent repaying debts.[6] Once husbands migrate, most women described being filled with worry. These worries include whether their husbands will survive the desert crossing and whether they will eventually abandon the family. All migrants' wives reported feelings of sadness in the absence of their husbands, and some women described how this immense sadness made them physically sick.[7] During the years men spend in the United States women worry about the additional monitoring they are subject to. Some women "choose" to restrict their movements because of such monitoring. Others find themselves no longer "allowed" to work outside the house even though they would like to.

The loss of husbands' presence in the household places women in economically and socially precarious situations.[8] Ana, age thirty-three, notes that without her husband in the house to run interference or defend her, she struggles: "No one takes care of the wife. You see, his being gone creates problems. I'm just here with his parents and his absence provokes uncertainty and lack of trust. There are negative effects for us wives. . . . It is better if your husband just doesn't go."

While female family members offered them words of "support" and "encouragement," very few felt as if they had someone they could talk to. Only one woman described such dialogues in a space in which she could *openly* talk about her feelings and frustrations associated with her husband's migration. Overwhelmingly, wives told me that they had no one that they could or wanted to share their feelings with. Talking with me was the only space they had to *desahogarse* (unburden themselves). Some revealed that I was the first person to ask them about their feelings of frustration, sadness, and even joy that arose from their husbands' migrations. They did not talk about these feelings with other community members, even with fellow wives of migrants.

In much the same way that gossip constrained the movements of migrants' wives (see chapter 4), a fear of gossip made women uncomfortable expressing their feeling about their husbands' migrations. For example, women told me that they did not want to form support groups because of the prevalence of local gossip.[9] This is in keeping with a general reluctance seen throughout communities in the Guatemala highlands to confide in those outside the immediate family.[10] This fear was tied to the local expectations for wives to demonstrate that their husbands had not undertaken the hardships of migration in vain.[11] Discussion of frustrations or dissatisfactions could be interpreted as lack of gratitude. Indeed, wives' suffering was unspoken outside of the context of my interviews; migrants' wives maintained a "public secret."[12] This chapter unveils this public secret by revisiting the stories of six women who have already been introduced in the book. These narratives reveal how, in the context of Kaqchikel transnational migration in a digital age, some ties remain strong while others break.

ROSA: BREAKING FREE FROM THE PAST

Before her husband migrated, Rosa's life was the embodiment of the enduring woman described in chapter 1. Rosa, age forty-three, had endured her husband's constant cheating and loss of love. She had gone through multiple (unplanned) pregnancies, making it impossible for them to divorce. Rosa had resigned herself to an unfulfilling life. She described trying to focus on her children to distract herself from the reality of her increasingly unhappy marriage.

Despite a courtship filled with love letters and flirtatious glances across Tecpán's main plaza, Rosa characterized her marriage as ultimately "without love." Her husband's constant infidelities had changed her feelings for him. Her lack of love and his "sexist attitude" had strained their relationship.

When her husband had the opportunity to go to the United States, Rosa welcomed his extended absence. Years after his initial migration in the late 2000s, Rosa characterized his absence as more of a relief than she could have imagined: "I hope he never comes back. It is like a storm when he is here. No one is happy—not me, not my children." Like Rosa, those wives who had experienced domestic violence at the hands of their husbands before their migrations described experiencing an intense sense of relief and often newfound happiness in their husbands' extended absence. Rosa and her husband only used cell phones to stay in touch. They did not use Facebook. The unspoken reality was that Rosa was not looking to maintain, much less improve, the intimacy of her marriage. Weekly cell phone conversations and the occasional WhatsApp messages were enough for her.

The physical absence (but continuing economic presence) of her abusive husband allowed Rosa to imagine a happier future for herself and her children. Several times Rosa talked to me about how the situation with her husband had taught her the value of education, especially for her daughters. She lamented that she had chosen to get married young instead of finishing school: "I went to high school with Doña Irma [a local teacher and mutual friend]. I didn't continue on, but she did. She became a teacher . . . if I had finished, I also could have been a professional." Rosa did not want her daughters to find themselves in the same situation she had experienced, unhappy in their marriages but without the economic means to leave. Of course, she hoped that all her children married people who were on the same path and contributed to the successes of the family. Her own experiences made her painfully aware of the fact that marriages often did not turn out as planned. She likewise knew that this reality would impact her daughters more than her son. Like many in Tecpán, Rosa saw education as the key to protecting her children's future.

Rosa still experienced pressures from her husband and his family. The physical absence of her migrant husband did not end his abuse. Rosa explained that her husband was still verbally abusive, calling only to fight or accuse her of cheating. In these calls he threatened to quit sending money for the children. Sometimes Rosa rebuked his accusations and sometimes she endured them. Rosa much preferred to endure these calls than to live with her husband, who she characterized as "a monster in disguise."

Rosa's husband constantly accused her of cheating (despite his own infidelities) and forbade Rosa from leaving the house without first asking his permission. Rosa described how this impacted her: "I was unhappy in this time because we fought a lot." Sometimes these fights escalated to physical violence, but she could not see an alternative available to her. She could not even look to her local Catholic Church for support or guidance because her husband accused her of having an affair with the priest when she told him she had spoken to him about their marital problems. As we chatted, Rosa conceded that she understood why migrants might be nervous about their wives' potential infidelities as local men tried to "take advantage" of the fact that husbands were away. Despite this inclination of local men, Rosa was adamant that most migrants' wives did not want to, much less actually have affairs. She posed a rhetorical question: "Why would a woman want to enter into a relationship with another man who will only mistreat her?"

Rosa found that dealing with the monitoring and pressure she felt from her in-laws was also difficult. Even as a middle-aged woman with four children, Rosa experienced intense pressure from her in-laws to not leave the house. Although she tried to brush it off, the constant pressure from her in-laws, who lived next door to her, was notable. Sometimes Rosa was afraid to leave the house: "It is the fear I have, leaving the house. They want me to be encerrada." Being at home made it easier to for them to monitor her, but it was also aspirational. Being encerrada requires financial stability. It is an outward demonstration that the family does not need to use female labor to make ends meet. I also imagine that her in-laws wanted her to be encerrada to prevent everyone from seeing how much happier she was in the absence of their son.

Dealing with the pressure to be encerrada was one of Rosa's primary worries. Her other worry was what would happen if she lost the economic support of her husband. These two preoccupations went together. Rosa saw her nominal compliance with her in-laws' desire to be encerrada as a way of keeping them, and by extension her husband, happy with her. Besides, she had come up with some ways of making their desires match hers, like quickly visiting friends when she took her kids to school or arranging to "run into" her friends from church when she went to the market.

By her calculations, making her in-laws feel as though they had some control was worth the sacrifices it required in her own life. Those sacrifices could potentially translate into their defense of her and longer economic support. Rosa further navigated her fears about losing her husband's economic support, noting, "I try to save money as much as I can. You never know what tomorrow will bring. He may quit sending money. Then what would we do?" The pregnant pause following this statement hinted at the fact that Rosa suspected that one day her husband would quit sending money. However, Rosa tried to not spend too much time worrying about the future.

Thinking back on the unhappiness of her life before her husband migrated made her lament how much time she had "lost." While Rosa still worried about her financial situation, especially regarding what would happen if her husband were to abandon her and her children, her life is happier with her husband in the United States. For the time being Rosa concentrates on the present, in which everyone is doing better and is happier because of his absence.

MARÍA: WHEN THE GOOD LIFE IS NOT SO GOOD

Unlike Rosa, whose husband's migration provided her with a chance to experience a happier life, María's world became extremely unhappy largely because of the malicious gossip and constant monitoring placed on her by her mother-in-law. María experienced a significant constriction of her world following her husband's migration. Before her husband left Tecpán, María, age thirty-four, worked outside the home. However, once her husband migrated, he forbade her from working. María explained, "I used to work outside the house. I was a maid in Guatemala City when my husband met me. Then, after we got married, I worked with him in a garment factory . . . I wanted to help [by working] when it was hard for him to find work there [in the United States], but he said, no. . . . He doesn't trust me. He doesn't believe what I say. Instead, well, he believes things that he hears, things his parents tell him."

Kaqchikel women like María often lose power in their households once their husbands migrate. Traditionally, power in Kaqchikel household is derived from age (with elders exerting more power) and gender (with men having more power than women). As such, younger women's power in a household, especially one that is shared, comes from their husbands. When men migrate, women like María experience a significant loss of their status in the household. Such a loss of power has been difficult for younger wives of migrants in the twenty-first century. These generations of women have experienced more years of education than previous generations and were more likely to have worked outside the home. The expectations that they will remain at home where they are subject to monitoring is stressful; it challenges how they conceive of themselves.

Whereas many wives conform to others' expectations of their being encerrada, María refused to be locked away in the house, despite surveillance and local gossip. She explained, "They want me to stay in the house, always in the house. But I won't let them control me. I go out when I want to." This refusal placed María in the center of local gossip. María's behavior was not scandalous. Indeed, migrants' wives often developed strategies that enabled them to leave the house, including running errands with children. The problem seemed to be that María did not even pretend to be encerrada. María ran errands with her children and by herself. Being out alone made her behavior more suspicious and exacerbated her husband's surveillance.

Further increasing this monitoring was María's acknowledgment that she had "male and female friends." In the Tecpán area, married women simply were not friends with men outside their families. Given this anomalous behavior, gossip of her "male friends" quickly traveled to her husband in the United States. In this context, it is unsurprising that María's husband charged his parents with monitoring María and making sure that she remained in the house, where her actions could be carefully monitored.

The surveillance of María's husband did little to increase his trust of María; nor did it increase María's "good behavior." Instead, the intensity of her husband's "electronic gaze" worsened their fights: "When he calls, he only says mean things to me, things he learned on the street . . . things like bitch. His mean words hurt more than when he used to hit me."

María's life as the wife of a migrant was not at all as she imagined. The couple's attempt at achieving the good life took a toll on María. "I'm depressed," she said. "I've started drinking some because I'm so sad. I feel like I can't breathe." Locally, Kaqchikel women, particularly those who are members of evangelical churches, rarely drink.[13] María's drinking, depression, and "sickness" (later determined to be heart palpitations from anxiety) prompted her to seek medical treatment. After a year of intermittent visits to several physicians in Guatemala City and Antigua, María was diagnosed with anxiety and depression. While María was the only wife of a migrant to be formally diagnosed as being depressed, anxious, and sad among the women I knew, it was a common experience.

DOLORES: ABANDONMENT

Despite the fact that Edwin left Dolores for her younger sister, Dolores was constantly subjected to surveillance by her mother-in-law. While Edwin and Dolores were being separated (though not legally divorced), Dolores's life was still influenced by expectations that she be a good wife. She worried what would happen to her if she did not comply with their wishes. Would they through her out of her house? How would she cover all the household expenses? Dolores revealed how the loss of her husband and his economic support (as well as the ongoing surveillance and mistreatment at the hands of her mother-in-law) negatively affected her mental health: "What I have experienced from him and his family has left a great sadness in my heart. It never goes away. I fight it every day." Ultimately, Dolores missed Edwin's economic support, but not him.[14] He had never really treated her with respect.

Dolores described the profound sadness and hopelessness she felt when her husband left both her and Guatemala: "When he left it was very hard, very, very hard for me. I was all alone. We didn't have anything. There wasn't money for food, for soap, for clothing . . . There isn't a way for me to make enough money . . . I harvest coffee when I can, but all a woman can do is pray . . . sometimes I hoped for death, but death didn't come."

Recognizing it was unhealthy for her children to see her in such a state, Dolores left her children with her in-laws for a couple of weeks while she returned to her parents' house, located on the edge of the aldea. All her parents could offer was emotional support; they could not afford for her to return to live in their home, nor could they afford to support Dolores and her children. With no financial support and realizing the added sadness that came from being away from her children, Dolores returned to live in the house she formerly shared with her husband on her in-laws' property.

Dolores has survived thanks to the meager financial support she receives from her siblings, especially her younger brothers. Dolores explained, "Instead it is my brothers and sisters who have helped me. I was like a mother to them . . . I am the one who cared for them when they were little." Their emotional and financial support helped her overcome the immense sadness she faced immediately following her separation. They encouraged her to dedicate herself to her children. Despite their "difficult" relationship, Dolores's in-laws also helped her by offering to let her stay in her house.

Dolores told me that she primarily focuses on her children. Periodically she looks for small jobs she can do in town that would let her make some money. She has resigned herself to the fact that she will always be subject to the whims of her in-laws. She does not have much hope for a future that includes romantic love. She characterized herself as too old for anyone to be interested in. Besides, "I don't have much faith that men are worth it."

JUANITA: HAPPINESS AFTER INFIDELITIES

Women's infidelities were rare, though not unheard of, in transnational households. A female aldea resident and wife of a current migrant noted, "There are only one or two who have cheated on their husbands, but it causes problems for the rest of us." These few were used to justify the need for the constant copresence of mothers-in-law. They also served as examples of the dissolution of families that was said to be the "inevitable" consequence of transnational migration. Upon hearing the topic of my research, one of the first comments (from both men and women) was about the prevalence of cheating among migrants' wives. For example, Julio, a neighbor in Tecpán, repeatedly corrected me when I suggested that migrants' wives had very little opportunity to cheat and that I found such rumors to be overstated. One afternoon he firmly said, "No, Meghan. I have heard talk about how women [migrants' wives] cheat. People say that women are taking injections of birth control, but they don't need it. Their husbands are gone."[15]

Women's infidelities did, on occasion, occur. I suspected that María might be having an affair, but she never confirmed my suspicions. I only knew one story of female infidelity to be more than gossip. Juanita, the young wife of Enselmo, cheated on him while he was in the United States. She had a brief affair with a man from a neighboring aldea (despite living with her mother-in-law). Juanita's infidelity became town and transnational fodder when she ended up pregnant.

Enselmo learned of Juanita's affair when he discovered she was pregnant through the mediation enabled by cell phones and encomienda photographs (see chapter 2). Juanita did not want to talk to me about her affair; most of my knowledge about it came from Enselmo himself and the locally circulating gossip. Enselmo had only returned from New Jersey a couple of months before I began my fieldwork and talk of what would become of the couple was very much at the forefront of local gossip. Overwhelmingly, town gossip centered on what would become of Juanita when Enselmo inevitably divorced her. While many community members expected Enselmo to throw her out of his house, as women's infidelities were culturally acceptable grounds for separation, Enselmo did not.[16] He and Juanita stayed married, rather happily.

Upon his return Enselmo gave the baby his last name and accepted her as his own daughter. Several local men commented that such behavior was uncommon, saying, "It is not just any man who would raise another man's child" and "I don't know of many who would do what Enselmo did. I couldn't do it. He is a good Christian." Enselmo revealed that he had the time to work out his anger and pain when he was in the United States. He and Juanita talked about their problems over the phone. When he returned home he wanted to have his family be whole and "complete." For Enselmo that meant that his children lived with their mother and father. Almost a year after Enselmo returned Juanita was pregnant with their fourth child. Enselmo and Juanita, each separately, told me how they were happy and had worked past their troubles. Enselmo saw the issues as related to his absence and not a lack of love in the couple. Since he has returned, he does not anticipate other infidelities. In addition, he is not planning to migrate again, regardless of economic need.

FLORA: IMAGINING NEW FUTURES AS MIGRANTS

In addition to navigating the economic challenges associated with transitional migration, migrants' wives also struggled to figure out their role in the transnational households. The extended absence of their migrant husbands results in a decrease in the number of children. In communities where women are still largely defined by their roles as mothers, men's migration and associated decrease in the number of children have left many women feeling without a purpose. Such feelings were common among younger women who looked to new means of "proving their worth" to their families. For example, Flora looked to migration to find a new place for herself in her transnational household.

Upon her husband Catirino's migration, Flora experienced a crisis of identity. She explained how she struggled to define the ways in which she contributed to the household. She and Catirino had only been married two years when he migrated. In that time, they had one child, but Flora had not yet found her place in her new household—that of her in-laws. Feelings of anxiety about her place in her husband's family were pronounced in comparison to Flora's sisters-in-law. They had more children than Flora, giving them additional responsibilities. They had also been part of the household for longer, giving them more status and agency.[17] Flora was disorientated by her seeming lack of purpose or ability to contribute to the household.

These were new feelings for Flora. As she explained to me, she had always excelled at school and had been active in her natal home, helping do domestic chores (typically associated with women's work) *and* working in the family's corner store. In Catirino's—more traditional—home, Flora was primarily expected to fulfill domestic chores like taking nixtamal to the mill, marking tortillas, weaving, and caring for children.

Catirino's absence meant that he and Flora would not have more children for several years. She realized that she could not define herself only as a mother. Additionally, she described that the domestic duties expected of women simply did not take up her day as they were shared among six women. Flora disliked not being busy because it gave her too much time to think. She was also overwhelmed by the thought of being "left alone with my in-laws," even though she liked them and thought they treated her fairly. After spending time with Flora I understood the weight of having so much of her day spent weaving in the courtyard, always with one of her in-laws. Someone was always there, potentially watching.

In many ways Flora's life was typical of that of most women in rural aldeas, except that Flora finished twelve years of school. She was not satisfied to be a housewife and always be at home. Flora explained, "I want to have my own business. Right now I sell huipiles to a middleman who takes them to the market. But I don't make much money . . . only about $300 Q. . . [Catirino] is fighting there [in the United States]; I want to fight here . . . If we had a business it could be an inheritance for our son." She hoped that a business would give her a way to contribute financially the household, to the larger goals she had for her and Catirino's lives.

Having fewer children created the time for women like Flora to work. Catirino, like many other Kaqchikel migrants, prohibited formal work outside the home. He told Flora she could not take a teaching job that had been offered to her in the aldea. When it became clear that formal-sector employment would not be available to her. Flora convinced Catirino to use some of their remittances to start a business. Several times Flora mentioned that it had not been easy to get Catirino to agree to the business idea. Flora explained, "I argued with my husband about how the store would help us in the future. Initially he didn't want me to have the store until he returned. He didn't want me to work at all, just weave [in the house]. When they offered me a job teaching, he said no . . . I had to struggle for him to agree [to starting a business]." Some enterprising women in the Tecpán area have used their husband's remittances as a means of financing informal economic ventures, the most common of which is opening a store, often in the front rooms of homes. Flora used these women as examples, both for her own imagining of her future and in her conversations with her husband. As Flora said, "The best women have businesses." Catirino's reluctance suggested that he (or his parents) and Flora had different ideas about whether "good" women worked.[18]

About a year later (in 2013), Flora and her husband had saved enough money to open a small store in the center of town. To my surprise the store was not the book and stationary store that Flora had wanted to open, but rather a shoe store. It was Catirino who had the idea for a shoe store. Flora made this compromise to start a business before he returned. She explained that the store was his, not hers, and that he would take over running it once he returned from New Jersey. Then, if there was enough money, they would talk about opening a store for her to run. Though unstated, Flora and I both knew that it was unlikely she would have the opportunity once he returned. More probable was that she would have more children and there would be neither the financial resources nor the time for her to run her own store.

The shoe store was in a wooden building with a pressed dirt floor. The building was not as impressive as other stores in the center of town, which were made of cinderblock. However, the store offered Flora "a chance to make money" and "work to do my part." For Flora, contributing to the well-being of her family, beyond domestic duties, was important. Once the store opened, Flora and her then two-year-old son spent the afternoons and Saturdays working in it, weaving when there were no customers to attend to. One afternoon we sat in her store, sharing a bag of sliced mango. Flora commented, "Not everyone here thinks about the future, how to save money and plan for the future, the future of our children. When I was a little girl my father taught me about saving money. It is a custom in our family to save money. It is not that way in my husband's house. I think that classes about budgeting money would be good for men . . . I explained to him that us having this business would let us earn more money that if we just saved it in the bank." It took many conversations for Catirino to see the store as a way of ensuring that they will have money for their son's education, "even [in] years the land doesn't give enough."

The shoe store was not the panacea Flora hoped it would be. While it enabled her financial contributions to the household and helped provide an outlet for her energies, it was not her own space. First, Flora had to struggle for her husband to agree to start a business. Her entrepreneurial aspirations were constrained. Furthermore, as the owner of the store the decisions about the business, including who should work in the store, were his to make. Catirino's decision-making process was greatly influenced by his parents, whom he trusted to provide an honest assessment of the family's needs. The second way that the store was not what Flora expected became evident when I looked up the hill: her in-laws had a clear view of the inside of the store from their patio. The store effectively became an extension of her in-laws' patio. Although Flora appeared to have a lot of freedom, her movements and behaviors were constantly under scrutiny. Flora described her in-laws as "fair" and she genuinely liked them. However, she found that the store did not offer her as much agency and direction as she had imagined it would.

After some "difficulties between family members," Flora and her husband decided that she would migrate to be with him. Catirino sold the shoe store to his brother to help finance his wife's border crossing. Flora described her migration as "extremely, extremely hard." But she was proud that she had made it all the way to New Jersey, where she lived with her husband in a small apartment for three, almost four, years. Flora told me this story over a WhatsApp call; her voice was happy as she described her time in New Jersey. She and Catirino renewed their vows in a church in the United States, as a symbol of starting their life there. They had two more children in the United States. But Flora was most excited about how much they were together. It was just them. As soon as Catirino finished work, the family was together. Again and again, Flora commented on the joy, happiness, and unity they felt as a family.

In January of 2020, a routine traffic stop led to Catirino's deportation. Flora decided to return with the children. This was just before the pandemic. She was glad that they were not stuck in their small apartment during the lockdowns, but Flora missed the life she and Catirino had made in New Jersey. She explained, "Now he works, and has errands, and checks on the fields. We aren't together like before . . . Yes, I miss it."

NOHEMY: STAYING IN TOUCH ON FACE

As discussed earlier, Nohemy used WhatsApp to stay in touch with her husband and Facebook to publicly perform her dedication to him. Her use of the two platforms meant that she stayed in close contact with her husband. She had few complaints about their relationship; they had created a pattern of communication that simulated the intimacy of everyday life together. However,

Nohemy was worried that the lines of communication that had been opened by his migration would not last once he returned. Nohemy had heard whispers from her extended family that once husbands returned, they were excited by the freedom of being back in Guatemala and filled their afternoons "running their own errands." Returned migrants are less inclined to dedicate time to talking with their wives.

Nohemy, like other young women described in this chapter, also struggled to define a role for herself once her husband migrated. However, in contrast to Flora, Nohemy was able to create a space in which she could establish her own role and identity within her household without migration. Nohemy's use of Facebook made her aware of a local NGO looking for bilingual staff members. With the permission of her husband and in-laws, she applied for the position and started a job, earning a regular paycheck. Nohemy and her husband used this money to cover all the household expenses, including school supplies for their child. Because of her work outside the home, the couple was able to dedicate all her husband's remittances to faster debt repayment. They were also saving money for future projects, including buying land in their aldea.

In addition to ensuring her substantial financial contributions, Nohemy's job at the NGO provided her with a sense of self and identity that is her own. Working as a community health representative for a women's health project requires that she visits homes around the Tecpán area. She has even made presentations to donors in Antigua and Guatemala City. These are experiences that she would not likely have had as a young married Kaqchikel women from an aldea. At the same time, mediating her relationship and her work on Facebook created a way for Nohemy to privilege images more typically associated with good womanhood. For example, Nohemy's posts pertaining to her work with the NGO showed her caring for other women and children.

Facebook facilitated her job and serves to mitigate local gossip and rumors about her working outside the home. The curation of Nohemy's posts, including family collage portraits and inspirational quotes, as well as the comments and likes on the posts themselves demonstrate her husband's approval of her working outside the home as a community health worker. Nohemy concedes, though, that there is always the space for gossip and malicious rumors.

CONCLUSION

All long-term relationships experience changes in dynamics. Writing about the United States, psychologist Harriet Learner notes that it is often best to think of a marriage as a series of marriages with different dynamics.[19] The women's stories demonstrate that Kaqchikel marriages are not so different. Discussion of the dynamics of their now transnational marriages show that they are equally filled with moments of both agreement and conflict, happiness and sadness. However, for transnational couples the stress of migration weighs heavily, altering the dynamics between the couple. These are complicated by local perceptions that it is men's lives, not women's lives, that change. Migrants' wives are expected to maintain the public secret that transnational migration results in a lot of private troubles. This chapter has described the outcomes of several women's stories in an effort to make public their secrets. Indeed, the public secret about transnational migration's impact on women is that pursuit of the good life often makes their lives not so good.

For a few wives, their husbands' migration provided them a means to envision a new life either by working outside the home or creating a business funded by remittances. However, the ability to create a business or work outside the home was only available to those wives who were already well established when their husband migrated or for small families with few expenses. Most wives did not establish a business as their remittances first went to buying land, to building a home, and for children's education. These economic needs made establishing businesses more attainable for older migrants who were already established, or for younger households with few children, like those of Flora and Nohemy, whose economic needs were not as great. However, the economic activities of these women were constrained by their husbands' authority.

Men's migration allowed some wives, such as Rosa, to envision an alternative, happier future because they were no longer subjected to the daily domestic abuse in the absence of their migrant husbands. Nevertheless, the majority of wives described their profound sadness at the personal change their husbands' migration had created. For some, there was a loss of companionship, both emotional and physical. Others lamented the loss of their husbands and the economic security that they provided. This was especially true of middle-aged women with lower education levels. They were aware that the loss of their husband's economic support left them and their children with few options for survival. Wives who had been abandoned by their husbands were among those who described experiencing extreme sadness, desperation, and hopelessness. For María and Dolores, this sadness was debilitating.

Conclusion

Today, Kaqchikel women experience greater gender parity when compared with previous generations. Like other women in Guatemala, they have completed more years of school and have worked outside the home, usually before marriage. They have entered into partnerships with spouses with whom they have imagined a future for themselves and their families. However, the conditions of daily life for Indigenous peoples in Guatemala mean that to achieve the life they want, to achieve "something more," their families have to engage in undocumented transnational migration to the United States. Overwhelmingly, in Tecpán it is men who undertake these migrations, as they fulfill local exceptions to provide economically for their families. But men's migrations result in entire families living transnational lives.

For Kaqchikel Maya women this transnationalism means that their worlds are simultaneously expanding and contracting. Transnational families have been at the forefront of mediation for more than thirty years. Mediation offers the potential to sustain intimacy, love, and unity in the five to seven years men are typically away. It is possible to reproduce the familiarity of sharing tortillas around the hearth. Although limited to the confines of screens, there is the belief that maintaining such connections and intimacy will ensure their shared future. Digital photo collages ensure that family and community members perceive the family as a loving unit. These mediated communications offer women an outlet from the constriction of their physical worlds. Women are increasingly able to build networks of support. The mediation of Facebook means that women have a place to do family and create a livable world.

Yet, the same technologies intended to enable love and intimacy can become tools of social control, as husbands use cell phones to monitor their wives, ensuring their fidelity and "good" behavior. To extend their electronic gaze men invoke their mothers to become local agents of surveillance. Patrilocal postmarital patterns and familial power dynamics facilitate suegra surveillance.

Migrants' wives lamented the intense pressure to be encerrada, whether motivated by protection or control, exerted on them by their mothers-in-law. A significant local culture of gossip and the pressure of in-laws result in a contraction of women's worlds. As one woman commented to me, "I was surprised that it was other women who judged me the most."

Changes in technology mean that different generations of migrants and their families have distinct experiences of mediation. The first technological generation of economic migrants left Tecpán in the 1990s. Payphones and letters were the primary forms of technology used by migrants in the first generation (1990–2005). The lack of personal phones in the United Stated and Guatemala presented logistical issues, such as coordinating weekly calls. This was accompanied by a lack of privacy, constraining genuine expressions of intimacy. However, as return migrant Eduardo explained, couples bonded over their shared frustrations with mediation. Families in this technological generation also looked to letters to keep in touch. Yet even here, migrant men lamented a lack of privacy, especially when writing letter to their wives, who were likely to be less literate.

The second technological generation (2005–2015) saw the expansion of cell phone usage. In the United States, migrants used smartphones; their family members in Tecpán used frijolitos. The digital divide gave husbands significantly more power to initiate communication and the monitoring of their wives. Encomiendas also mediated transnational lives. The photographs, videos, and letters sent in encomiendas served as testimony of behavior of both migrants and their wives. Additionally, these items were treasured because of their physicality. They were tangible representations of intimacy during extended absences.

The current technological generation (2015 to the present) is characterized by the expansion of smartphone technologies and the use of social media platforms. The new forms of mediation associated with smartphone and social media usage have created new spaces for the nurturing of intimacy and friendship. WhatsApp messages allow for daily communication and an economical means of sharing photographs as well as audio and video messages. Photographs shared through WhatsApp and other platforms serve as the "truth," the "testimony" of what is really going on. For example, Alicia sends me pictures of her school receipts and her grades as testimony. They serve as proof in a way that a message does not.

Transnational families use social media sites like Facebook to do the affective labor of marriage. Making family photos using collage-making apps is not solely for wives in Guatemala and their husbands in the United States.

Wives, the primary creators of such collages, could easily create the digitally constructed family photo and simply send it to their husbands via WhatsApp. Indeed, these images are also shared between family members in just that way. However, most digital collages and especially inspirational posts are shared not privately between individuals but are meant to be seen by all of their Facebook friends, acquaintances, and possibly strangers. The porous boundaries of social media, where the private is always at least a little public, provides an ideal space for these presentations of self and constructions of identity.

Men and women share inspirational posts to imagine a happier future and nurture it into being in the present. For women, social media is also a place for doing the affective work of self-definition. Social media provides migrants' wives a novel way to do the affective work of marriage and personhood. These women look to Facebook to perform their femininity, demonstrate that they are "good" Kaqchikel women, and to define themselves. As women use social media posts to construct their identities in the five to seven years their husbands are away, these posts overwhelmingly mobilize traditional images of Kaqchikel femininity. Deployment of such images of femininity is not about reifying patriarchal gender roles. Instead, these images garner respect and protect the women from malicious gossip. In the absence of their migrant husbands women must be especially mindful to protect their reputations as their behavior is under extra scrutiny. However, local expectations of good womanhood—being a mother, responsibly managing household needs, speaking Kaqchikel—are overwhelmingly practiced in the intimate spaces of the home, rendering them invisible to community members and migrant husbands.

Social media presents migrants' wives with a way of proving their goodness in a way other digital technologies do not. Additionally, social media becomes a key space of these definitions of self because migrant's wives often experience a constriction of their physical worlds as they find themselves subject to additional scrutiny and local monitoring, often at the hands of their mothers-in-law.

The use of Facebook to do family is a precarious enterprise. Just as sharing posts creates the space for imagining the good life and performing good womanhood, it also makes the private public. Gossip and familial monitoring are among the key forces shaping the worlds of contemporary Kaqchikel women. These parallel forms of social control operate for all Kaqchikel women, but the intersection of men's transnational migration with the increased use of information communication technologies, namely smartphones, results in increased monitoring and entrenchment of traditional gender norms. Suegras emerge as a key actor in the surveilling of migrants' wives, demonstrating that women, especially older ones, actively participate in the subjugation of other women. This monitoring can be experienced as caring protection as in the cases of Glenda and Diana or controlling punishment as in the cases of María and Dolores.

For transnational couples the stress of migration weighs heavily, altering the dynamics between the couple. These dynamics are complicated by local expectations of good womanhood and the perception that it is men's lives, not women's lives, that change with migration. The reality of transnational migration is that it often results in private troubles, including fear of abandonment and profound sadness. This reality lies at the crux of what Lauren Berlant terms cruel optimism. In perhaps the cruelest moment, wives are expected to not complain about the difficulties they experience; they are to maintain the public secret.

Men's migration allowed some wives to envision an alternative, happier future because they were no longer subjected to the daily domestic abuse in the absence of their migrant husbands. Rosa reported that both she and her children were happier when her husband was gone. For a few wives, their husbands' migration provided them a means to envision a new life either by working outside the home or creating businesses funded by remittances. However, the ability to create a business or work outside the home was only available to those wives who were already well established when their husband migrated or for small families with few expenses like those of Flora and Nohemy. Yet, even the economic activities of these women were constrained by their husbands' authority.

Along the Pan-American Highway just outside Tecpán, billboards featuring a light-skinned woman laughing on the phone promote Tigo, Guatemala's largest cell phone provider. The words "Estoy contigo" grace the bottom of the two-story image. The phrase is a play on words; it means both "I'm with you" and "I'm with Tigo." Smartphones shape the lives of Tecpanecos at home in Guatemala and abroad. They play a special role in the lives of migrants' wives who endure the social and economic precarity of their husbands' undocumented migration to the United States in the hopes of achieving the good life. These transnational women use technology to prove to their husbands that they are indeed *contigo* (with you).

Glossary

Unless noted, terms are in Spanish.

achi'ia' (Kaq.): men (achin, singular)
agricultor: farmer
aguantar: to endure, to put up with
ajq'ij (Kaq.): day-keeper
alab'oni' (Kaq.): boys (alab'on, singular)
aldea: rural community
ama de casa: homemaker
ánimo: spirit; energy
atol: corn-gruel drink
auxiliatura: community government committee
b'ey (Kaq.): the street, the path
campesino: farmer
caserío: rural town
ch'at (Kaq.): bed
cofradia: local religious brotherhood
encerrada: closed off, remaining at home
encomienda: service for sending items between the United States and Guatemala
evangélico: evangelical, protestant
feria: fair for the patron saints feast day
frijol: bean
huipil: traditional woven blouse worn by Maya women (see po't)
indígena: Indigenous person
indio: historical, now derogatory term, for an Indigenous person
Iximché (Kaq.): preconquest capital of Kaqchikel kingdom; archaeological ruins outside city of Tecpán
ixoqi' (Kaq.): women (ixöq, singular)
jay (Kaq.): the house

jornalero: agricultural day-laborer
kaketa' (Kaq.): God wills it
kanäj (Kaq.): to remain
kulubik (Kaq.): courtship (see noviazgo)
la violencia: "the violence," the most brutal years of the Guatemalan civil war (1980–1982)
ladino: non-Indigenous, mixed race
machismo: Sexism
masa: ground corn dough
mayon (Kaq.): to think; to worry
municipio: Municipality
nixtamal: corn cooked with lime for tortillas
noviazgo: courtship (see kulubik)
novios: a dating/engaged couple
nuera: daughter-in-law
pa's (Kaq.): woven belt worn by women
pila: water source in home or community
po't (Kaq.): traditional woven blouse worn by Maya women (see huipil)
primero Dios: God wills it (see kaketa')
rodillero: traditional clothing worn by Maya men (see xerka)
saldo: prepaid cell phone minutes
sedalina: silky thread used for weaving
suegra: mother-in-law
Tecpaneco: person from Tecpán
tiendita: corner store
traje: traditional clothing [comprised of a huipil (blouse), faja (belt), and corte (skirt)] worn by Maya women
tuj (Kaq.): traditional sauna
tuk-tuk: three-wheel motorized taxi
xerka (Kaq.): traditional clothing worn by Maya men (see rodillero)
xtani' (Kaq.): girls (xtän, singular)

Notes

Preface

1. Paul Farmer, *Infections and Inequalities: The Modern Plagues* (Berkeley: University of California Press, 2001).

2. I use pseudonyms throughout the book.

3. Rachel Ann Hall-Clifford, "Oral Rehydration Therapy in Highland Guatemala: Long-Term Impacts of Public Health Intervention on the Self" (PhD diss., Boston University, 2009); Jennifer S. Hirsch, *Courtship after Marriage: Sexuality and Love in Mexican Transnational Families* (Berkeley: University of California Press, 2003).

Introduction

1. Often huipil designs are associated with a specific town and/or region.

2. Organización Internacional para las Migraciones (OIM), *Encuesta sobre migración internacional de personas guatemaltecas en el exterior y remesas 2022* (2023) (website).

3. Los Angeles: Nora Hamilton and Norma Stoltz Chinchilla, *Seeking Community in a Global City: Guatemalans and Salvadorans in Los Angeles* (Philadelphia: Temple University Press, 2001); James Loucky, "Maya in a Modern Metropolis: Establishing New Lives in Los Angeles," in *The Maya Diaspora: Guatemalan Roots, New American Lives*, ed. James Loucky and Marilyn M. Moors (Philadelphia: Temple University Press, 2000), 214–22. North Carolina: Leon Fink, *The Maya of Morgantown: Work and Community in the Nuevo New South* (Chapel Hill: University of North Carolina Press, 2003). Texas: Susanne Jonas and Nestor Rodríguez, *Guatemala-U.S. Migration: Transforming Regions* (Austin: University of Texas Press, 2015). New England: Patricia Foxen, *In Search of Providence: Transnational Mayan Identities* (Nashville: Vanderbilt University Press, 2007); Patricia Foxen and Debra H. Rodman, "Guatemalans in New England: Transnational Communities through Time and Space," *Practicing Anthropology* 34, no. 1 (2012): 17–26; Debra Hain Rodman, "Gender, Migration, and Transnational Identities: Maya and Ladino Relations in Eastern Guatemala" (PhD diss., University of Florida, 2006). Florida: Allan F. Burns, "Indiantown, Florida: The Maya Diaspora and Applied Anthropology," in Loucky and Moors, *Maya Diaspora*, 152–71; Allan F. Burns, *Maya in Exile: Guatemalans in Florida* (Philadelphia: Temple University Press, 1993).

4. Joyce Bennett and Ambrocia Cuma, "Maya-americanos en casa: Los efectos de la migración de Guatemala a los EEUU en la Región Kaqchikel [Maya-Americans at Home: The

Effects of Migration from Guatemala to the United States in the Kaqchikel Region]," *Maya America: Journal of Essays, Commentary, and Analysis* 2, no. 1 (2020); Meghan Farley Webb, "Yojkanäj Wawe' (We Remain Here): Kaqchikel Migrants's Wives under Surveillance" (PhD diss., University of Kansas, 2015).

5. I will use Tecpán to refer to the municipality. I will note when I am referring to the city of Tecpán (to the exclusion of the municipality).

6. Edward F. Fischer, *The Good Life: Aspiration, Dignity, and the Anthropology of Wellbeing* (Stanford: Stanford University Press, 2014); Edward F. Fischer and Peter Benson, *Broccoli and Desire: Global Connections and Mayan Struggles in Postwar Guatemala* (Stanford: Stanford University Press, 2006).

7. Fischer, *Good Life*, 119.

8. "In-home garment factory": Kedron Thomas, "An Ethnography of Brand Piracy in Guatemala" (PhD diss., Harvard University, 2011); "crops": Fischer and Benson, *Broccoli and Desire*.

9. "in 2022": Instituto Nacional de Estadística, *Canasta básica alimentaria (Cba) y ampliada (ca), febrero de 2022* [Basic food basket and amplifed, February 2022], Guatemala City, March 2022, (website); "making it the most expensive": Sandra Vi, "Cómo está la Canasta básica en Guatemala, precios y evolución durante 2022 [What is the Canasta básica like in Guatemala, costs and their evolution in 2022]," *La Republica* (Guatemala), August 8, 2022; Dolfi Gómez García, "Canasta básica en LatAm: Esto le cuesta a cada país conseguir alimentos [The Canasta básica in Latin America: This is what it costs to buy basic food stuffs in each country]," Bloomberg (website), May 13, 2022.

10. Kelly Brown et al., "Mixed-Methods Study Identifies Key Strategies for Improving Infant and Young Child Feeding Practices in a Highly Stunted Rural Indigenous Population in Guatemala," *Maternal and Child Nutrition* (2014): online, n.p.; Thomas E. Davis et al., "Chronic Malnutrition, Breastfeeding, and Ready to Use Supplementary Food in Guatemalan Maya Town," *Human Organization* 73, no. 1 (2014): 72–81; Meghan Farley Webb et al., "Exploring Mechanisms of Food Insecurity in Indigenous Agricultural Communities in Guatemala: A Mixed Methods Study," *BMC Nutrition* 2, no. 1 (2016): 1–11.

11. Severo Martínez Peláez, *La Patria del Criollo: An Interpretation of Colonial Guatemala*, ed. W. George Lovell and Christopher H. Lutz, trans. Susan M. Neve and W. George Lovell (Durham: Duke University Press, 2009).

12. Though largely outside the region where coffee, sugar, and bananas are grown, Tecpán was well integrated into coffee's labor recruiting practices. Coffee requires intensive labor, but only at harvest time. David McCreery, "State Power, Indigenous Communities, and Land in Nineteeth-Centruy Guatemala, 1820–1920," in *Guatemalan Indians and the State, 1540–1988*, ed. Carol A. Smith (Austin: University of Texas Press, 1990), 96–115.

13. The vagrancy law required 150 days per year of work from the "unemployed" and those with little land, typically Indigenous men. While Ubico's vagrancy law resulted in brutal treatment of Guatemala's Indigenous peoples, it was tame compared with Decree 1816, which eliminated the consequences landowners faced from any action they undertook while protecting their property and goods. This meant that there were no consequences for killing Indigenous peoples who were causing trouble.

14. Nina Glick Schiller, Linda Basch, and Cristina Blanc-Szanton, "Transnationalism: A New Analytic Framework for Understanding Migration," *Annals of the New York Academy of Sciences* 645 (1992): 1.

15. Jorgen Carling, "The Human Dynamics of Migrant Transnationalism," *Ethnic and Racial Studies* 31, no. 8 (2008): 1452–77.

16. David Stoll, *El Norte or Bust!: How Migration fever and Microcredit Produced a Financial Crash in a Latin American Town* (Lanham, MD: Rowman and Littlefield, 2013); Matthew J. Taylor, Michell J. Moran-Taylor, and Debra Rodman Ruiz, "Land, Ethnic, and Gender Change: Transnational Migration and Its Effects on Guatemalan Lives and Landscapes," *Geoforum* 37 (2006): 41–61.

17. Patricia Foxen, *In Search of Providence: Transnational Mayan Identities* (Nashville: Vanderbilt University Press, 2007).

18. Joyce N. Bennett, *Good Maya Women: Migration and Revitalization of Clothing and Language in Highland Guatemala* (Tuscaloosa: University of Alabama Press, 2022).

19. Rodman, "Gender, Migration, and Transnational Identities." See also Carolina Rosas, *Varones al son de la migración internacional y masculinidades de Veracruz a Chicago* (México, D.F.: El Colegio de México, 2008); Jocelyn Skolnik, Sandra Lazo de la Vega, and Timothy Steigenga, "*Chisme* across Borders: The Impact of Gossip in a Guatemalan Transnational Community," *Migraciones Internacionales* 6, no. 3 (2012): 9–38.

20. Foxen, *In Search of Providence*; Rodman, "Gender, Migration, and Transnational Identities."

21. Mirca Madianou and Daniel Miller, *Migration and New Media: Transnational Families and Polymedia* (New York: Routledge, 2012).

22. Heather A. Horst and Daniel Miller, *The Cell Phone: An Anthropology of Communication* (Oxford: Berg, 2006).

23. Heather A. Horst and Daniel Miller, "From Kinship to Link-Up: Cell Phones and Social Networking in Jamaica," *Current Anthropology* 46, no. 5 (2005): 755–78.

24. Baird Campbell and Nell Haynes, "Constructing the Digital Self in the Global South," *Journal of Language and Sexuality* 9, no. 1 (2020): 1–13; Baird Campbell, "The Archive of the Self: Trans Self-Making and Social Media in Santiago de Chile" (PhD diss., Rice University, 2021).

25. Heather A. Horst and Daniel Miller, eds., *Digital Anthropology* (New York: Routledge, 2020 [2012]).

26. Ilana Gershon, *The Breakup 2.0: Disconnecting over New Media* (Ithaca, NY: Cornell University Press, 2010); Madianou and Miller, *Migration and New Media.*

27. See chapter 9 in Madianou and Miller, *Migration and New Media.*

28. Deborah A. Boehm, *Intimate Migrations: Gender, Family, and Illegality among Transnational Mexicans* (New York: New York University Press, 2012); Rhacel Salazar Parreñas, *Children of Global Migration: Transnational Families and Gendered Woes* (Stanford: Stanford University Press, 2005); Joanna Dreby, *Divided by Borders: Mexican Migrants and Their Children* (Berkeley: University of California Press, 2010); Paolo Boccagni, "Practising Motherhood at a Distance: Retention and Loss in Ecuadorian Transnational Families," *Journal of Ethnic and Migration Studies* 38, no. 2 (2012): 261–77.

29. Lauren Berlant, *Cruel Optimism* (Durham, NC: Duke University Press, 2011), 21.

30. Berlant, *Cruel Optimism*; Zoë H. Wool, *After War: The Weight of Life at Walter Reed* (Durham, NC: Duke University Press, 2015).

31. Joanna Dreby, "Gender and Transnational Gossip," *Qualitative Sociology* 32, no. 1 (2009): 33–52; Heike Drotbohm, "Gossip and Social Control across the Seas: Targeting Gender, Resource Inequalities and Support in Cape Verdean Transnational Families," *African and Black Diasporas: An International Journal* 3, no. 1 (2010): 51–68; Skolnik, Lazo de la Vega, and Steigenga, "*Chisme* across Borders."

32. Christian Fuchs, *Social Media: A Critical Introduction*, 3rd ed. (London: Sage, 2021 [2014]).

33. Anna-Maria Walter, *Intimate Connections: Love and Marriage in Pakistan's High Mountains* (New Brunswick, NJ: Rutgers, 2022).

34. Instituto Nacional de Estadística (INE), "Resultados Departamento de Chimaltenango," 2019 (website), accessed June 3, 2021.

35. INE, "Resultados Departamento de Chimaltenango."

36. Fluency in Kaqchikel is beginning to decrease among younger people. Some residents in their thirties did not learn Kaqchikel because of fear of persecution during the civil war (1960–1996). Younger children are not learning Kaqchikel because English, not Kaqchikel, is seen as the language of the future. My ability to speak Kaqchikel was often pointed to as motivator for young people to learn to speak Kaqchikel. For more on linguistic shifts, see Brigittine M. French, *Maya Ethnolinguistic Identity: Violence, Cultural Rights, and Modernity in Highland Guatemala* (Tucson: University of Arizona Press, 2010).

37. Some young Kaqchikel girls prefer to wear jeans and shirts after changing out of their school uniforms, which have a traje and *vestido* (Western style) version. However, for special occasions and going to church, traje remains the preferred clothing item. For ethnography of traje in Tecpán, see Carol Hendrickson, *Weaving Identities: Construction of Dress and Self in Highland Guatemala* (Austin: University of Texas Press, 1995).

38. Diane Nelson, *A Finger in the Wound: Body Politics in Quincentennial Guatemala* (Berkeley: University of California Press, 1999).

39. Charles R. Hale, *Más Que Un Indio (More than an Indian): Racial Ambivalence and The Paradox of Neoliberal Multiculturalism in Guatemala* (Santa Fe: School of American Research Press, 2006).

40. See preface for a more detailed discussion of my ethnographic methods.

41. Several local entrepreneurs have capitalized on this beauty by building restaurants along the Pan-American highway, just beyond the city limits. While these restaurants (like Kape Paulinos and Hacienda Tecpán) are well visited, they are not the city of Tecpán. Tecpán is not visible from either of the city's exits from the highway.

42. Only two buildings, one being the large Catholic church, remained standing after the earthquake. See Edward F. Fischer and Carol Hendrickson, *Tecpán, Guatemala: Global Connections and Mayan Struggles in Postwar Guatemala* (Boulder: Westview, 2003), 63.

43. In 1525 Pedro de Alvarado established Santiago de los Caballeros, the first capital of Guatemala, just outside Ixmiché. Fighting between the Spanish and the Kaqchikel and an alliance between the K'iche' and the Kaqchikel prompted the Spanish to move the colonial capital to the Panchoy Valley (Cuidad Vieja), relegating Tecpán to another tribute-paying town in the highlands. See Judith Maxwell and Robert M. Hill II, *Kaqchikel Chronicles: The*

Definitive Edition (Austin: University of Texas Press, 2006); Robert M. Hill II, *Colonial Cakchiquels: Highland Maya Adaptation to Spanish Rule, 1600–1700*, ed. George Spindler and Louise Spindler (New York: Holt, Rinehart, and Winston, 1992).

44. Cristobal Mardoqueo Arriola Mairen, "Historia y actualidad de Tecpan Guatemala" (MA thesis, Universdidad de San Carlos, 2004).

45. More recently, Tecpán's garment producers have purchased computerized sewing machines and begun making school uniforms and pirated clothing, including "Ralph Lauren" polo shirts and "Columbia" vests. See Kedron Thomas, *Regulating Style: Intellectual Property Law and the Business of Fashion in Guatemala* (Oakland: University of California Press, 2016).

46. A local *ajq'ij* (daykeeper) told me that contemporary Tecpanecos' business acumen is a new incarnation of the renown that the men of Iximché had as warriors. This is demonstrative of the exceptionalism Tecpanecos express.

47. Fischer and Hendrickson, *Tecpán, Guatemala*, 8.

48. Both men and women may work in fields, but agriculture is seen as the domain of men. Agricultural lands are primarily controlled by men, with elder men owning land and being the primary decision-makers regarding crops.

49. Growing nontraditional agricultural exports has primarily benefited aldea families of higher socioeconomic status, who own larger plots and the transportation needed to sell their products at market. Most residents of aldeas farmers sell their products to middlemen, who earn the majority of profits. See Webb et al., "Exploring Mechanisms of Food Insecurity."

50. Fischer and Benson, *Broccoli and Desire*; Webb et al., "Exploring Mechanisms of Food Insecurity."

51. Peter Rohloff, Florencio Calí, and José Frederico Calí, *Xejuyu: Demographic Survey*, Wuqu' Kawoq|Maya Health Alliance, Guatemala, 2011.

52. The domain of the house was not linguistically marked in Spanish. More effort was directed toward marking those things that were *de la calle*. Private domains were defined in opposition to those defined as public.

53. I was honored after three years when the great-grandmother who lived across the patio from me invited me into her kitchen to share coffee and tamalitos with her.

54. Margit Ystanes, "Unfixed Trust: Intimacy, Blood Symbolism, and Porous Boundaries in Guatemala," in *Trusting and Its Tribulations: Interdisciplinary Engagements with Intimacy, Sociality, and Trust*, ed. Vigdis Broch-Due and Margit Ystantes (New York: Berghahn Books, 2016), 44.

55. The building of multiple-story homes reflects the scarcity and rising cost of land in the city center.

56. Multigenerational households may have multiple kitchens. Secondary "kitchens" belong to married couples who live in the household. These kitchens are made by the placement of one to two gas burners and a container of potable water in the room. They often lack a working sink and/or a wood-burning stove.

57. Nikki Craske, *Women and Politics in Latin America* (Malden, MA: Polity Press, 2005 [1999]).

58. Helen Icken Safa, "Economic Restructuring and Gender Subordination," *Latin American Perspectives* 22, no. 2 (1995): 32–52; Carol A. Smith, "Race-Class-Gender Ideology in

Guatemala: Modern and Anti-Modern Forms," *Comparative Studies in Society and History* 37 (1995): 723–49.

59. Fischer, *Good Life.*

60. Tracy Bachrach Ehlers, *Silent Looms: Women and Production in a Guatemalan Town* (Austin: University of Texas Press, 2000).

61. Setaç Sehlikoglu and Asli Zengin, "Introduction: Why Revisit Intimacy?" *Cambridge Journal of Anthropology* 33, no. 2 (2015): 20–25.

62. Ann Laura Stoler, *Carnal Knowledge and Imperial Power: Race and the Intimate in Colonial Rule* (Berkely: University of California Press, 2010 [2002]), 16.

63. Stoler, *Carnal Knowledge and Imperial Power*, 79–81.

64. Marta Elena Casaús Arzú, *Guatemala: Linaje y racismo* [Guatemala: lineage and racism] (Guatemala City, Guatemala: F & G Editores, 2007).

65. Nelson, *Finger in the Wound*; Andrew Canessa, *Intimate Indigeneities: Race, Sex, and History in the Small Spaces of Andean Life* (Durham, NC: Duke University Press, 2012).

66. Canessa, *Intimate Indigeneities.*

67. Laurel Herbenar Bossen, *The Redivision of Labor: Women and Economic Change in Four Guatemalan Communities* (Albany: State University of New York Press, 1984); Ehlers, *Silent Looms*; Liliana R. Goldín and Brenda Rosenbaum, "Culture and History: Subregional Variation among the Maya," *Comparative Studies in Society and History* 35, no. 1 (1993): 110–32; Hendrickson, *Weaving Identities.*

68. Maud Oakes, *Beyond the Windy Place: Life in the Guatemalan Highlands* (New York: Farrar, Straus, 1951).

69. Lois Paul, "The Mastery of Work and the Mystery of Sex in a Guatemalan Village," in *Women, Culture, and Society*, ed. Michelle Zimblast Rosaldo and Louise Lamphere (Stanford: Stanford University Press, 1974), 281–99.

70. Lourdes de León, "Texting Amor: Emerging Intimacies in Textually Mediated Romance among Tzotzil Mayan Youth," *Ethos* 45, no. 4 (2017): 462–88.

71. Brent E. Metz, "Politics, Population, and Family Planning in Guatemala: Ch'orti' Maya Experiences," *Human Organization* 60, no. 3 (2001): 259–71.

72. David Carey, *Engendering Mayan History: Kaqchikel Women as Agents and Conduits of the Past, 1875–1970* (London: Routledge, 2006); Brigittine M. French, "The Maya Movement and Modernity: Local Kaqchikel Linguistic Ideologies and the Problem of Progress," *Proceedings of the Tenth Annual Symposium about Language and Society* (2002); Greg Grandin, *The Blood of Guatemala: A History of Race and Nation* (Durham, NC: Duke University Press, 2000).

73. From the *testimonios* (testimonies) collected by UN workers, anthropologists, and others it is estimated that fifty thousand people were disappeared and two hundred thousand were killed during the war. Nearly one million Maya fled or were displaced by counterinsurgency tactics. See Recovery of Historical Memory Project (REMHI), *Guatemala Never Again!: The Official Report of the Human Rights Office* (New York: Maryknoll, 1999).

74. In May 1981, Father Carlos Alberto Gálvez was assassinated by "unknowns" on motorcycles outside the Catholic parish in the chaos of the Thursday market. Several leaders of Círculo Cultural Ixmukane, a local Indigenous youth group, were disappeared around the same time. This violence prompted the dissolution of the group and the migration of several

members. In response to these killings, guerrillas bombed Tecpán's municipal building in November of 1981. As a result, the military established a garrison in town that would remain there for eight years. Many people who were taken to the garrison were never seen again. Tecpanecos recalled hearing screams coming from the garrison at night. The military also punished those aldeas it determined to be colluding with the guerrillas. As in other parts of the highlands, this punishment involved massacring entire villages. The survivors I spoke to described surviving the massacres by hiding under the bodies of their murdered loved ones until the military left or fleeing into the mountains. See Edward F. Fischer, *Cultural Logics and Global Economies: Maya Identity in Thought and Practice* (Austin: University of Texas Press, 2001), 7; Fischer and Hendrickson, *Tecpán, Guatemala*, 58.

75. Burns, "Indiantown, Florida." See also Bennett and Cuma, "Maya-americanos en casa."

76. It was not until 2013 that Ríos Montt stood trial for war crimes. The trials were a lightning rod for an unhealed nation, with some ladinos, primarily in the capital, claiming there never was a genocide and that the Ixil (primarily women) who testified against him were being manipulated by outsiders. Ríos Montt was convicted of genocide, crimes against humanity, and war crimes and sentenced to eighty years in prison. But this victory was short-lived. A mere ten days later the verdict was annulled, and a second trail was ordered to take place. However, the court declared Ríos Montt mentally unable to stand trial. He died in 2018 having never been held accountable for the genocidal violence that he engineered. Although a few military officers have been convicted, most continue to operate with impunity.

77. Guatemala has one of the highest rates of NGOs per capita in the Western Hemisphere. See Peter Rohloff, Anne Kraemer Díaz, and Shom Dasgupta, "'Beyond Development': A Critical Appraisal of the Emergence of Small Health Care Non-governmental Organizations in Rural Guatemala," *Human Organization* 70, no. 4 (2011): 427–37.

78. Taylor, Moran-Taylor, and Rodman Ruiz, "Land, Ethnic, and Gender Change."

Chapter 1

1. I have translated *vida* as "destiny" rather than "life." This reflects the way women describe "enduring" to me. In much the same way that *nahuales* (days of the Maya calendar round) predict personality traits or the fate of individuals, gender predicts women's fate. Women are destined to endure.

2. Laurel Herbenar Bossen, *The Redivision of Labor: Women and Economic Change in Four Guatemalan Communities* (Albany: State University of New York Press, 1984); Marion C. Carter, "Gender and Community Context: An Analysis of Husband's Household Authority in Rural Guatemala," *Sociological Forum* 19, no. 4 (2004): 633–52; Tracy Bachrach Ehlers, "Debunking Marianismo: Economic Vulnerability and Survival Strategies among Guatemalan Wives," *Ethnology* 30, no. 1 (1998): 1–6; Ehlers, *Silent Looms: Women and Production in a Guatemalan Town* (Austin: University of Texas Press, 2000); Shelton Annis, *God and Production in a Guatemalan Town* (Austin: University of Texas Press, 1987).

3. Bossen, *Redivision of Labor*; Ehlers, *Silent Looms*.

4. Emma Delfina Chirix García, *Una aproximación sociológica a la sexulaidad kaqchikel hoy* (Guatemala: FLASCO, 2008).

5. Autonomy is a complicated though important metric. For national and departmental data on female autonomy, including decision-making power, see chapter 14 of Ministerio de Salud Pública y Asistencia Social (MSPAS), Instituto Nacional de Estadística (INE), and ICF International, *Encuesta nacional de salud maternoinfantil 2014–2015: Informe final* (Guatemala: MSPAS/INE/ICF, 2017).

6. Throughout Latin America, this model is often described throughout the lens of machismo and marianismo. While no one I talked to in Guatemala, was aware of the term "marianismo," all were aware—and largely critical of—machismo. For more discussion of machismo and marianismo, see Matthew C. Gutmann, *The Meanings of Macho: Being a Man in Mexico City* (Berkeley: University of California Press, 1996); Matthew C. Gutmann and Mara Viveros Vigoya, "Masculinities in Latin America," in *Handbook of Studies on Men and Masculinity*, ed. Michael S. Kimmel, Jeff Hearn, and R. W. Connell (Thousand Oaks, CA: Sage Publications, 2005), 114–28; Evelyn P. Stevens, "Machismo and Marianismo," *Society* 10 (1973): 57–63.

7. Ehlers, *Silent Looms.*

8. Throughout the chapter I focus on local conceptions of Kaqchikel femininity rather than Kaqchikel masculinity. Even though it is impossible for Kaqchikel femininity to exist in isolation of masculinity, I privilege women's voices and experiences. For discussion of contemporary Kaqchikel masculinities, see Brent E. Metz and Meghan Farley Webb, "Historical Sediments of Competing Gender Models in Indigenous Guatemala," in *Masculinities in a Global Era*, ed. Joseph Gelfer (New York: Springer, 2013), 192–213.

9. Chirix García, *Una aproximación sociológica.*

10. Chirix García, *Una aproximación sociológica.*

11. Despite a decrease in subsistence farming in urban areas, milpa production continues to have great symbolic importance.

12. Bossen, *Redivision of Labor.*

13. Meghan Farley Webb, "Transnational Migration's Psychosocial Impacts for Kaqchikel Maya Migrants' Wives," *Human Organization* 77, no. 1 (2018): 32–41.

14. Deniz Kandiyoti, "Bargaining with Patriarchy," *Gender and Society* 2, no. 3 (1988): 274–90; Serena Nanda, *Love and Marriage: Cultural Diversity in a Changing World* (Long Grove, IL: Waveland Press, 2019).

15. *Encuesta nacional de salud*, 94.

16. In a discussion on courtship and marriage, one woman suggested that economic considerations, like owning land, were formerly framed in romantic terms.

17. For a description of arranged marriage traditions in Tecpán, see Carol Hendrickson, *Weaving Identities: Construction of Dress and Self in Highland Guatemala* (Austin: University of Texas Press, 1995).

18. Nathaniel Tarn and Martín Prechtel, "'Comiéndose la fruta': Metáforas sexuales e inciaciones en Santiago Atitlán," *Mesoamérica* 19 (1990): 73–82.

19. Lourdes de León, "Texting Amor: Emerging Intimacies in Textually Mediated Romance among Tzotzil Mayan Youth," *Ethos* 45, no. 4 (2017): 462–88.

20. Gloria Gonzalez-Lopez, *Erotic Journeys: Mexican Immigrants and Their Sex Lives* (Los Angeles: University of California Press, 2005).

21. Locally, there was disagreement about this euphemism. All agreed that the phrase

came from Kaqchikel. Most suggested that *tururú* referenced to the verb *tür* (to pull down) given the command *taturu'*. The verb *turin* (to spin) was also suggested as the origin of the phrase. Some said it referred to *tur* (a fungus that grows on diseased corn), although they noted that this word was primarily used only by elders. Still others suggested that the phrase originated from the word *tukr* (owl).

22. Typically, such behaviors merely generate local gossip, not a series of Facebook posts.

23. *Encuesta nacional de salud.*

24. The age of first sexual encounter has increased. Women (aged twenty to forty-nine) reported their first sexual experience at the age of 18.7 and men (twenty to forty-nine) reported their first sexual experience at the age of 17.4. See Ministerio de Salud Pública y Asistencia Social, Instituto Nacional de Estadística, and ICF International, *Encuesta nacional de salud*, 95.

25. See also Lois Paul, "The Mastery of Work and the Mystery of Sex in a Guatemalan Village," in *Women, Culture, and Society*, ed. Michelle Zimblast Rosaldo and Louise Lamphere (Stanford: Stanford University Press, 1974), 281–99.

26. For other examples in the ethnographic literature, see Ehlers, *Silent Looms*, and Marc Rosenblum, "Immigration and U.S. National Interests: Historical Cases and the Contemporary Debate," in *Immigration Policy and Security: U.S., European, and Commonwealth Perspectives*, ed. Terri E. Givens, Gary P. Freeman, and David L. Leal (New York: Routledge, 2009), 13–38.

27. Beatriz Palomo de Lewin, "Vida conyugal de las mujeres en Guatemala (1741–1871) [Married life of Guatemalan Women 1741–1871)]," in *Mujeres, genero e historia en América Central durante los siglos XVIII, XIX y XX* [Women, gender, and history in Central America during the 18th, 19th, and 20th centuries], ed. Eugenia Rodríguez Sáenz (San José, Costa Rica: UNIFEM Oficina Regional para México, Centroamérica, Cuba y República Dominicana and Plumsock Mesoamerican Studies, 2002), 25–34.

28. David Carey and M. Gabriela Torres, "Precursors to Femicide: Guatemalan Women in a Vortex of Violence," *Latin American Research Review* 45, no. 3 (2010): 142–64.

29. *Encuesta nacional de salud*, 469.

30. Nicole S. Berry, *Unsafe Motherhood: Mayan Maternal Mortality and Subjectivity in Post-War Guatemala* (New York: Berghahn Books, 2010).

31. *Encuesta nacional de salud*, ix.

32. *Encuesta nacional de salud*, 121.

33. Kirsten Austad, Pooja Shah, and Peter Rohloff, "Correlates of Long-Acting Reversible Contraception Uptake among Rural Women in Guatemala," *PLoS One* 13, no. 6 (2018).

34. *Encuesta nacional de salud*, 157.

35. *Encuesta nacional de salud.*

36. Catholic families are more likely to use day keepers. Many Evangelical churches discourage their parishioners from engaging in "pagan" rituals.

37. Edward F. Fischer, *Cultural Logics and Global Economies: Maya Identity in Thought and Practice* (Austin: University of Texas Press, 2001).

38. Joyce N. Bennett, "Comadre Work: Grassroots Feminism in a Kaqchikel Maya Town," *Journal of International Women's Studies* 20, no. 6 (2019): 60–74.

39. Stevens, "Machismo and Marianismo."

40. Berry, *Unsafe Motherhood*; Marta Elena Casaús Arzú, *Guatemala: Linaje y racismo* [Guatemala: lineage and racism] (Guatemala City, Guatemala: F & G Editores, 2007); Cecilia Menjívar, *Enduring Violence: Ladina Women's Lives in Guatemala* (Berkeley: University of California Press, 2011).

41. Maren Christensen Bjune, "Religious Change and Political Continuity: The Evangelical Church in Guatemalan Politics" (PhD diss., University of Bergen, 2016); David Stoll, *Is Latin America Turning Protestant?: The Politics of Evangelical Growth* (Berkeley: University of California Press, 1990).

42. David Stoll, "'Jesus Is the Lord of Guatemala': Evangelical Reform in a Death-Squad State," in *Accounting for Fundamentalism: The Dynamic Character of Movements*, ed. Martin E. Marty and R. Scott Appleby (Chicago: University of Chicago Press, 1994).

43. Bjune, "Religious Change and Political Continuity," 77.

44. David Carey, *Our Elders Teach Us: Maya-Kaqchikel Historical Perspectives* (Tuscaloosa: University of Alabama Press, 2001); Maria Elena Garcia, *Making Indigenous Citizens: Identity, Development, and Multicultural Activism in Peru* (Stanford: Stanford University Press, 2005).

45. Carey, *Our Elders Teach Us.*

46. *Encuesta nacional de salud*, 31.

47. For more on the dynamics of gender and selling in the market, see Walter Little, *Mayas in the Marketplace: Tourism, Globalization, and Cultural Identity* (Austin: University of Texas, 2004); S. Ashley Kistler, *Maya Market Women: Power and Tradition in San Juan Chamelco, Guatemala* (Urbana: University of Illinois Press, 2014).

48. For example, Luisa occasionally sent me WhatsApp messages, but they were more frequent when it was time for me to send her money to pay her school fees. Luisa would send a message saying, "Hi Meghan I hope you're having a good day." Luisa never asked for money or reminded me that it was time for me to pay her school fees, despite my repeatedly saying it wouldn't offend me. Instead, these messages gave me the opportunity to volunteer my support. This parallels the ways Horst and Miller describe the use of cell phones among Jamaican women. See Heather A. Horst and Daniel Miller, "From Kinship to Link-Up: Cell Phones and Social Networking in Jamaica," *Current Anthropology* 46, no. 5 (2005): 755–78.

49. Ehlers, *Silent Looms*, xxxv.

50. Ehlers, *Silent Looms.*

51. Irma's economic status comes from both her steady income as a teacher and from the fact that she—not her husband—owns the land on which their family home stands.

52. Susan A. Berger, *Guatemaltecas: The Women's Movement 1986–2003* (Austin: University of Texas Press, 2006), 24; Liliana R. Goldín, *Global Maya: Work and Ideology in Rural Guatemala* (Tucson: University of Arizona, 2009), 70; Hendrickson, *Weaving Identities*, 132.

53. Berger, *Guatemaltecas*, 95.

54. *Encuesta nacional de salud*, 109–11.

Chapter 2

1. The winter correlates with the rainy season, typically May through October.

2. All the people whom we met with were her either his or her relatives.

3. William Mazzarella, "Culture, Globalization, Mediation," *Annual Review of Anthropology* (2004): 347–67.

4. Jay David Bolter and Richard Grusin, *Remediation: Understanding New Media* (Cambridge, MA: MIT Press, 2000); Sarah Kember and Joanna Zylinska, *Life after New Media: Mediation as a Vital Process* (Cambridge: Massachusettes Institute of Technology Press, 2015).

5. Tiffany Creegan Miller, *The Maya Art of Speaking Writing: Remediating Indigenous Orality in the Digital Age* (Tuscon: University of Arizona Press, 2022).

6. Traditional huipil designs are unique to different towns. Huipils are one of many mediations in Maya women's worlds. Such mediations can be as complicated as navigating Guatemala's ongoing racism (described in the introduction) and being denied entry into "elite" spaces or as simple as trying to catch a bus. For example, a friend from the neighboring town of Comalapa described the difficulty she had catching a bus to Tecpán because none of the buses traveling up the Pan-American Highway were stopping. She then realized she was wearing the huipil traditional to Patzún, a town whose exit on the Pan-American highway was very close to Comalapa's. She suspected that the buses did not want to stop for such a short ride (and low fare).

7. Gonzalo Bacigalupe and Susan Lambe, "Virtualizing Intimacy: Inforamtion Communication Technologies and Transnational Families in Therapy," *Family Process* 50, no. 1 (2011): 14.

8. "Mobile Cellular Subscriptions (per 100 people)-Guatemala," World Bank (website), 2022.

9. Instituto Nacional de Estadística, *Poblacion de 7 años o más por uso de celular, compu, y/o internet* (website) 2019.

10. Often local stores are painted either blue or red. These colors correspond to the colors of Guatemala's two cell- phone companies, Tigo and Claro. While stores are painted the colors of a particular associated with a particular cell phone provider, the stores are independently owned. Their painting is purely an advertisement that store owners seek out as a free coat of paint. There is little rhyme or reason to which stores are painted which color. Nor does the color indicate what types of cell phone minutes can be purchased at that store. You can buy Tigo recarga from a Claro store, as I did nearly once a week while I lived in Guatemala.

11. For a Guatemala-wide division of waves of migrants see Susanne Jonas and Nestor Rodríguez, *Guatemala-U.S. Migration: Transforming Regions* (Austin: University of Texas Press, 2015).

12. The most detailed explorations of mediation come from the two periods that most overlapped with my fieldwork. Discussion of the first wave of Tecpán's transnational migrants comes from interviews with individuals who migrated at the time and the available ethnographic literature. My discussion of mediation in the subsequent waves of transnational migration comes from interviews and participant observation.

13. Heather A. Horst, "The Blessings and Burdens of Communication: Cell Phones in Jamaican Transnational Social Fields," *Global Networks* 6, no. 2 (2006): 143–59; Heather A. Horst and Daniel Miller, "From Kinship to Link-Up: Cell Phones and Social Networking in Jamaica," *Current Anthropology* 46, no. 5 (2005): 755–78; Bolter and Grusin, *Remediation*.

14. Those who left before the 1990s were more likely to be individuals and families fleeing the violence of the civil war.

15. Guatemala has two major daily papers in circulation in Tecpán: *Prensa Libre* and *Nuestro Diario*. *Prensa Libre* is a well-respected newspaper covering departmental, national, and international news. On Sundays, the paper features the front page of the *New York Times* in Spanish. It is widely read throughout the country, especially among educated Guatemalans. *Nuestro Diario* is very popular in the countryside because it is cheaper and has more sensationalized news coverage. The paper also features daily photographs of ladina models and beauty queens in bikinis. This was the most "read" feature by many in Tecpán.

16. Edward F. Fischer and Carol Hendrickson, *Tecpán, Guatemala: Global Connections and Mayan Struggles in Postwar Guatemala* (Boulder: Westview, 2003), 8. By the early 2010s there was only one parlor that had a TV and several old arcade games. I never entered the parlor as it seemed to be the domain of men and boys. However, its location near the Dispensa Familiar meant that it was visible when I walked to the store. I mostly saw teenage boys playing arcade games and never noticed pornographic movies playing on the TV screen.

17. Bruce Wydick, Harmony Karp Hayes, and Sarah Hilliker Kempf, "Social Networks, Neighborhood Effects, and Credit Access: Evidence from Rural Guatemala," *World Development* 39, no. 5 (2011): 974–82.

18. Landlines, which are still uncommon in rural homes in the municipio, were especially rare in the 1990s.

19. Even in 2013, when I conducted my longest period fieldwork, it was common to see signs advertising the service and to see individuals using it. I have a distinct memory of hurriedly running to a large corner store in Tecpán's Patacabaj neighborhood. I was on a short break from the Kaqchikel language program and needed to purchase supplies, including a piñata, for the week's activities. When I arrived at the store a man of about forty was arranging to make a phone call on the rented phone. His straw cowboy hat and worn button-down shirt suggested that he was from an aldea and was taking advantage of a trip into the city center to make purchases and rent a telephone to make a call. Despite my efforts to not listen to the conversation, it was impossible to not hear an occasional bit of information as I waited for the store owner to retrieve the items I needed.

20. Eduardo commented that the only noticeable difference was the trip—crossing the desert versus getting on a plane to Canada.

21. Jonas and Rodríguez, *Guatemala-U.S. Migration*, 147; Laura M. Ahearn, *Invitations to Love: Literacy, Love Letters, and Social Change in Nepal* (Ann Arbor: University of Michigan Press, 2012 [2001]).

22. Debra Hain Rodman, "Gender, Migration, and Transnational Identities: Maya and Ladino Relations in Eastern Guatemala" (PhD diss., University of Florida, 2006); Patricia Foxen, *In Search of Providence: Transnational Mayan Identities* (Nashville: Vanderbilt University Press, 2007).

23. Return migrants had difficult remembering the exact costs of these cards. They recalled that it was cheaper to call at night.

24. Rodman, "Gender, Migration, and Transnational Identities," 138.

25. Steven Vertovec, "Cheap Calls: The Social Glue of Migrant Transnationalism," *Global Networks* 4, no. 2 (2004): 219–24.

26. See also Rhacel Salazar Parreñas, "Long Distance Intimacy: Class, Gender, and

Intergenerational Relations between Mothers and Children in Filipino Transnational Families," *Global Networks* 5, no. 4 (2005): 317–36.

27. Rodman, "Gender, Migration, and Transnational Identities."

28. I purchased my frijolito in 2010 and it accompanied every round of fieldwork. It was sturdy and could easily be carried in my bra during trips on buses and through the market. It finally died in 2016.

29. Cell phone calls threatening kidnapping in particular and/or demanding bribes were a common method of extorting money in Guatemala in the late 1990s through the early 2010s. See Kedron Thomas, "An Ethnography of Brand Piracy in Guatemala" (PhD diss., Harvard University, 2011).

30. See also Mirca Madianou and Daniel Miller, *Migration and New Media: Transnational Families and Polymedia* (New York: Routledge, 2012), 110.

31. Meghan Farley Webb, "Transnational Migration's Psychosocial Impacts for Kaqchikel Maya Migrants' Wives," *Human Organization* 77, no. 1 (2018): 32–41; Dinah Hannaford, "Technologies of the Spouse: Intimate Surveillance in Senegalese Transnational Marriages," *Global Networks* 15, no. 1 (2015): 43–59.

32. Madianou and Miller, *Migration and New Media*.

33. Meghan Farley Webb, "Yojkanäj Wawe' (We Remain Here): Kaqchikel Migrants' Wives under Surveillance" (PhD diss., University of Kansas, 2015).

34. Hannaford, "Technologies of the Spouse."

35. The cost to *desfrijolízarse* listed in the advertisement only covered the cost of the phone. It did not include the cost of any data or saldo following the initial promotional period (usually a month).

36. I was never able to get my Alcatel OT-385 to connect to WiFi networks in Tecpán or Antigua. The only time I was able to use the phone to get on Facebook was during the promotional period.

37. During my time in Guatemala, I alternated between using my frijolito and my knockoff Blackberry, moving my chip between phones. I never worried that using my frijolito on buses would make me a target for robbery.

38. The website of one encomienda that served the Los Angeles region actively discouraged its use if one were not living in the area.

39. Some aldeas have their own encomienda services, and others have a local "branch" of one of the larger encomienda services located in Tecpán.

40. Cati Coe, "What Is Love?: The Materiality of Care in Ghanain Transnational Families," *International Migration* 49, no. 6 (2011): 7–24; Pierrette Hondagneu-Sotelo, *Domestica: Immigrant Workers Cleaning and Caring in the Shadows of Affluence* (Berkeley: University of California Press, 2001); Rhacel Salazar Parreñas, *Servants of Globalization: Women, Migration, and Domestic Work* (Stanford: Stanford University Press, 2001); Rhacel Salazar Parreñas, *Children of Global Migration: Transnational Families and Gendered Woes* (Stanford: Stanford University Press, 2005).

41. Raelene Wilding, "Viritual" Intimacies?: Families Communicating across Transnational Contexts," *Global Networks* 6, no. 2 (2006): 125–42.

42. Ilana Gershon, *The Breakup 2.0: Disconnecting over New Media* (Ithaca, NY: Cornell University Press, 2010).

43. See also Miller, *Maya Art of Speaking Writing.*

44. Lourdes de León, "Texting Amor: Emerging Intimacies in Textually Mediated Romance among Tzotzil Mayan Youth," *Ethos* 45, no. 4 (2017): 462–88.

45. Jillian Moore et al., "Aid and Gendered Subjectivity in Rural Guatemala," *Journal of Development Studies* 53, no. 12 (2017): 2164–78; Shom Dasgupta-Tsikinas and Paul Wise, "'Mi Familia Probreza': Conditional Cash Transfers and Materal-Child Health in Rural Guatemala," in *Privatization and the New Medical Pluralism: Shifting Healthcare Landscapes in Maya Guatemala*, ed. Anita Chary and Peter Rohloff (Lanham, MD: Lexington Books, 2015), 19–34.

46. Anita Chary, "'A Poor Woman's Disease' in the Time of Global Health: An Ethnography of Cervical Cancer in Guatemala" (PhD diss., Washington University, 2015).

47. For a discussion of precarious networks and the pursuit of medical service in Guatemala see: Anita Chary and Peter Rohloff, eds., *Privatization and the New Medical Pluralism: Shifting Healthcare Landscapes in Maya Guatemala* (Lanham, MD: Lexington Books, 2015).

48. Even though I have known men to share an already-made post on their own Facebook pages, I have never known a man to make one.

49. In 2020, Facebook (WhatsApp's parent company) reported that there were more than two billion users worldwide. "WhatsApp: Two Billion Users—Connecting the World Privately," Facebook (website) 2020.

50. Laura M. Ahearn, *Invitations to Love: Literacy, Love Letters, and Social Change in Nepal* (Ann Arbor: University of Michigan Press, 2012 [2001]).

51. In 2018, a community Facebook page was created as a place for *denuncias* (complaints).

52. John Vincent Clary, "Digital Geographies of Transnational Spaces: A Mixed-Methods Study of Mexico-US Migration" (MA thesis, University of Texas, 2014).

53. I use the term "inspirational post" to describe the photographs and quotations commonly posted on Facebook pages throughout Latin America. Many speak about friendship and love. They often have a religious theme or undertone.

Chapter 3

1. Christian Fuchs, *Social Media: A Critical Introduction*, 3rd ed. (London: Sage, 2021 [2014]).

2. Fuchs, *Social Media*; Jacob Johannsen, *Psychoanalysis and Digital Culture: Audiences, Social Media, and Big Data* (New York: Routledge, 2019); Verónica Gómez-Urrutia and Felipe Tello-Navarro, "Gender, Love and the Internet: Romantic Online Interactions in Chilean Young People," *Journal of Youth Studies* 24, no. 6 (2020): 731–45.

3. Baird Campbell and Nell Haynes, "Constructing the Digital Self in the Global South," *Journal of Language and Sexuality* 9, no. 1 (2020): 1–13.

4. Nancy A. Naples, "A Member of the Funeral: An Introspective Ethnography," in *Queer Families, Queer Politics: Challenging Culture and the State*, ed. Mary Bernstein and Renate Reinmann (New York: Columbia University Press, 2001), 21–43; Margaret K. Nelson, "Single Mothers 'Do' Family," *Journal of Marriage and Family* 68 (2006): 781–95; Candace West and Sarah Fenstermaker, "Doing Difference," *Gender and Society* 9, no. 1 (1995): 8–37; Candace West and Don H. Zimmerman, "Doing Gender," *Gender and Society* 45, no. 2 (1987):

125–51; Candace West and Don H. Zimmerman, "Doing Gender," in *Doing Gender, Doing Difference: Inequality, Power, and Institutional Change*, ed. Sarah Fernstermaker and Candace West (New York: Routledge, 2002), 3–25.

5. Gómez-Urrutia and Tello-Navarro, "Gender, Love and the Internet."

6. Campbell and Haynes, "Constructing the Digital Self."

7. Carol Hendrickson, *Weaving Identities: Construction of Dress and Self in Highland Guatemala* (Austin: University of Texas Press, 1995).

8. Virginia Garrard-Burnett, "Aftermath: Women and Gender Issues in Postconflict Guatemala," Center for Development Information and Evaluation, U.S. Agency for International Development (Washington, DC, 2000); Linda Green, *Fear as a Way of Life: Mayan Widows in Rural Guatemala* (New York: Columbia University Press, 1999); Victoria Sanford, *Buried Secrets: Truth and Human Rights in Guatemala* (New York: Palgrave, 2003); Judith N. Zur, "The Psycholsocial Effects of 'la Violencia' on Widows of El Quiché, Guatemala," *Focus on Gender* 1, no. 2 (1993): 27–30; Judith N. Zur, *Violent Memories: Mayan War Widows in Guatemala* (Boulder: Westview, 1998).

9. Meghan Farley Webb, "Transnational Migration's Psychosocial Impacts for Kaqchikel Maya Migrants' Wives," *Human Organization* 77, no. 1 (2018): 32–41.

10. For a discussion of how female migrants demonstrate their status as "good women" in Kaqchikel communities, see Joyce N. Bennett, *Good Maya Women: Migration and Revitalization of Clothing and Language in Highland Guatemala* (Tuscaloosa: University of Alabama, 2022).

11. Elisabeth Stasser et al., "Doing Family: Response to the Constructions of 'The Migrant Family' across Europe," *History of the Family* 14, no. 2 (2009): 165–76.

12. Thomas E. Davis et al., "Chronic Malnutrition, Breastfeeding, and Ready to Use Supplementary Food in Guatemalan Maya Town," *Human Organization* 73, no. 1 (2014): 72–81.

13. Zoë H. Wool, *After War: The Weight of Life at Walter Reed* (Durham, NC: Duke University Press, 2015), 157.

14. In 2009, Guatemala had one of the lowest rates of Facebook usage in the world. See Summer Harlow, "Social Media and Social Movements: Facebook and an Online Guatemalan Justice Movement that Moved Offline," *New Media and Society* 14, no. 2 (2011): 228.

15. It was not so much that men had "extra" money as it was that men were more likely to be in charge of money and have the discretion to spend it on a leisure activity like going to an internet café.

16. Brent E. Metz and Meghan Farley Webb, "Historical Sediments of Competing Gender Models in Indigenous Guatemala," in *Masculinities in a Global Era*, ed. Joseph Gelfer (New York: Springer, 2013), 192–213.

17. Mestizo is an uncommon ethnoracial identification in Guatemala. See Emilio del Valle Escalante, *Maya Nationalisms and Postcolonial Challenges in Guatemala: Coloniality, Modernity, and Identity Politics*, ed. James F. Brooks, Global Indigenous Politics (Santa Fe: School for Advanced Research, 2009).

18. Tomás's daughter died of complications from an unmanaged chronic disease in 2015. It is unclear how technological changes may have altered the communication between her and her brother.

19. Johannsen, *Psychoanalysis and Digital Culture.*

20. Tiffany Creegan Miller, *The Maya Art of Speaking Writing: Remediating Indigenous Orality in the Digital Age* (Tuscon: University of Arizona Press, 2022).

21. Anne Allison, "Cuteness as Japan's Millenial Product," in *Pikachu's Global Adventure: The Rise and Fall of Pokémon*, ed. Joseph J. Tobin (Durham, NC: Duke University Press, 2004), 34–49.

22. Lourdes de León, "Texting Amor: Emerging Intimacies in Textually Mediated Romance among Tzotzil Mayan Youth," *Ethos* 45, no. 4 (2017): 462–88.

23. Brent E. Metz, *Ch'orti'-Maya Survival in Eastern Guatemala: Indigeneity in Transition* (Albuquerque: University of New Mexico Press, 2006).

24. Metz and Webb, "Historical Sediments."

25. Cartas de Amor y Pasion (website).

26. The Saint-Exupéry quotation reads, "Love does not consist of gazing at each other, but in looking outward together in the same direction."

27. Margaret K. Nelson and Anita Ilta Garey, eds., *Who's Watching?: Daily Practices of Surveillance among Contemporary Families* (Nashville: Vanderbilt University Press, 2009).

28. Emily W. Kane, "Policing Gender Boundaries: Monitoring of Preschool Children's Gender Nonconformity," in Nelson and Garey, *Who's Watching?* 239–60.

29. Nelson, "Single Mothers 'Do' Family," 783.

30. Margaret K. Nelson and Anita Ilta Garey, "Who's Watching?: An Introductory Essay," in Nelson and Garey, *Who's Watching?* 2.

Chapter 4

1. David Lyon, *Surveillance Studies: An Overview* (Maldan, MA: Polity Press, 2007), 14.

2. Michel Foucault, *Discipline and Punish: The Birth of the Prison*, trans. Alan Sheridan (New York: Pantheon Books, 1977).

3. As "professional gossips," anthropologists have long had an interest in the topic. See Max Gluckman, "Gossip and Scandal," *Current Anthropology* 4 (1963): 307–16; Robert Paine, "What Is Gossip About?: An Alternative Hypothesis," *Man* 2, no. 2 (1967): 278–85; Niko Bresnier, *Gossip and the Everyday Production of Politics* (Honolulu: University of Hawaii Press, 2009); John K. Campbell, *Honour, Family, and Patronage: A Study of Institutions and Moral Values in a Modern Greek Community* (Oxford: Oxford University Press, 1964); Gary Alan Fine, "Rumor," in *Folklore: An Encyclopedia of Beliefs, Customs, Tales and Art*, ed. Thomas A. Green (Santa Barbara, CA: ABC-CLIO, 1997); Trinh T. Minh-Ha, *Woman, Native, Other: Writing Postcoloniality and Feminism* (Bloomington: Indiana University Press, 2009 [1989]); David Samper, "Cannibalizing Kids: Rumor and Resistance in Latin America," *Journal of Folklore Research* 39, no. 1 (2002): 1–32; Pamela J. Stewart and Andrew Strathern, *Witchcraft, Sorcery, Rumors and Gossip* (New York: Cambridge University Press, 2004); Cass R. Sunstein, *On Rumors: How Falsehoods Spread, Why We Believe Them, and What Can Be Done* (Princeton: Princeton University Press, 2014); Sarah R. Wert and Peter Salovey, "A Social Comparison Account of Gossip," *Review of General Psychology* 8, no. 2 (2004): 122–37; Luise White, *Speaking with Vampires: Rumor and History in Colonial Africa* (Berkeley: University of California Press, 2008).

4. Linda Green, *Fear as a Way of Life: Mayan Widows in Rural Guatemala* (New York: Columbia University Press, 1999), 55.

5. Officially, membership in PACs was for men aged eighteen to sixty. In practice, there was much more variability, and the ages range from approximately twelve to seventy. See Patricia Foxen, *In Search of Providence: Transnational Mayan Identities* (Nashville: Vanderbilt University Press, 2007); Virginia Garrard-Burnett, *Terror in the Land of the Holy Spirit: Guatemala under General Efraín Ríos Montt, 1982–1983* (New York: Oxford University Press, 2010); Victor Montejo, *Testimony: Death of a Guatemalan Village* (East Haven, CT: Cornerstone Press, 1987).

6. Edward F. Fischer, *Cultural Logics and Global Economies: Maya Identity in Thought and Practice* (Austin: University of Texas Press, 2001); Edward F. Fischer and Carol Hendrickson, *Tecpán, Guatemala: Global Connections and Mayan Struggles in Postwar Guatemala* (Boulder: Westview, 2003).

7. Community justice takes a variety of forms in Guatemala, ranging from neighborhood and church watch programs to extrajudicial lynchings. See Jennifer L. Burrell, "In and Out of Rights: Security, Migration, and Human Rights Talk in Postwar Guatemala," *Journal of Latin American and Caribbean Anthropology* 15, no. 1 (2010): 90–115; Kevin Lewis O'Neill and Kedron Thomas, eds., *Securing the City: Neoliberalism, Space, and Insecurity in Postwar Guatemala* (Durham, NC: Duke University Press, 2011).

8. Other local rumors included that the robberies were in fact justified because the owners (of the thread distributor) were known to be involved in nefarious business practices and perhaps had even used witchcraft to ensure their success. For an extensive and insightful description of envy and gossip as a regulatory model in Tecpán's apparel industry, see Kedron Thomas, *Regulating Style: Intellectual Property Law and the Business of Fashion in Guatemala* (Oakland: University of California Press, 2016.

9. Fischer, *Cultural Logics and Global Economies*; Thomas, *Regulationg Style.*

10. Brent E. Metz and Meghan Farley Webb, "Historical Sediments of Competing Gender Models in Indigenous Guatemala," in *Masculinities in a Global Era*, ed. Joseph Gelfer (New York: Springer, 2013), 192–213.

11. Elective abortion is illegal in Guatemala except when deemed medically necessary to save the woman's life. Therefore, most abortions performed in the country are performed in clandestine and unsafe settings. Unsafe abortion accounts for 10 percent of maternal mortality in the country. Nicole S. Berry, *Unsafe Motherhood: Mayan Maternal Mortality and Subjectivity in Post-War Guatemala* (New York: Berghahn Books, 2010); Edgar Kestler et al., "Scaling Up Post-Abortion Care in Guatemala: Initial Successes at National Level," *Reproductive Health Matters* 14, no. 27 (2006): 138–47.

12. For an examination of the value of being at home for Indigenous women in Oaxaca, Mexico, see Lynn Stephen, "Women's Weaving Cooperatives in Oaxaca: An Indigenous Response to Neoliberalism," *Critique of Anthropology* 25, no. 3 (2005): 253–78.

13. S. Ashley Kistler, *Maya Market Women: Power and Tradition in San Juan Chamelco, Guatemala* (Urbana: University of Illinois Press, 2014), 48.

14. It is estimated that a woman spends four hours a day cooking alone. See Tracy Bachrach Ehlers, *Silent Looms: Women and Production in a Guatemalan Town* (Austin: University of Texas Press, 2000), 73. More recently, authors have described women spending nearly 8.8 hours a day cooking and/or tending fires. Wood-burning stoves are more common in aldeas than they are in the city center. Jillian Moore et al., "Aid and Gendered

Subjectivity in Rural Guatemala," *Journal of Development Studies* 53, no. 12 (2017): 5. In the city of Tecpán, kitchens usually have both a wood stove, which also serves as the kitchen table and a set of two to four gas burners. Wood-burning stoves are still widely used, especially in the raining season, as the source of heat for homes. Additionally, some staple foods, like beans, are rarely cooked on gas stoves. Beans are usually cooked in clay pots on wood-burning stoves both for their taste and because it would be too expensive (and wasteful) to use the gas stove for the hours needed to cook dried beans.

15. The expansion of cell phones has not diminished the importance of older forms of social control. Suegras, for example, use constant co-presence to monitor their daughters-in-law.

16. While Flora characterized Eugenia as fair in her delegation of duties, it is not unusual for suegras to be described as taking advantage of their daughters-in-law's labor. This is one of the reasons that unmarried teenage girls fear suegras.

17. Many husbands look to migration to build their own homes. This increases the likelihood that nueras in transnational households are under the control of their mother in-law (see the continuation of Dolores's story in this chapter).

18. Carol Hendrickson, *Weaving Identities: Construction of Dress and Self in Highland Guatemala* (Austin: University of Texas Press, 1995).

19. Anita Chary et al., *Formative Assessment of Infant and Young Child Nutrition in Two Indigenous Communities in Guatemala*, Wuqu' Kawoq/Maya Health Alliance (2013).

20. The monitoring of daughters-in-law is not purely selfless. Sons generally remit a portion of their earnings to their parents, especially when sons have yet to build their own houses.

21. See also Mary Alice Scott, "La Mujer Se Va Pa'bajo: Women's Health at the Intersections of Nationality, Class, and Gender" (PhD diss., University of Kentucky, 2010).

22. Metz and Webb, "Historical Sediments."

23. In her discussion of familial surveillance and gender (non)conformity in the United States Kane suggests that parental monitoring of children's gender identities reinforces parents' own gender identity. Emily W. Kane, "'No Way My Boys Are Going to Be Like That!': Parents' Responses to Children's Gender Nonconformity," *Gender and Society* 20 (2006): 149–76.

24. In addition to María's mother and father-in-law, María's brothers-in-law and sisters-in-law live in the house.

25. She also blamed the fact that he "had fallen into vices" and "forgot about his children."

26. Sixty percent of interviewees said that migrants' parents are responsible for protecting nueras. Thirty percent said that it is up to daughters-in-law to protect themselves. As one wife (who lived with her in-laws) explained, "There is no one to protect me. It is just me."

27. Margaret K. Nelson and Anita Ilta Garey, "Who's Watching?: An Introductory Essay," in *Who's Watching?: Daily Practices of Surveillance among Contemporary Families*, ed. Nelson and Garey (Nashville: Vanderbilt University Press, 2009), 239–60.

Chapter 5

1. Treadle foot looms are usually operated by men. Carol Hendrickson, *Weaving Identities: Construction of Dress and Self in Highland Guatemala* (Austin: University of Texas Press, 1995), 44–45.

2. See Kedron Thomas, *Regulating Style: Intellectual Property Law and the Business of Fashion in Guatemala* (Oakland: University of California Press, 2016.

3. Meghan Farley Webb, "Transnational Migration's Psychosocial Impacts for Kaqchikel Maya Migrants' Wives," *Human Organization* 77, no. 1 (2018): 32–41.

4. Webb, "Transnational Migration's Psychosocial Impacts for Migrants' Wives."

5. Michael Taussig, *Defacement: Public Secrecy and the Labor of the Negative* (Stanford: Stanford University Press, 1999).

6. David Stoll, *El Norte or Bust!: How Migration Fever and Microcredit Produced a Financial Crash in a Latin American Town* (Lanham, MD: Rowman and Littlefield, 2013).

7. Deborah A. Boehm, "Deseos y Dolores: Mapping Desire, Suffering, and (Dis)loyalty within Transnational Partnerships," *International Migration* 49, no. 6 (2011): 95–106.

8. Linda Green, *Fear as a Way of Life: Mayan Widows in Rural Guatemala* (New York: Columbia University Press, 1999).

9. Webb, "Transnational Migration's Psychosocial Impacts Migrants' Wives."

10. Carla Pezzia, "The Sober Self: Discourse and Identity of Recovering Alcoholics in the Western Highlands of Guatemala" (PhD diss., University of Texas at San Antonio, 2013).

11. Boehm, "Deseos y Dolores"; Cecilia Menjívar, *Enduring Violence: Ladina Women's Lives in Guatemala* (Berkeley: University of California Press, 2011).

12. Taussig, *Defacement.*

13. Virginia Garrard-Burnett, "Community Culture and Control in Guatemala," in *Distilling the Influence of Alcohol: Aguardiente in Guatemalan History*, ed. David Carey (Gainsville: University Press of Florida, 2012).

14. Tracy Bachrach Ehlers, "Debunking Marianismo: Economic Vulnerability and Survival Strategies among Guatemalan Wives," *Ethnology* 30, no. 1 (1998): 1–6.

15. Later I found out from Julio's wife that she had caught him sending sexually explicit texts to another woman.

16. Men's infidelities were only grounds for separation and/or divorce if they resulted in the husband's failures to economically provide for the family.

17. S. Ashley Kistler, *Maya Market Women: Power and Tradition in San Juan Chamelco, Guatemala* (Urbana: University of Illinois Press, 2014).

18. It is hard to know whether Catirino's reluctance was his genuine opinion or whether he was heavily influenced by the ideas of his parents.

19. Harriet Lerner, *Marriage Rules: A Manual for the Married and Coupled Up* (New York: Gotham Books, 2013).

References

Ahearn, Laura M. *Invitations to Love: Literacy, Love Letters, and Social Change in Nepal.* Ann Arbor: University of Michigan Press, 2012 [2001].

Allison, Anne. "Cuteness as Japan's Millenial Product." In *Pikachu's Global Adventure: The Rise and Fall of Pokémon,* edited by Joseph J. Tobin, 34–49. Durham, NC: Duke University Press, 2004.

Annis, Shelton. *God and Production in a Guatemalan Town.* Austin: University of Texas Press, 1987.

Arriola Mairen, Cristobal Mardoqueo. "Historia y actualidad de Tecpan Guatemala." MA thesis, Universdidad de San Carlos, 2004.

Austad, Kirsten, Pooja Shah, and Peter Rohloff. "Correlates of Long-Acting Reversible Contraception Uptake among Rural Women in Guatemala." *PLoS One* 13, no. 6 (2018).

Bacigalupe, Gonzalo, and Susan Lambe. "Virtualizing Intimacy: Information Communication Technologies and Transnational Families in Therapy." *Family Process* 50, no. 1 (2011): 12–26.

Bennett, Joyce N. "Comadre Work: Grassroots Feminism in a Kaqchikel Maya Town." *Journal of International Women's Studies* 20, no. 6 (2019): 60–74.

———. *Good Maya Women: Migration and Revitalization of Clothing and Language in Highland Guatemala.* Tuscaloosa: University of Alabama Press, 2022.

Bennett, Joyce, and Ambrocia Cuma. "Maya-Americanos en casa: Los efectos de la migración de Guatemala a los EEUU en la Región Kaqchikel [Maya-Americans at Home: The Effects of Migration from Guatemala to the United States in the Kaqchikel Region]." *Maya America: Journal of Essays, Commentary, and Analysis* 2, no. 1 (2020): 51–71.

Berger, Susan A. *Guatemaltecas: The Women's Movement 1986–2003.* Austin: University of Texas Press, 2006.

Berlant, Lauren. *Cruel Optimism.* Durham, NC: Duke University Press, 2011.

Berry, Nicole S. *Unsafe Motherhood: Mayan Maternal Mortality and Subjectivity in Post-War Guatemala.* New York: Berghahn Books, 2010.

Bjune, Maren Christensen. "Religious Change and Political Continuity: The Evangelical Church in Guatemalan Politics." PhD diss., University of Bergen, 2016.

Boccagni, Paolo. "Practising Motherhood at a Distance: Retention and Loss in Ecuadorian Transnational Families." *Journal of Ethnic and Migration Studies* 38, no. 2 (2012): 261–277.

Boehm, Deborah A. "Deseos y Dolores: Mapping Desire, Suffering, and (Dis)Loyalty within Transnational Partnerships." *International Migration* 49, no. 6 (2011): 95–106.

———. *Intimate Migrations: Gender, Family, and Illegality among Transnational Mexicans*. New York: New York University Press, 2012.

Bolter, Jay David, and Richard Grusin. *Remediation: Understanding New Media*. Cambridge, MA: MIT Press, 2000.

Bossen, Laurel Herbenar. *The Redivision of Labor: Women and Economic Change in Four Guatemalan Communities*. Albany: State University of New York Press, 1984.

Bresnier, Niko. *Gossip and the Everyday Production of Politics*. Honolulu: University of Hawaii Press, 2009.

Brown, Kelly, Nicole Henretty, Anita Chary, Meghan Farley Webb, Heather Wehr, Jillian Moore, Caitlin Baird, Anne Kraemer Díaz, and Peter Rohloff. "Mixed-Methods Study Identifies Key Strategies for Improving Infant and Young Child Feeding Practices in a Highly Stunted Rural Indigenous Population in Guatemala." *Maternal and Child Nutrition* 12, no. 2 (2016): 262–77.

Burns, Allan F. "Indiantown, Florida: The Maya Diaspora and Applied Anthropology." In Loucky and Moors, *Maya Diaspora*, 152–71.

———. *Maya in Exile: Guatemalans in Florida*. Philadelphia: Temple University Press, 1993.

Burrell, Jennifer L. "In and out of Rights: Security, Migration, and Human Rights Talk in Postwar Guatemala." *Journal of Latin American and Caribbean Anthropology* 15, no. 1 (2010): 90–115.

Campbell, Baird. "The Archive of the Self: Trans Self-Making and Social Media in Santiago De Chile." PhD diss., Rice University, 2021.

Campbell, Baird, and Nell Haynes. "Constructing the Digital Self in the Global South." *Journal of Language and Sexuality* 9, no. 1 (2020): 1–13.

Campbell, John K. *Honour, Family, and Patronage: A Study of Institutions and Moral Values in a Modern Greek Community*. Oxford: Oxford University Press, 1964.

Canessa, Andrew. *Intimate Indigeneities: Race, Sex, and History in the Small Spaces of Andean Life*. Durham, NC: Duke University Press, 2012.

Carey, David. *Engendering Mayan History: Kaqchikel Women as Agents and Conduits of the Past, 1875–1970*. London: Routledge, 2006.

———. *Our Elders Teach Us: Maya-Kaqchikel Historical Perspectives*. Tuscaloosa: University of Alabama Press, 2001.

Carey, David, and M. Gabriela Torres. "Precursors to Femicide: Guatemalan Women in a Vortex of Violence." *Latin American Research Review* 45, no. 3 (2010): 142–64.

Carling, Jorgen. "The Human Dynamics of Migrant Transnationalism." *Ethnic and Racial Studies* 31, no. 8 (2008): 1452–77.

Carter, Marion C. "Gender and Community Context: An Analysis of Husband's Household Authority in Rural Guatemala." *Sociological Forum* 19, no. 4 (2004): 633–52.

Casaús Arzú, Marta Elena. *Guatemala: Linaje y racismo* [Guatemala: Lineage and Racism] . Guatemala City, Guatemala: F & G Editores, 2007.

Chary, Anita. "'A Poor Woman's Disease' in the Time of Global Health: An Ethnography of Cervical Cancer in Guatemala." PhD diss., Washington University, 2015.

Chary, Anita, Kelly Brown, Meghan Farley Webb, Heather Wehr, Jillian Moore, Caitlin Baird, Anne Kraemer Díaz, Nicole Henretty, and Peter Rohloff. *Formative Assessment of Infant and Young Child Nutrition in Two Indigenous Communities in Guatemala.* Report produced by Wuqu' Kawoq/Maya Health Alliance, 2013.

Chary, Anita, and Peter Rohloff, eds. *Privatization and the New Medical Pluralism: Shifting Healthcare Landscapes in Maya Guatemala.* Lanham, MD: Lexington Books, 2015.

Chirix García, Emma Delfina. *Una aproximación sociológica a la sexulaidad Kaqchikel hoy.* Guatemala: FLASCO, 2008.

Clary, John Vincent. "Digital Geographies of Transnational Spaces: A Mixed-Methods Study of Mexico-Us Migration." MA thesis, University of Texas, 2014.

Coe, Cati. "What Is Love?: The Materiality of Care in Ghanain Transnational Families." *International Migration* 49, no. 6 (2011): 7–24.

Craske, Nikki. *Women and Politics in Latin America.* Malden, MA: Polity Press, 2005 [1999].

Dasgupta-Tsikinas, Shom, and Paul Wise. "'Mi Familia Probreza': Conditional Cash Transfers and Materal-Child Health in Rural Guatemala." In *e Pluralism: Shifting Healthcare Landscapes in Maya Guatemala,* edited by Anita Chary and Peter Rohloff, 19–34. Lanham, MD: Lexington Books, 2015.

Davis, Thomas E. , Edward F. Fischer, Peter J. Rohloff, and Douglas C. Heimburger. "Chronic Malnutrition, Breastfeeding, and Ready to Use Supplementary Food in Guatemalan Maya Town." *Human Organization* 73, no. 1 (2014): 72–81.

de León, Lourdes. "Texting Amor: Emerging Intimacies in Textually Mediated Romance among Tzotzil Mayan Youth." *Ethos* 45, no. 4 (2017): 462–88.

del Valle Escalante, Emilio. *Maya Nationalisms and Postcolonial Challenges in Guatemala: Coloniality, Modernity, and Identity Politics.* Global Indigenous Politics. Edited by James F. Brooks. Santa Fe: School for Advanced Research, 2009.

Dreby, Joanna. *Divided by Borders: Mexican Migrants and Their Children.* Berkeley: University of California Press, 2010.

———. "Gender and Transnational Gossip." *Qualitative Sociology* 32, no. 1 (2009): 33–52.

Drotbohm, Heike. "Gossip and Social Control across the Seas: Targeting Gender, Resource Inequalities and Support in Cape Verdean Transnational Families." *African and Black Diasporas: An International Journal* 3, no. 1 (2010): 51–68.

Ehlers, Tracy Bachrach. "Debunking Marianismo: Economic Vulnerability and Survival Strategies among Guatemalan Wives." *Ethnology* 30, no. 1 (1998): 1–16.

———. *Silent Looms: Women and Production in a Guatemalan Town*. Austin: University of Texas Press, 2000.

Farmer, Paul. *Infections and Inequalities: The Modern Plagues*. Berkeley: University of California Press, 2001.

Fine, Gary Alan. "Rumor." In *Folklore: An Encyclopedia of Beliefs, Customs, Tales and Art*, edited by Thomas A. Green, 741–44. Santa Barbara, CA: ABC-CLIO, 1997.

Fink, Leon. *The Maya of Morgantown: Work and Community in the Nuevo New South*. Chapel Hill: University of North Carolina Press, 2003.

Fischer, Edward F. *Cultural Logics and Global Economies: Maya Identity in Thought and Practice*. Austin: University of Texas Press, 2001.

———. *The Good Life: Aspiration, Dignity, and the Anthropology of Wellbeing*. Stanford: Stanford University Press, 2014.

Fischer, Edward F., and Peter Benson. *Broccoli and Desire: Global Connections and Mayan Struggles in Postwar Guatemala*. Stanford: Stanford University Press, 2006.

Fischer, Edward F., and Carol Hendrickson. *Tecpán, Guatemala: Global Connections and Mayan Struggles in Postwar Guatemala*. Boulder: Westview, 2003.

Foucault, Michel. *Discipline and Punish: The Birth of the Prison*. Translated by Alan Sheridan. New York: Pantheon Books, 1977.

Foxen, Patricia. *In Search of Providence: Transnational Mayan Identities*. Nashville: Vanderbilt University Press, 2007.

Foxen, Patricia, and Debra H. Rodman. "Guatemalans in New England: Transnational Communities through Time and Space." *Practicing Anthropology* 34, no. 1 (2012): 17–26.

French, Brigittine M. *Maya Ethnolinguistic Identity: Violence, Cultural Rights, and Modernity in Highland Guatemala*. Tucson: University of Arizona Press, 2010.

———. "The Maya Movement and Modernity: Local Kaqchikel Linguistic Ideologies and the Problem of Progress." *Proceedings of the Tenth Annual Symposium about Language and Society*, 2002, 58–68.

Fuchs, Christian. *Social Media: A Critical Introduction*. 3rd ed. London: Sage, 2021 [2014].

Garcia, Maria Elena. *Making Indigenous Citizens: Identity, Development, and Multicultural Activism in Peru*. Stanford: Stanford University Press, 2005.

Garrard-Burnett, Virginia. "Aftermath: Women and Gender Issues in Post Conflict

Guatemala." Washington, DC: Center for Development Information and Evaluation, US Agency for International Development, 2000.

———. "Community Culture and Control in Guatemala." In *Distilling the Influence of Alcohol: Aguardiente in Guatemalan History*, edited by David Carey, 157–80. Gainsville: University of Florida Press, 2012.

———. *Terror in the Land of the Holy Spirit: Guatemala under General Efraín Ríos Montt, 1982–1983*. New York: Oxford University Press, 2010.

Gershon, Ilana. *The Breakup 2.0: Disconnecting over New Media*. Ithaca, NY: Cornell University Press, 2010.

Glick Schiller, Nina, Linda Basch, and Cristina Blanc-Szanton. "Transnationalism: A New Analytic Framework for Understanding Migration." *Annals of the New York Academy of Sciences* 645 (1992): 1–24.

Gluckman, Max. "Gossip and Scandal." *Current Anthropology* 4 (1963): 307–16.

Goldín, Liliana R. *Global Maya: Work and Ideology in Rural Guatemala*. Tucson: University of Arizona, 2009.

Goldín, Liliana R., and Brenda Rosenbaum. "Culture and History: Subregional Variation among the Maya." *Comparative Studies in Society and History* 35, no. 1 (1993): 110–32.

Gómez García, Dolfi. "Canasta básica en LatAm: Esto le cuesta a cada país conseguir alimentos [The Canasta Básica in Latin America: This is what it costs to buy basic food stuffs in each country]." *Bloomberg*, May 13, 2022. Web.

Gómez-Urrutia, Verónica, and Felipe Tello-Navarro. "Gender, Love and the Internet: Romantic Online Interactions in Chilean Young People." *Journal of Youth Studies* 24, no. 6 (2020): 731–45.

Gonzalez-Lopez, Gloria. *Erotic Journeys: Mexican Immigrants and Their Sex Lives*. Los Angeles: University of California Press, 2005.

Grandin, Greg. *The Blood of Guatemala: A History of Race and Nation*. Durham, NC: Duke University Press, 2000.

Green, Linda. *Fear as a Way of Life: Mayan Widows in Rural Guatemala*. New York: Columbia University Press, 1999.

Gutmann, Matthew C. *The Meanings of Macho: Being a Man in Mexico City*. Berkeley: University of California Press, 1996.

Gutmann, Matthew C., and Mara Viveros Vigoya. "Masculinities in Latin America." In *Handbook of Studies on Men and Masculinity*, edited by Michael S. Kimmel, Jeff Hearn and R. W. Connell, 114–28. Thousand Oaks, CA: Sage Publications, 2005.

Hale, Charles R. *Más Que Un Indio (More Than an Indian): Racial Ambivalence and the Paradox of Neoliberal Multiculturalism in Guatemala*. Santa Fe: School of American Research Press, 2006.

Hall-Clifford, Rachel Ann. "Oral Rehydration Therapy in Highland Guatemala: Long-Term Impacts of Public Health Intervention on the Self." PhD diss., Boston University, 2009.

Hamilton, Nora, and Norma Stoltz Chinchilla. *Seeking Community in a Global City: Guatemalans and Salvadorans in Los Angeles*. Philadelphia: Temple University Press, 2001.

Hannaford, Dinah. "Technologies of the Spouse: Intimate Surveillance in Senegalese Transnational Marriages." *Global Networks* 15, no. 1 (2015): 43–59.

Harlow, Summer. "Social Media and Social Movements: Facebook and an Online Guatemalan Justice Movement That Moved Offline." *New Media and Society* 14, no. 2 (2011): 225–43.

Hendrickson, Carol. *Weaving Identities: Construction of Dress and Self in Highland Guatemala*. Austin: University of Texas Press, 1995.

Hill, Robert M., II. *Colonial Cakchiquels: Highland Maya Adaptation to Spanish Rule, 1600–1700*. Case Studies in Cultural Anthropology. Edited by George Spindler and Louise Spindler. New York: Holt, Rinehart, and Winston, 1992.

Hirsch, Jennifer S. *Courtship after Marriage: Sexuality and Love in Mexican Transnational Families*. Berkeley: University of California Press, 2003.

Hondagneu-Sotelo, Pierrette. *Domestica: Immigrant Workers Cleaning and Caring in the Shadows of Affluence*. Berkeley: University of California Press, 2001.

Horst, Heather A. "The Blessings and Burdens of Communication: Cell Phones in Jamaican Transnational Social Fields." *Global Networks* 6, no. 2 (2006): 143–59.

Horst, Heather A., and Daniel Miller. *The Cell Phone: An Anthropology of Communication*. Oxford: Berg, 2006.

———. "From Kinship to Link-Up: Cell Phones and Social Networking in Jamaica." *Current Anthropology* 46, no. 5 (2005): 755–78.

Horst, Heather A., and Daniel Miller, eds. *Digital Anthropology*. New York: Routledge, 2020 [2012].

Instituto Nacional de Estadística (INE). *Canasta básica alimentaria (Cba) y ampliada (Ca), febrero de 2022* [Basic food basket and amplifed, February 2022]. Guatemala City: Instituto Nacional de Estadística, March 2022.

———. *Poblacion de 7 años o más por uso de celular, compu, y/o internet*, 2019.

———. "Resultados Departamento de Chimaltenango," 2019.

Johannsen, Jacob. *Psychoanalysis and Digital Culture: Audiences, Social Media, and Big Data*. New York: Routledge, 2019.

Jonas, Susanne, and Nestor Rodríguez. *Guatemala-U.S. Migration: Transforming Regions*. Austin: University of Texas Press, 2015.

Kandiyoti, Deniz. "Bargaining with Patriarchy." *Gender and Society* 2, no. 3 (1988): 274–90.

Kane, Emily W. "'No Way My Boys Are Going to Be Like That!': Parents' Responses to Children's Gender Nonconformity." *Gender and Society* 20 (2006): 149–76.

———. "Policing Gender Boundaries: Monitoring of Preschool Children's Gender Nonconformity." In Nelson and Garey, *Who's Watching?* 239–60.

Kember, Sarah, and Joanna Zylinska. *Life after New Media: Mediation as a Vital Process*. Cambridge, MA: MIT Press, 2015.

Kestler, Edgar, Linda Valencia, Vincio Del Valle, and Alejandro Silva. "Scaling up Post-Abortion Care in Guatemala: Initial Successes at National Level." *Reproductive Health Matters* 14, no. 27 (2006): 138–47.

Kistler, S. Ashley. *Maya Market Women: Power and Tradition in San Juan Chamelco, Guatemala*. Urbana: University of Illinois Press, 2014.

Lerner, Harriet. *Marriage Rules: A Manual for the Married and Coupled Up*. New York: Gotham Books, 2013.

Little, Walter. *Mayas in the Marketplace: Tourism, Globalization, and Cultural Identity*. Austin: University of Texas, 2004.

Loucky, James. "Maya in a Modern Metropolis: Establishing New Lives in Los Angeles." In Loucky annd Moors, *Maya Diaspora*, 214–22.

Loucky, James, and Marilyn M. Moors, eds. *The Maya Diaspora: Guatemalan Roots, New American Lives*. Philadelphia: Temple University Press, 2000.

Lyon, David. *Surveillance Studies: An Overview*. Maldan, MA: Polity Press, 2007.

Madianou, Mirca, and Daniel Miller. *Migration and New Media: Transnational Families and Polymedia*. New York: Routledge, 2012.

Martínez Peláez, Severo. *La Patria del Criollo: An Interpretation of Colonial Guatemala*. Translated by Susan M. Neve and W. George Lovell. Edited by W. George Lovell and Christopher H. Lutz. Durham, NC: Duke University Press, 2009.

Maxwell, Judith, and Robert M. Hill II. *Kaqchikel Chronicles: The Definitive Edition*. Austin: University of Texas Press, 2006.

Mazzarella, William. "Culture, Globalization, Mediation." *Annual Review of Anthropology* (2004): 345–67.

McCreery, David. "State Power, Indigenous Communities, and Land in Nineteeth-Centruy Guatemala, 1820–1920." In *Guatemalan Indians and the State, 1540–1988*, edited by Carol A. Smith, 96–115. Austin: University of Texas Press, 1990.

Menjívar, Cecilia. *Enduring Violence: Ladina Women's Lives in Guatemala*. Berkeley: University of California Press, 2011.

Metz, Brent E. *Ch'orti'-Maya Survival in Eastern Guatemala: Indigeneity in Transition*. Albuquerque: University of New Mexico Press, 2006.

———. "Politics, Population, and Family Planning in Guatemala: Ch'orti' Maya Experiences." *Human Organization* 60, no. 3 (2001): 259–71.

Metz, Brent E., and Meghan Farley Webb. "Historical Sediments of Competing Gender Models in Indigenous Guatemala." In *Masculinities in a Global Era*, edited by Joseph Gelfer, 193–213. New York: Springer, 2013.

Miller, Tiffany Creegan. *The Maya Art of Speaking Writing: Remediating Indigenous Orality in the Digital Age*. Tuscon: University of Arizona Press, 2022.

Minh-Ha, Trinh T. *Woman, Native, Other: Writing Postcoloniality and Feminism*. Bloomington: Indiana University Press, 2009 [1989].

Ministerio de Salud Pública y Asistencia Social (MSPAS), Instituto Nacional de Estadística (INE), and ICF International. *Encuesta nacional de salud materno infantil 2014–2015: Informe final.* Guatemala: MSPAS/INE/ICF, 2017.

"Mobile Cellular Subscriptions (Per 100 People)-Guatemala." World Bank Data, 2022. Web.

Montejo, Victor. *Testimony: Death of a Guatemalan Village.* East Haven, CT: Cornerstone Press, 1987.

Moore, Jillian, Meghan Farley Webb, Anita Chary, Anne Kraemer Díaz, and Peter Rohloff. "Aid and Gendered Subjectivity in Rural Guatemala." *Journal of Development Studies* 53, no. 12 (2017): 2164–78.

Nanda, Serena. *Love and Marriage: Cultural Diversity in a Changing World.* Long Grove, IL: Waveland Press, 2019.

Naples, Nancy A. "A Member of the Funeral: An Introspective Ethnography." In *Queer Families, Queer Politics: Challenging Culture and the State,* edited by Mary Bernstein and Renate Reinmann, 21–43. New York: Columbia University Press, 2001.

Nelson, Diane. *A Finger in the Wound: Body Politics in Quincentennial Guatemala.* Berkeley: University of California Press, 1999.

Nelson, Margaret K. "Single Mothers 'Do' Family." *Journal of Marriage and Family* 68 (2006): 781–95.

Nelson, Margaret K., and Anita Ilta Garey. "Who's Watching?: An Introductory Essay." In Nelson and Garey, *Who's Watching?* 1–16.

Nelson, Margaret K., and Anita Ilta Garey, eds. *Who's Watching?: Daily Practices of Surveillance among Contemporary Families.* Nashville: Vanderbilt University Press, 2009.

O'Neill, Kevin Lewis, and Kedron Thomas, eds. *Securing the City: Neoliberalism, Space, and Insecurity in Postwar Guatemala.* Durham, NC: Duke University Press, 2011.

Oakes, Maud. *Beyond the Windy Place: Life in the Guatemalan Highlands.* New York: Farrar, Straus, 1951.

Organización Internacional para las Migraciones (OIM). *Encuesta sobre migración internacional de personas guatemaltecas en el exterior y remesas 2022.* 2023. Web.

Paine, Robert. "What Is Gossip About?: An Alternative Hypothesis." *Man* 2, no. 2 (1967): 278–85.

Palomo de Lewin, Beatriz. "Vida conyugal de las mujeres en Guatemala (1741–1871) [Married life of Guatemalan women 1741–1871)]." In *Mujeres, genero e historia en América Central durante los siglos XVII, XIX y XX* [Women, Gender, and History in Central America During the 18th, 19th, and 20th Centuries], edited by Eugenia Rodríguez Sáenz, 25–34. San José, Costa Rica: UNIFEM Oficina Regional para México, Centroamérica, Cuba y República Dominicana and Plumsock Mesoamerican Studies, 2002.

Parreñas, Rhacel Salazar. *Children of Global Migration: Transnational Families and Gendered Woes*. Stanford: Stanford University Press, 2005.

———. "Long Distance Intimacy: Class, Gender, and Intergenerational Relations between Mothers and Children in Filipino Transnational Families." *Global Networks* 5, no. 4 (2005): 317–36.

———. *Servants of Globalization: Women, Migration, and Domestic Work*. Stanford: Stanford University Press, 2001.

Paul, Lois. "The Mastery of Work and the Mystery of Sex in a Guatemalan Village." In *Women, Culture, and Society*, edited by Michelle Zimblast Rosaldo and Louise Lamphere, 281–99. Stanford: Stanford University Press, 1974.

Pezzia, Carla. "The Sober Self: Discourse and Identity of Recovering Alcoholics in the Western Highlands of Guatemala." PhD diss., University of Texas at San Antonio, 2013.

Recovery of Historical Memory Project (REMHI). *Guatemala Never Again!: The Official Report of the Human Rights Office*. New York: Maryknoll, 1999.

Rodman, Debra Hain. "Gender, Migration, and Transnational Identities: Maya and Ladino Relations in Eastern Guatemala." PhD diss., University of Florida, 2006.

Rohloff, Peter, Florencio Calí, and José Frederico Calí. *Xejuyu: Demographic Survey*. Wuqu' Kawoq|Maya Health Alliance. Guatemala, 2011.

Rohloff, Peter, Anne Kraemer Díaz, and Shom Dasgupta. "'Beyond Development': A Critical Appraisal of the Emergence of Small Health Care Non-Governmental Organizations in Rural Guatemala." *Human Organization* 70, no. 4 (2011): 427–37.

Rosas, Carolina. *Varones al son de la migración internacional y masculinidades de Veracruz a Chicago*. Mexico City: El Colegio de México, 2008.

Rosenblum, Marc R. "Immigration and U.S. National Interests: Historical Cases and the Contemporary Debate." In *Immigration Policy and Security: U.S., European, and Commonwealth Perspectives*, edited by Terri E. Givens, Gary P. Freeman, and David L. Leal, 13–38. New York: Routledge, 2009.

Safa, Helen Icken. "Economic Restructuring and Gender Subordination." *Latin American Perspectives* 22, no. 2 (1995): 32–50.

Samper, David. "Cannibalizing Kids: Rumor and Resistance in Latin America." *Journal of Folklore Research* 39, no. 1 (2002): 1–32.

Sanford, Victoria. *Buried Secrets: Truth and Human Rights in Guatemala*. New York: Palgrave, 2003.

———. "From Genocide to Feminicide: Impunity and Human Rights in Twenty-First Century Guatemala." *Journal of Human Rights* 7 (2008): 104–22.

Scott, Mary Alice. "La Mujer Se Va Pa'bajo: Women's Health at the Intersections of Nationality, Class, and Gender." PhD diss., University of Kentucky, 2010.

Sehlikoglu, Setaç, and Asli Zengin. "Introduction: Why Revisit Intimacy?" *Cambridge Journal of Anthropology* 33, no. 2 (2015): 20–25.

Skolnik, Jocelyn, Sandra Lazo de la Vega, and Timothy Steigenga. "*Chisme* across Borders: The Impact of Gossip in a Guatemalan Transnational Community." *Migraciones Internacionales* 6, no. 3 (2012): 9–38.

Smith, Carol A. "Race-Class-Gender Ideology in Guatemala: Modern and Anti-Modern Forms." *Comparative Studies in Society and History* 37 (1995): 723–49.

Stasser, Elisabeth, Albert Kraler, Saskia Bonjour, and Veronika Bilger. "Doing Family: Response to the Constructions of 'the Migrant Family' across Europe." *History of the Family* 14, no. 2 (2009): 165–76.

Stephen, Lynn. "Women's Weaving Cooperatives in Oaxaca: An Indigenous Response to Neoliberalism," *Critique of Anthropology* 25, no. 3 (2005): 253–78.

Stevens, Evelyn P. "Machismo and Marianismo." *Society* 10 (1973): 57–63.

Stewart, Pamela J., and Andrew Strathern. *Witchcraft, Sorcery, Rumors and Gossip*. New York: Cambridge University Press, 2004.

Stoler, Ann Laura. *Carnal Knowledge and Imperial Power: Race and the Intimate in Colonial Rule*. Berkely: University of California Press, 2010 [2002].

Stoll, David. *El Norte or Bust!: How Migration Fever and Microcredit Produced a Financial Crash in a Latin American Town*. Lanham, MD: Rowman and Littlefield, 2013.

———. *Is Latin America Turning Protestant?: The Politics of Evangelical Growth*. Berkeley: University of California Press, 1990.

———. "'Jesus Is the Lord of Guatemala': Evangelical Reform in a Death-Squad State." In *Accounting for Fundamentalism: The Dynamic Character of Movements*, edited by Martin E. Marty and R. Scott Appleby, 99–123. Chicago: University of Chicago Press, 1994.

Sunstein, Cass R. *On Rumors: How Falsehoods Spread, Why We Believe Them, and What Can Be Done*. Princeton: Princeton University Press, 2014.

Tarn, Nathaniel, and Martín Prechtel. "'Comiéndose la fruta': Metáforas sexuales e inciaciones en Santiago Atitlán." *Mesoamérica* 19 (1990): 73–82.

Taussig, Michael. *Defacement: Public Secrecy and the Labor of the Negative*. Stanford: Stanford University Press, 1999.

Taylor, Matthew J., Michell J. Moran-Taylor, and Debra Rodman Ruiz. "Land, Ethnic, and Gender Change: Transnational Migration and Its Effects on Guatemalan Lives and Landscapes." *Geoforum* 37 (2006): 41–61.

Thomas, Kedron. "An Ethnography of Brand Piracy in Guatemala." PhD diss., Harvard University, 2011.

———. *Regulating Style: Intellectual Property Law and the Business of Fashion in Guatemala*. Oakland: University of California Press, 2016.

Vertovec, Steven. "Cheap Calls: The Social Glue of Migrant Transnationalism." *Global Networks* 4, no. 2 (2004): 219–24.

Vi, Sandra. "Cómo está la Canasta básica en Guatemala, precios y evolución durante

2022 [What is the Canasta Básica like in Guatemala, costs and their evolution in 2022]." *La Republica* (Guatemala), August 8, 2022.

Walter, Anna-Maria. *Intimate Connections: Love and Marriage in Pakistan's High Mountains*. New Brunswick, NJ: Rutgers University Press, 2022.

Webb, Meghan Farley. "Transnational Migration's Psychosocial Impacts for Kaqchikel Maya Migrants' Wives." *Human Organization* 77, no. 1 (2018): 32–41.

———. "Yojkanäj Wawe' (We Remain Here): Kaqchikel Migrants' Wives under Surveillance." PhD diss., University of Kansas, Lawrence, 2015.

Webb, Meghan Farley, Anita N. Chary, Thomas T. De Vries, Samantha Davis, Michael Dykstra, David Flood, Margaret Haley Rhodes, and Peter Rohloff. "Exploring Mechanisms of Food Insecurity in Indigenous Agricultural Communities in Guatemala: A Mixed Methods Study." *BMC Nutrition* 2, no. 1 (2016). Web.

Wert, Sarah R., and Peter Salovey. "A Social Comparison Account of Gossip." *Review of General Psychology* 8, no. 2 (2004): 122–37.

West, Candace, and Sarah Fenstermaker. "Doing Difference." *Gender and Society* 9, no. 1 (1995): 8–37.

West, Candace, and Don H. Zimmerman. "Doing Gender." In *Doing Gender, Doing Difference: Inequality, Power, and Institutional Change*, edited by Sarah Fernstermaker and Candace West, 3–25. New York: Routledge, 2002.

———. "Doing Gender." *Gender and Society* 45, no. 2 (1987): 125–51.

"WhatsApp: Two Billion Users—Connecting the World Privately." About Facebook News, 2020. Web.

White, Luise. *Speaking with Vampires: Rumor and History in Colonial Africa*. Berkeley: University of California Press, 2008.

Wilding, Raelene. "'Viritual' Intimacies?: Families Communicating across Transnational Contexts." *Global Networks* 6, no. 2 (2006): 125–42.

Wool, Zoë H. *After War: The Weight of Life at Walter Reed*. Durham, NC: Duke University Press, 2015.

Wydick, Bruce, Harmony Karp Hayes, and Sarah Hilliker Kempf. "Social Networks, Neighborhood Effects, and Credit Access: Evidence from Rural Guatemala." *World Development* 39, no. 5 (2011): 974–82.

Ystanes, Margit. "Unfixed Trust: Intimacy, Blood Symbolism, and Porous Boundaries in Guatemala." In *Trusting and Its Tribulations: Interdisciplinary Engagements with Intimacy, Sociality, and Trust*, edited by Vigdis Broch-Due and Margit Ystantes, 37–59. New York: Berghahn Books, 2016.

Zur, Judith N. "The Psycholsocial Effects of 'La Violencia' on Widows of El Quiché, Guatemala." *Focus on Gender* 1, no. 2 (1993): 27–30.

———. *Violent Memories: Mayan War Widows in Guatemala*. Boulder: Westview, 1998.

Index

Page numbers in italics refer to figures.